Best Restaurants®
Chicago & Environs

PUBLISHER
Robert J. Dolezal

EDITORIAL DIRECTOR
Christine Robertson

NATIONAL SALES MANAGER
Charles H. Aydelotte

PRODUCTION DIRECTOR
Ernie S. Tasaki

SYSTEM MANAGER
Katherine L. Parker

PROJECT DIRECTOR
Karin Shakery

PROJECT COORDINATOR
Laurie A. Prather

SERIES FORMAT DESIGNER
Thomas Ingalls & Associates

MAP DESIGNER
Marti Walton Design

PRODUCTION
Studio 165

PRINTING
W. A. Krueger Company

*Photograph on front cover
Michael LaMotte*

Copyright © 1982, 1986 Sherman Kaplan
Copyright © 1989 Chevron Chemical Company

All rights reserved under international and Pan-American copyright conventions.
No part of this book may be reproduced in any form without the written permission of 101 Productions.
Printed and bound in the U.S.A.
Published by 101 Productions and distributed by Ortho Information Services, Box 5047, San Ramon, CA 94583.

Library of Congress Catalog Card Number 88-72347
ISBN 0-89721-186-3

Best Restaurants®
Chicago & Environs

Sherman Kaplan

**PUBLISHED BY 101 PRODUCTIONS
DISTRIBUTED BY ORTHO INFORMATION SERVICES**

PREFACE

EACH TIME I FINISH a wonderful meal and am stretched to the groaning point, I recall the counseling of a friend on the subject of being hungry. "No matter how much you eat," he told me, "the hunger always comes back." Well, like hunger, *Best Restaurants Chicago* is back.

This fifth edition is the biggest yet. Some restaurants found in the very first book back in 1977 are still here, though all have been updated with the very latest information on hours, credit cards, and so on. So, you will find some Chicago landmarks here, plus dozens of new restaurants trying to make a lasting impression on the local dining scene.

The listings are as current as possible, but restaurants do come and go, or change hours, reservation policy, or credit card acceptability. Some information cannot be exact. For example, the city of Chicago has a new no-smoking ordinance on the books, but just how widely applied it will be remains unknown at this writing. And there is no legal definition of "handicap accessible" in Illinois. The designation is based on a given restaurateur's claims, so if such access is important to you, I suggest you call the restaurant to ask for details. In other words, no matter how new this edition may be, a phone call will put you even more up-to-date.

Once again I have included my exclusive K/Rating system. The K/Rating is an effort to quantify just how successful a restaurant can be in giving you good service, appetizing food, pleasant surroundings, and value for money. The very best of the best have a K/Rating of 20/20, but no restaurant has a rating under 15/20.

Like its previous editions, *Best Restaurants Chicago* continues to guide you according to price. Generally, those restaurants classified as inexpensive offer dinners for $10 or less per person. Moderate restaurants are in the $10–$20 range, while those described as expensive are over $20 per person. Add on tax, tip, and drinks to those basic figures. If in doubt about a restaurant's prices, call ahead for specifics.

Chicagoans continue to demonstrate a tremendous interest in American cooking. You will find that several of the newer listings are dedicated to the cuisine of the heartland. At the same time, there has been the introduction of moderately priced, better restaurants where two people can dine rather well for $40 or $50 per couple, including wine, tax, and tip. And there are more ethnic restaurants than ever. Sometimes, restaurants can be so ethnic that there is a language barrier. But take that situation as part of the fun of discovering a new way of dining.

Chances are you will find some familiar restaurants in these pages, plus scores that will be new to you. If I have overlooked a favorite, please write to the publisher and let me know. I will consider it for future editions.

As with my earlier restaurant guides, this new volume would not have been possible without the cooperation of WBBM Newsradio 78, where I have been news anchor and restaurant critic for twenty years. I also want to thank the News Voice Newspapers, which publish my reviews each week. Though all opinions are mine, and mine alone, thanks must go to several people, including the friends who have been willing accomplices in my tastings. My children Joshua and Shawna have endured more than their share of meals that do not include burgers, fries, and pop, for the sake of reviewing a new ethnic eatery. The most thanks goes to my wife Eileen, with whom, as always, I share not only my meals, but my love and my life.

—Sherman Kaplan

CONTENTS

CHICAGO	**9**
Downtown & Loop	10
CHICAGO: NORTH	**31**
Near North	32
Midnorth	73
North	98
Far North	108
SUBURBS: NORTH	**119**
CHICAGO: WEST & NORTHWEST	**147**
West	148
Northwest	155
SUBURBS: WEST & NORTHWEST	**159**
CHICAGO: SOUTH	**177**
Near South	178
South	182
SUBURBS: SOUTH	**189**
INDEX	199

Chicago: Downtown & Loop

Don Roth's River Plaza

American

405 North Wabash, Chicago
Telephone: (312) 527-3100

Lunch: Monday–Friday 11–3. Dinner: Monday–Friday, Sunday 5–10, Saturday 5–11. Cards: AE, CB, DC, MC, V. Reservations only for dining room. Casual, but neat dress; jackets requested for gentlemen. No-smoking section. Valet parking after 5; garage parking all hours. Full bar service; good wines by the glass. Handicap accessible. Semiprivate party rooms for small groups. Troubleshooter: Richard L. Valente (owner). Moderate.

Famed restaurateur Don Roth is no longer at the helm here, but the new management seems particularly adept at catching the wave of contemporary dining tastes. The menu emphasizes New Orleans and Cajun cuisines. Specials change daily and have included sautéed crawfish tails with fettuccine, grilled pork chop with Creole mustard sauce, and white sea bass with red bell pepper sauce. Other choices might include Creole mixed grill, chicken and andouille stew and Key lime pie or Louisiana bread pudding for dessert. Versions of blackened sirloin steak and blackened red fish are also given prominent treatment. Along conventional lines are such dishes as grilled swordfish, roast prime rib of beef, and barbecued baby back ribs. As the name suggests, River Plaza has a handsome view of the Chicago River and busy north Loop commerce. In addition to the main dining room, there is the adjoining River Plaza Cafe for lighter luncheon fare in a more casual setting.

K/Rating of 18/20: Decor 4/4, Service 4/5, Food 8/9, Value 2/2

Binyon's

American

327 South Plymouth Court, Chicago
Telephone: (312) 341-1155

Hours: Monday–Saturday 11:30–10. Cards: AE, CB, DC, MC, V. Reservations suggested. No-smoking section. Valet parking after 5 and garage parking. Full bar service. Four private party rooms for 10–120 people. Troubleshooter: Hal Binyon (owner). Moderate.

Binyon's is built on a foundation of tradition stretching back to Prohibition days. The black enamel paint on the front door handle is worn away by the touches of thousands of hungry and thirsty Chicagoans over the decades. Inside, the restaurant looks like an old-fashioned men's club or taproom, although the human interaction is more bustling here than in those hushed halls. More than a thousand people can be served at once from a basic American menu.

Fish, chops, and steaks provide the bulk of sustenance at Binyon's. True, you could order sautéed veal kidney or sweetbreads with bacon and mushrooms, but grilled walleyed pike, brook trout, and a selection of steaks seem more in keeping with what Binyon's is all about. The house recommendation is good old American roast prime rib, an ample but not gargantuan portion of tender beef. When turtle soup is offered as the broth of the day, don't miss its rich flavors. Full dinners also include potatoes, vegetables, and a house salad. Binyon's has always been a favorite with Loop lawyers and local gadabouts. Chances are that as many big deals have been carved out over the tables here as have steaks and chops. And while regulars number in the hundreds, there always seems to be room for one more.

K/Rating of 16/20: Decor 3.5/4, Service 3.5/5, Food 7/9, Value 2/2

GORDON

American

500 North Clark, Chicago
Telephone: (312) 467-9780

Lunch: Monday–Saturday 11:30–2:30. Dinner: Sunday–Thursday 5:30–9:30, Friday–Saturday late supper until 12:30. Sunday brunch: 11:30–2:30. Cards: AE, CB, DC, MC, V, house accounts. Reservations required. Jackets required for gentlemen. No-smoking section. Valet parking and parking lots across the street. Full bar service; extensive list of cognacs and ports; wine list recognized as one of the best in the country. Handicap accessible. Private party rooms. Troubleshooter: Gordon Sinclair (owner). Expensive.

If there is a cafe society in Chicago, its gathering place is Gordon. In its previous location up a few doors, I once called Gordon's interior "steamroom Gothic." Now, the large L-shaped dining area is even more sybaritic, swathed in swag draperies and bold flesh- and earth-toned murals. It is a restaurant that speaks of self-indulgence and fashion, characteristics manifest in the foods that come from the Gordon kitchen.

Smoked salmon for an appetizer is given more than usual treatment with the addition of thin pasta noodles fashioned not only with semolina and egg, but with bits of black caviar and a touch of chive. The restaurant's nod to the popularity of pasta also extends to parsley tagliatelle, less than pale green and dressed in a touch of olive oil with the flavor of basil and garlic. The coup of the day recently was a seafood cream soup, more spicy than might be expected.

Gordon, for all its hedonism, wisely offers diners the opportunity to order half-portion entrées at half the cost of the entrée plus one dollar. It's a good way to trim calories and the budget or have a more rococo go at things by ordering double entrées. Seared tuna with a coarse chop of tomato and chive in execution of calamari fritters. He coats the small squid with beer batter, but a light vinaigrette is a satisfying choice, though tuna can be a bit stronger than I prefer. More on the mark is roasted grouper. A square of polenta accompanies the fish, bringing a touch of the land to this seafood. The roasting works fine with the meaty grouper, as it does with an order of sweetbreads. These come with chanterelles and bits of prosciutto in a chardonnay wine sauce. The garnish is appropriate, a retiring afterstatement that does not intrude on the lovely flavor of the sweetbreads. It might seem that roasting would be too harsh a cooking method. Yet it works, actually enhancing the buttery softness of this silken meat by contrasting it with the seared exterior.

Other entrées on the menu might include some oriental influences, such as grilled salmon with Chinese mustard glaze, or duck with ginger slaw, soy, and scallion. A grilled beef tenderloin comes with cabernet sauce and braised mushrooms. Rack of lamb is indulged with honey, dates, and cumin.

To return to Gordon after a much-too-long absence reminded me again of just how refined this excellent restaurant is. Expect to spend about $60 a couple, plus wine, tax, and tip.

K/Rating 19.5/20: Decor 4/4, Service 5/5, Food 8.5/9, Value 2/2

FOLEY'S

American

211 East Ohio, Chicago
Telephone: (312) 645-1261

Lunch: Monday–Friday 11:30–2:30. Dinner: Monday–Thursday 5:30–10, Friday–Saturday 5:30–11. Cards: AE, CB, DC, MC, V. Reservations required. No-smoking section. Parking available in building. Full bar service. Handicap accessible. Small party room. Troubleshooter: Michael Foley (chef-owner). Expensive.

Chef Michael Foley is doing the kinds of things with domestic and imported ingredients not seen in Chicago before on such a grand, yet at the same time logical scale. He does not combine diverse ingredients merely for the sake of shock value, but his menu seems unlimited in imagination. Consider a Brazilian chowder with salmon, shrimp, mussels, and other seafood, accented with the bite of jalapeños, sharp or mild as you wish. Grilled chicken breast, the crosshatching of the grill stamped boldly on the poultry, comes with mushroom slices and the bite of cracked pepper sautéed together in a reduced sauce of butter and pinot noir. Not as heady as a port wine sauce might be, it serves to support, not overwhelm.

Seafood choices can be as simple as a grilled tuna steak garnished with nothing more than enoki mushrooms or fresh catfish with sesame seeds and lemon butter. A more exquisite presentation showcases bay scallops. These tiny pearls are sautéed with pieces of orange and cilantro and come with sun-dried tomato concasse. Foley's technique with a frypan is made apparent in his instead of deep frying them, he works in a shallow pan, constantly agitating and stirring to get all squid surfaces golden. The result is an airy, cloudlike creation.

Desserts include fresh ice creams and a luscious shortcake with a mix of fruits, all bedded in a rasberry purée.

K/Rating of 19.5/20: Decor 4/4, Service 5/5, Food 3.5/9, Value 2/2

MICHAEL STUART'S

American Nouvelle

140 South Wells, Chicago
Telephone: (312) 558-4700

Power Breakfast: Monday–Friday 6:30–10. Lunch: 11:30–4. Dinner: Monday–Friday 5–10, Saturday 5–11. Cards: AE, CB, DC, DISC, MC, V. Reservations suggested. Jackets and ties requested for gentlemen. No-smoking section. Free parking in lot at 145 South Wells after 5. Courtesy limo service to and from nearby cultural events. Full bar service; excellent wine list. Handicap accessible. Private party rooms for 15–125 people. Troubleshooter: Michael Lieberman (owner). Expensive.

There are dark woods and high-backed banquettes framing starched, immaculate white tablecloths. Waiters and waitresses are tuxedoed, obviously eager to please and seemingly well informed about the menu. Michael Stuart's is serving some of the most creative food currently found in Chicago. For example, a recent appetizer among daily specials was snails with slivers of red and green peppers surrounding a circle of goat cheese. (It is amazing how symbiotic the flavors and textures of snails and goat cheese can be.) More conventional, but no less delicious, is steamed mussels in a light saffron broth. Carpaccio, no longer the novelty it was a few years ago, is served with an herbed mayonnaise.

As delicate as some entrée selections can be, a large steak au poivre is substantial in both portion and flavor, lavish with its cracked-pepper goodness. And roast duckling in a sweet currant cream sauce is as satisfying as can be. Similarly, seafood fettuccine in a cream sauce is a lovely balance of texture and nautical flavors. Even a breaded veal chop takes the ordinary to a new plateau of satisfaction. Such enhancements as Minnesota wild rice soup are hard to pass up, as are the desserts, which include a chocolate turtle pie among several tantalizing selections.

K/Rating of 18/20: Decor 4/4, Service 3.5/5, Food 3.5/9, Value 2/2

CRICKET'S

100 East Chestnut, Chicago
Telephone: (312) 280-2100

Lunch: Monday–Friday noon–2:30. Dinner: Sunday–Thursday 6–10:30, Friday–Saturday 6–11:30. Brunch: Saturday noon–2:30, Sunday 11–2:30. Cards: AE, CB, DC, MC, V. Reservations mandatory. Jackets and ties required for gentlemen. Valet parking. Full bar service; cocktail lounge; extensive wine list. Handicap accessible. Private party room for up to 120 people. Troubleshooter: Jean Pierre Lutz (maître d'). Expensive.

American/Continental

This Chicago version of New York's 21 Club is a masculine, almost clublike sort of restaurant. The place reminds me of taverns that used to be called "tack rooms." At Cricket's, it's not so much horse racing memorabilia as it is artifacts of Chicago commerce, including baseball, football, newspaper paraphernalia, even earth-moving toys suspended from the ceiling. Food and service are exceptional. Waiters and captains seem to anticipate every need from replenishing an inexhaustible supply of hot rolls to topping off a goblet of wine. The à la carte menu, which changes seasonally, holds some wonderful selections. Saucing is virtually perfect, with just the correct nap of meat and fish. Among early courses, crème Senegalese has become a signature soup for the restaurant. Desserts include crêpes suzette, fresh fruits of the season, even rice pudding.

K/Rating 18.5/20: Decor 4/4, Service 5/5, Food 8/9, Value 1.5/2

GRAND & WELLS TAP

531 North Wells, Chicago
Telephone: (312) 645-1255

Lunch: Monday–Saturday 11:30–3. Dinner: Monday–Thursday 5-11, Friday–Saturday 5–11:30, Sunday 4–10. Cards: AE, CB, DC, MC, V. Reservations required. No-smoking section. Handicap accessible. Private party room for 300 or more people. Full bar service. Troubleshooter: Fran Lucatotoro (general manager). Expensive.

American/Italian

At Grand & Wells Tap, the steaks are as thick as a stick of butter and just about as smooth. A round loaf of warm bread and a scoop of butter are brought to each table as diners are seated. The menu comes next, straightforward about what's being offered. From the appetizers be sure to try focaccia—only bread and olive oil as described by the menu, but when matched with Tuscan garlic marinara, it's great for anyone with an advanced case of the munchies. The stuffed zucchini isn't so great, nor is the similarly prepared artichoke. But Grand & Wells Tap has some dandy pasta dishes. Try the house special: pasta and seafood with delicious nuggets of shrimp, crabmeat, and scallops in the marinara that puts this restaurant on my food map.

Among the entrées aside from pasta, breast of chicken Grand & Wells is a sautéed boneless breast of chicken in egg batter, served on a pasta bed with plum tomatoes, black olives, and plenty of seasoning. The best things on the menu, however, are the steaks. There are only three, but they are as good as they come. You can order your steak plain, al forno with grated parmesan broiled on top, or Tuscan style with that great marinara showing up again. Keeping in step with popular tastes, Grand & Wells Tap has begun featuring limited choices of daily fresh seafood. Ask your waiter for what's current and how it's being prepared. All dinners include a complimentary selection of fresh fruits and Italian cookies for dessert, although there are some fine à la carte choices, too. Friendly service and a comfortable atmosphere make Grand & Wells Tap a welcome addition to Chicago restaurants.

K/Rating 18.5/20: Decor 3.5/4, Service 5/5, Food 8/9, Value 2/2

CITY TAVERN

American/Eclectic

33 West Monroe, Chicago
Telephone: (312) 280-2740

Hours: Monday–Friday 7 am–9 pm, Saturday (Labor Day to spring) 11–9. Cards: AE, DC, MC, V. Reservations accepted. No-smoking section. Valet parking in evening; parking available in nearby garages. Full bar service. Handicap accessible. Troubleshooter: Mark Leavy (co-owner). Moderate.

There are times when you need a restaurant that just offers good food, reasonable prices, and quick service. That's particularly the case for a pre-theater supper, which raises the curtain on City Tavern, just across the street from Chicago's Schubert Theater. But this is more than just a restaurant for theatergoers. In addition to seating for 180 people, City Tavern houses a large circular bar, which gets especially busy after office hours.

The restaurant opens early enough to serve breakfast, stays open for lunch and dinner, and provides sustenance in between. Snackers will enjoy such appetizers as onion loaf, nachos, quesadillas, and even chicken tempura. Full dinners come with salad, rice or potatoes, and crusty, round loaves of bread. A light meal may also be made with any of several dinner-sized salads. The seafood salad features shredded crabmeat and whole shrimp among its mix of greens. City Tavern offers a variety of pasta dishes that come close to those served in ethnic Italian restaurants. Other dinners include excellent fresh choices. Among desserts is the same cappuccino ice cream served at Chestnut Street Grill (see page 16), and several attractions for dedicated chocoholics.

K/Rating of 16.5/20: Decor 3.5/4, Service 4/5, Food 7.5/9, Value 1.5/2

Chestnut Street Grill

American/Seafood

845 North Michigan (Water Tower Place Mezzanine Level), Chicago
Telephone: (312) 280-2720

Hours: Monday–Thursday 11:30–10:30, Friday–Saturday 11:30–midnight, Sunday 4:30–9:30. Sunday brunch: 11:30–2:30. Cards: AE, CB, DC, DISC, MC, V. Reservations only for parties of 6 or more evenings, all sizes for lunch. Discount parking in Water Tower garage. Full bar service. Handicap accessible. Troubleshooters: Terry Dixon (general manager) and Mark and Larry Levy (owners). Expensive.

The grill is attractively designed to capture a turn-of-the-century feeling: an effective use of wood moldings and a mosaic tile floor in a black-and-white pattern. Cafe curtains graciously separate the booths. Above all else, Chestnut Street Grill is a seafood restaurant with a difference: Most items are charcoal grilled over mesquite wood. This generally limits the menu to shellfish or firmer-fleshed fish that can stand up to searing heat and a ribbed grill surface.

I have sampled a number of specials and always come away impressed with the thought that this is consistently one of the city's better fish eateries. Swordfish, usually available, comes off particularly well when treated to charcoal grilling. Diners with light appetites will enjoy the quiche or the selection of omelets. Desserts include a fantastically delicious cappuccino ice cream; if you love coffee and chocolate, you'll rave about this after-dinner indulgence. For dieters, the grill has been serving a spa menu of sorts, with foods prepared sans butter, sans salt. In addition to the usual cocktails, there is a fine selection of beers, including stouts, plus an assembly of better California wines. Short of that, house wines by the carafe will not lead you to disaster.

K/Rating 18/20: Decor 4/4, Service 4.5/5, Food 8/9, Value 1.5/2

Cape Cod Room

Seafood

140 East Walton in the Drake Hotel, Chicago
Telephone: (312) 787-2200

Hours: daily noon–11. Cards: AE, CB, DC, MC, V. Reservations required. Jackets and ties required for gentlemen. Valet parking. Full bar service. Private party room for up to 20 people. Troubleshooter: Pat Bredin (maître d'). Expensive.

When people think of seafood in Chicago, the first place that comes to mind is the Cape Cod Room. There was a period a few years back when the restaurant's success seemed to interfere with the pleasures of fine dining. It was as if the place had been taken over by former U-boat captains who treated customers as if they were so much bilge. But that scourge has been lifted and the Cape Cod Room is right back up there among Chicago's top-notch restaurants.

There is some splendid eating here, from the selection of fresh bluepoints at the oyster bar to the pastries from the Drake Hotel's kitchen. Begin with a soup, perhaps the seafood gumbo, the creamy New England clam chowder, or the famous Bookbinder's snapper soup with an accent of sherry. The selection of whole fish is excellent. In addition to the printed menu, there are always daily specials. Among shellfish choices, I like the shrimp à l'indienne with its complementary curry accent. Crabmeat Maryland will attract diners with a taste for buttery richness.

The restaurant is a nautical vision, practically awash with artifacts from Davy Jones's locker. You will think that you are dining in a New England whaling village a century or more ago, when in fact you are just steps from Michigan Avenue and stylish Oak Street on Chicago's Magnificent Mile.

K/Rating 19/20: Decor 4/4, Service 5/5, Food 9/9, Value 1/2

SHAW'S CRAB HOUSE

Seafood

21 East Hubbard, Chicago
Telephone: (312) 527-2722

Lunch: Monday–Friday 11:30–2:30. Dinner: Monday–Friday 5:30–11, Saturday 5–11, Sunday 5–10. Blue Crab Lounge hours: Monday–Thursday 11:30–10, Friday until 11:30, Saturday 5–11. Cards: AE, CB, DC, MC, V, LEYE. Reservations for lunch only in main dining room. Jackets requested for men. No-smoking section. Parking across street. Two large bar areas, including the immensely popular and likable Blue Crab Lounge, serve a variety of wines, beers, and cocktails. Handicap accessible. Private party room for up to 52 people. Troubleshooter: Kevin Brown (manager). Expensive.

There may be nothing between here and the Atlantic coastline like Shaw's Crab House. I have the feeling it took designers quite a while to find just the right pieces and adornments. The same care and attention that went into the studied decor has obviously gone into preparation of the food. Dinner should begin with an appetizer, and, if you are lucky, it will be soft-shell crab season. These delectable little critters are quickly sautéed in butter and finished with toasted almonds or garlic as you choose. They come two to the appetizer or four to the dinner portion and are unbeatable.

Since dining is à la carte, and very pricy at that, you may want to move right on to a main course, although skipping something like the clam chowder or seafood gumbo may be hard to do. You might want one of the namesake crabs. The crab cakes are large, meaty, perfectly seasoned, and served with a spicy mustard and milder tartarlike sauce. The Nawlins'-style shrimp is a spicy rice casserole influenced by today's popular Cajun cuisine. This particular dish offers five medium-sized shrimp on a bed of highly seasoned, very spicy rice. For better than $12, it's not going to win recognition as one of the best values around town. And, in fact, that is the major flaw at Shaw's Crab House. Prices are simply too high for what is offered, good as it may be. Desserts are quite good and more fairly priced. Key lime pie has all the gusto of the real thing; a chocolate, caramel, and nut tart is worth every delicious calorie.

Service is friendly and well informed. Tables are rather close together, so if it's quiet intimacy you want, Shaw's Crab House is not the place. Otherwise, cash in a share or two of IBM and enjoy the authentic decor and, in most cases, unquestionably good food.

K/Rating of 15/20: Decor 4/4, Service 2.5/5, Food 8/9, Value .5/2

NICK'S FISHMARKET

Seafood

1 First National Bank Plaza, Chicago
Telephone: (312) 621-0200
Other location is listed opposite

Lunch: Monday–Friday 11:30–3. Dinner: Monday–Thursday 5:30–11, Friday–Saturday 5:30–11:30. Cards: AE, CB, DC, MC, V. Reservations required. Jackets requested for gentlemen. No-smoking section. Valet parking after 6 at Monroe Street entrance. Full bar service. Private party facilities for 20–250 people. Troubleshooter: Nick Nicholas (owner). Expensive.

Two things are usually said about Nick's Fishmarket. First, it is exceptionally good. Second, it is expensive. Both assertions are correct. Thirty dollars per person including a modest wine and tip is not an unusual check. However, portions are large, and the menu includes some seafoods not served in Chicago before Nick's opened. For instance, consider abalone in any of four preparations. The basic abalone dore is coated in an egg wash, floured, and sautéed in lemon butter. For an added flourish you may have abalone Ricci, the same preparation topped with sautéed asparagus spears, sliced mushrooms, and small shrimp. Other preparations offer the abalone with butter and capers or with almonds.

House specialties include mahimahi Veronique and good old American catfish. Opakapaka is a fish new to Chicago, thanks to Nick's. It works well with a lemony hollandaise. Bouillabaisse à la maison is appropriately seasoned with saffron and includes cut-up chunks of mahimahi, snapper, mussels, and other delectables in its broth. But the soup has a somewhat gelatinous quality that I find unappealing and totally out of character with fish stews. If you like scallops you will love the little morsels of fresh sautéed bay scallops; not a trace of sand or grit can be found.

You can begin dinner at Nick's with such excellent appetizers as softshell crabs or fried baby squid, which also come in dinner portions. Soups include thick, rich New England clam chowder, consommé, and gazpacho. And do not miss Nick's special salad, with one of the freshest-tasting spinach dressings I have ever enjoyed. Should you want dessert, savor cheesecake or mousse cake.

Nick's Fishmarket has a second location at 10275 West Higgins Road in Rosemont (312-298-8200).

K/Rating 19.5/20: Decor 4/4, Service 5/5, Food 9/9, Value 1.5/2

LINDO MEXICO RESTAURANT

Mexican

2642 North Lincoln, Chicago
Telephone: (312) 871-4832
Other location is listed below.

Hours: daily 11 am–2 am. Cards: AE, MC, DC, V. Reservations only for parties of 6 or more. No-smoking section. Valet parking Thursday–Saturday; street parking only on other nights. Full bar service; Mexican cocktails and beers. Handicap accessible. Troubleshooter: Roberto Martinez (owner). Inexpensive.

Although its large size makes this appear to be just another commercial Mexican restaurant, Lindo Mexico is about as authentic as they come. The diversity of the menu includes the so-called border foods, tacos, enchiladas, and the like. And they serve delicious fajitas, strips of steak or chicken, grilled with poblano peppers and wrapped with onions and tomatoes in the warmth of a soft tortilla. For burrito fans, the headliner is the large-size burrito stuffed to the brim with your choice of meats, plus vegetables, rice, frijoles, and a topping of guacamole, chopped tomatoes, a large dollop of sour cream, and shreds of lettuce. For a real change of pace, try the chicken or enchilada mole. It may look and even have the roughness of leftover coffee grounds, but mole is one of the great contributions to the enjoyment of Mexican cuisine.

If your idea of tongue comes from the corner delicatessen meat counter, try menudo, a variation of the classic Mexican stew with a rich tomato gravy and tender sliced tongue instead of tripe. Lindo Mexico has a couple of vegetarian choices as well as fish for nonmeat eaters.

Lindo Mexico Restaurant has a second location at 1934 Maple (312-475-3435), Evanston.

K/Rating of 17/20: Decor 4/4, Service 4/5, Food 7/9, Value 2/2

ZAVEN'S

260 East Chestnut, Chicago
Telephone: (312) 787-8260

Lunch: Monday–Friday 11:30–2:30. Dinner: daily 5:30–10:30. Cards: AE, CB, DC, MC, V, house accounts. Reservations suggested. Jackets required for gentlemen. Parking in public lots near building. Full bar service; cocktail lounge. Handicap accessible. Semiprivate balcony for up to 40 people. Troubleshooter: Zaven Kodjayan (owner). Expensive.

Continental

Zaven's makes no effort to be trendy. It is a reflection of a more traditional approach to food and ingredients. The taste combinations and textures remind me of the way restaurant chefs used to cook before nouvelle became the gastronomic byword. Soups and sauces are abundant with cream or butter. A lobster bisque is decadently rich in flavor and beautifully smooth.

From among entrées, I love the steak armagnac, which is a must for any lover of pepper steak. The waiter works tableside with his preparation cart, melting a chunk of butter as he heats the skillet. Then in goes the large cut of meat, perhaps fourteen ounces, sizzling on both sides, sauced with Worcestershire and Dijon mustard and, of course, heavily seasoned with freshly cracked pepper. Next comes a sizable splash of armagnac, flaming the meat and its unfinished sauce. To complete the dish, a thick bordelaise sauce is poured into the pan and is then joined by a large dollop of sour cream. It's the kind of cooking that might give cardiologists a fit, but it does make for satisfying dining.

Zaven's is one of the city's more romantic hideaways, perfect for a dinner for two where pampering should be part of the total dining experience. Handsome appointments add to the overall feeling of warmth and comfort that envelops diners.

K/Rating of 19/20: Decor 4/4, Service 5/5, Food 8.5/9, Value 1.5/2

CHEZ PAUL

660 North Rush, Chicago
Telephone: (312) 944-6680

Lunch: Monday–Friday 11:30–2:30. Dinner: Monday–Sunday 5:30–10:30. Cards: AE, CB, DC, MC, V. Reservations suggested. Jackets required for gentlemen. Full bar service. Private party facilities. Troubleshooters: Jean Pierre Sire (maître d') and Bill Contos (owner). Expensive.

French

Chez Paul continues year after year retaining old friends and winning new ones. Not a restaurant that chases a trend, Chez Paul offers diners a classic approach to French service and cuisine. A glance at the menu shows few changes, except for the inevitably higher prices. The food and service are on a par with the lovely old mansion decor. From the à la carte appetizer menu enjoy the seafood crêpe, a luscious balance of small firm shrimp and other edibles in a butter-rich sauce. Escargots are delicious little morsels tucked in their curved shells waiting to be drenched in melted butter. The hot and cold appetizers number about a dozen other choices. Seafood main courses are always exquisite. Or try the house specialty rack of lamb (single or double cut for two), carved tableside and perfectly garnished. Flamed pepper steak with armagnac is one of the more potent samples of beef. The fillet is studded with peppercorns and the bold sauce makes a stunning underpinning. Desserts are equally flamboyant in their own way, while the award-winning wine list provides a phenomenal collection for great drinking.

K/Rating 17/20: Decor 4/4, Service 4/5, Food 7.5/9, Value 1.5/2

THE EVEREST ROOM

French

440 South La Salle
(One Financial Place), Chicago
Telephone: (312) 663-8920

Lunch: Monday–Friday 11:30–2. Dinner: Tuesday–Friday 5:30–8:30, Saturday 6–9:30. Cards: AE, MC, V, La Salle Club membership, LEYE. Reservations required. Jackets required for gentlemen. No-smoking section. Free parking in building garage. Full bar service. Handicap accessible. Private party room for 75–100 people for sit-down dinner, 150 for cocktails. Troubleshooter: Jean Joho (chef). Expensive.

Drawing upon Mt. Everest as a metaphor for the pinnacle of greatness, The Everest Room has showcased chef Jean Joho's talent in a handsome blend of rich furnishings, extravagant chandeliers, and even a touch of big game hunting ambience. The chef first made his mark on the city at Maxim's, literally cooking in a basement; now forty floors above the street, diners look out on a cityscape as they await each dinner course.

The printed menu lists half a dozen appetizer choices headed by a lovely ballottine of quail on a purée of mushroom truffle mousse with an evanescent taste that only hints of its substance. Another top-of-the-line choice is foie gras from New York State with a dark port sauce and garnish of Belgian endive. The garniture of all the platters is especially effective, the foods imaginatively presented on oversized dinnerware. A prime example of visual artistry at its summit would be the evening special of shrimp sachet, an uncanny creation of thin phyllolike pastry, each sheet formed into the petal of a flower centered around a bulb. Inside the bulb are delicious whole shrimp at rest on a ragout of leeks and mushrooms, the whole napped in an intense lobster sauce. An appetizer to make even the most jaded palate curious was a recent offering of escargot mousse with escargot caviar, the roe of the snail.

Speaking of intense, that's the word to describe chef Joho's soups. Cream of mushroom is a deceptively thin broth that explodes in the kind of flavor that bites at the back of your throat in the same way a fine, old well-aged claret does. Among à la carte salads is one described on the menu as being served with Illinois goat cheese. The fact of the matter is that the supply is irregular, though the goat cheese is always domestic and without the tang characteristic of French chèvre. Still, it makes a refreshing salad of stylish greens in a light vinaigrette.

The parade that makes up the main-course options is almost too tempting. From the printed menu, the choice includes John Dory wrapped in a pastry crust, then roasted with potatoes and fresh thyme. Chef Joho's signature creation, salmon soufflé Paul Haeberlin, is a tribute to his mentor. Roast breast of duck comes with oriental nappa cabbage, though the recipe seems more inspired by the chef's native Alsace.

There are some small problems. Boned whole Dover sole may still retain enough tiny bones to be annoying. But fillet of beef, which could be ordinary, is enhanced by the handsome bouquet of delicate vegetable accompaniment and the ragout of scallions and chives upon which the fillet rests.

Desserts are highlighted by a superb pear brûlée. In contrast, chocolate fondant is hardly more entrancing than ordinary pudding. Service is excellent; the descriptions of presentations are positively sensual.

By the way, recent topological research has shown that Everest's Himalayan neighbor, K2, is a higher peak. But who would want to name a restaurant K2?

K/Rating of 19.75/20: Decor 4/4, Service 5/5, Food 8.75/9, Value 2/2

THE BERGHOFF

German

17 West Adams, Chicago
Telephone: (312) 427-3170

Hours: Monday–Saturday 11–10. Cards: AE, MC, V. Reservations only for parties of 5 or more. No-smoking section. Parking at adjacent garage after 5 ($3). Full bar service; 75-foot-long standup bar plus two service bars feature the restaurant's own label whiskey and beers plus call brands; full wine list. Private party rooms for 25–175 people. Troubleshooter: Herman Berghoff (owner). Inexpensive.

After a day of shopping along the State Street Mall, The Berghoff is a great place for a quick and inexpensive dinner. At lunchtime the restaurant is certain to be crowded with attorneys and judges taking a break from the busy schedule of cases at the nearby Dirksen Federal Building. Either time, lunch or dinner, you will find efficient service and some top-notch German-style foods.

The menu changes daily, but certain standards such as sauerbraten, German pot roast, and kassler rippchen (smoked loin of pork) are available all the time. Though some fish and steaks are listed on the menu at somewhat higher cost than many of the German preparations, the broiled strip steak could be one of the better values in this town of top-quality steak restaurants. Many dinners include salad and potato or vegetable. You will find appetizers as exotic as French snails, but Bismarck herring for a dollar is more in keeping with the character of this sprawling restaurant.

Waiters are of the old school: Black trousers and white shirts and aprons are their dress; service is efficient, if lacking familiarity until you become a regular. The Berghoff is noted for its special blended whiskey as well as its house beer, dark and light. This restaurant has been around for 80 years; I hope it goes strong for at least 180 more.

K/Rating 17/20: Decor 4/4, Service 3.5/5, Food 7.5/9, Value 2/2

La Gondola

Italian

2425 North Ashland, Chicago
Telephone: (312) 248-4433

Hours: Tuesday–Sunday 4–11. Cards: AE, D, MC, V. Reservations suggested. No-smoking section. Full bar service. Handicap accessible. Private party room available Monday only for up to 30 people. Troubleshooters: Luciano Librire and Dominic Amodeo (owners). Moderate.

La Gondola is the first Italian restaurant in Chicago I've found that genuinely encourages people to dine in the Italian manner. The key to real Italian dining has to do not only with what foods are ordered, but how they are ordered. The idea is to let each preceding course dictate the next. In other words, order a first course and when that is done, a second, and when that is done, a third, and so on until the end of the meal.

The economics of the restaurant business dictate that a dinner table should turn over two to three times in an evening. My guest and I at La Gondola were encouraged to ignore that demand of time, to linger, to order as we were ready and not by some schedule. Begin dinner with wine; a semidry Orvieto complements a large serving platter practically overflowing with lightly breaded, deep-fried zucchini slices, baked clams, deep-fried baby calamari, and stuffed whole calamari. Whole calamari often come out with the texture of a sponge; La Gondola prepares them carefully.

Next, choose a pasta course. La Gondola does not make their own noodles, but that hardly seems to matter. Once selected, your waitress brings a platter, presented family style.

The logic to ordering course by course suggests that only a glutton could choose too much food. Having finished two courses, plus steaming bowls of minestrone, take some time before main course selections. Though the menu is rather standard-issue Italian, you are certain to find several items that will please. The most difficult part is deciding which ones.

Having been moderate about main course selections, you can still look forward to dessert. Bisque tortoni and cannoli are the perfect finishing touches. I have yet to find the restaurant that makes its bisque from scratch; at least La Gondola has a good supplier. Although the cannoli shells come from outside, the kitchen does do the sweet filling.

K/Rating 16.5/20: Decor 3/4, Service 5/5, Food 6.5/9, Value 2/2

THE VILLAGE

Italian

71 West Monroe, Chicago
Telephone: (312) 332-7005

Lunch: Monday–Saturday 11–3. Dinner: Monday–Thursday 4:30–12:30 am, Friday–Saturday 4:30–1:30 am, Sunday noon–midnight. Cards: AE, CB, DC, MC, V. Reservations accepted. Casual dress, but no shorts. No-smoking section. Valet parking after 5:30 ($3). Full bar service; 987 bottlings on wine list. Private party room for up to 30 people. Troubleshooter: Ray Capitanini (owner). Moderate.

In the restaurant industry where the average lifespan of any establishment is perhaps five years, it is worth noting that The Village is more than sixty years old and still going strong. This restaurant has even spawned two others in its building, the casual La Cantina and the posh Florentine Room.

The Village is the antithesis of trendy. Yes, it is noisy, a condition favored by many new restaurateurs, but this noise just happens because of the crowds, not because of design or marketing strategy. Service may lack some of the finesse of more expensive restaurants, but you won't ever be troubled by a waiter who marches up and announces, "Hi, my name is Bruce!" And if the noise sometimes makes The Village less than romantic, the decor makes up for it. The rear wall is complete with crescent moon hanging low in the night sky, as if one is looking at a small Italian village perched up in the Tuscan hills.

The menu is vast, not especially innovative, but easily satisfying. You probably could find some two hundred different items or more among the legion of courses. A full dinner can be ordered by adding $1.50 to your dining price; this surcharge brings an appetizer, soup, salad, dessert, and beverage to your table. But even ordering à la carte, dining is not catastrophically expensive.

There is room for improvement with some menu choices. For instance, an order of fried calamari is not only too expensive, but not all that well prepared. The squid can sometimes be a bit tough, and the accompanying sauce is rather bland. On top of that, considering the price, the portion is small.

Nothing else I have had here seems small portioned, however. A pasta course was easily enough for two and was graciously presented split. From a selection that includes perhaps three dozen choices, we chose linguine with scallops in a pesto sauce. I would have liked the pasta to have been a tad less oily, but otherwise the pesto sauce was perfect and the small bay scallops tender. This is the kind of pasta to wrap around your fork and savor for flavor and texture.

Skipping over soup and salad, we moved on to our main courses, chicken Vesuvio and veal piccante. The menu describes the veal as sautéed with capers, pepperoncini (small red peppers), onions, and the always-present garlic. The scallops came in a creamy vegetable sauce reminiscent of that served with chicken à la king; it was not any veal dish I know. The chicken Vesuvio was a powerhouse of garlicky, buttery flavor, the disjointed chicken half crisp on the outside and hot and moist inside. The roasted potatoes absorbed all the flavors of the butter and garlic in which they were served.

The menu goes on and on with pastas, chops, pizza, and even sandwiches. Bisque tortoni for dessert smoothed out any rough edges from earlier courses. And I would have preferred brewed decaffeinated coffee, instead of instant.

The Village is a landmark of its kind, usually busy and boisterous, reminiscent of earlier days in the Chicago restaurant business. I suspect it will carry on for another sixty years . . . maybe more.

K/Rating of 16/20: Decor 3.5/4, Service 4/5, Food 7/9, Value 1.5/2

LA STRADA

Northern Italian

155 North Michigan (at Randolph), Chicago
Telephone: (312) 565-2200

Lunch: Monday–Friday 11:30–2:30. Dinner: Monday–Thursday 5–10, Friday–Saturday 5–10:30. Cards: AE, CB, DC, MC, V. Valet parking at night or parking adjacent to Grant Park garage. Full bar service; cocktail lounge; wine list with 200 selections. Private party accommodations available on 38th floor, Top of the Plaza. Troubleshooter: Alberto (maître d'). Expensive.

In richly appointed surroundings, La Strada has joined the top rank of restaurants in and around Chicago. Service is lavish, with enough space between tables for a degree of privacy and for waiters and captains to do whatever tableside preparation may be demanded for a given order. While the restaurant serves foods from most regions of Italy, the emphasis is on the north, where cream-based sauces replace tomato and where more subtle seasonings are not overpowered by garlic.

Veal gets prominent treatment, as is fitting in better Italian dining. Veal piccata is the expected thin scallops finished in butter and lemon sauce. The house namesake, scaloppine di vitello della Strada, comes from Italy's middle region; scallops of veal are cooked with prosciutto, fontina cheese, and the bite of lemon. The highlights are mussels in an excellent light tomato, wine, and herb sauce; exceptional rolled eggplant stuffed with cheese, lightened with eggs, and given a touch of tomato sauce glaze; and carpaccio, the Italian version of steak tartare in which thin strips of raw fillet are splattered with a dash or two of olive oil and lemon juice and garnished with small pieces of parmesan. Soups include a clear chicken broth with eggs (stracciatella romano), tortellini in capon broth, and fresh minestrone. If you like to make a meal of pasta, La Strada offers several pleasures. One special of the day was imported rigatoni stuffed with parmesan, bits of tomato, and a light cream binder. Or try linguine in pesto, the rich basil sauce that adds so much flavor to dining.

The restaurant has an excellent wine list, deep with reasonably priced Italian reds and whites. The dessert selection seems rather thin by comparison, although strawberries served with a touch of sugar and imported Italian white vinegar is a surprisingly fresh way of livening up the ordinary.

K/Rating 17.5/20: Decor 4/4, Service 4.5/5, Food 7.5/9, Value 1.5/2

MAMA DESTA'S RED SEA RESTAURANT

Ethiopian

3216 North Clark, Chicago
Telephone: (312) 935-7561

Hours: Tuesday–Sunday 11:30–11:30, Monday 4:30–10:30. Cards: AE, DC, MC, V. No reservations. No-smoking section. Discount parking available. No alcoholic beverages. Handicap accessible. Private party facilities except Saturday. Troubleshooter: Tekle W. Gabriel (owner). Inexpensive.

Mama Desta's Red Sea Restaurant serves Ethiopian food, and though the owners may have left their homeland, they have not deserted its heritage. The restaurant is decorated with photographs and various other arts and crafts; especially interesting is a large frieze showing the Ethiopian version of the story of Solomon and the Queen of Sheba. The foods are quite flavorful and the presentation is classic Ethiopian. There are no knives and forks. Instead, the various foods are served on flat, bread rounds called injera; they look much like large pancakes and have a slightly fermented taste. (This may be the world's first sourdough bread, even though San Franciscans are more famous for it.)

The menu ranges through exotic fashionings of chicken, lamb, beef, fish, and vegetables. Unless you already know the difference between yebig alitcha and zilzil wat, you'll need some personal assistance from the waiter. As with so many ethnic cuisines, a combination platter gives the best introduction.

A waiter will bring out six or seven small bowls and platters, each holding a different creation. These are arranged in front of you on the injera. Before you tear off a piece of the bread and wrap it around some meat or vegetable, take a moment to look at what is displayed at your table. You will see a beautiful array of colors and textures, what might be set out for a guest of honor at an East African banquet.

K/Rating 18/20: Decor 3/4, Service 5/5, Food 8/9, Value 2/2

HUE

Vietnamese

1138 West Argyle, Chicago
Telephone: (312) 275-4044

Hours: Tuesday–Friday 11:30–10, Saturday–Sunday 1–11. Cards: DISC, MC, V. Reservations accepted. Street parking difficult; parking lot available after 6 weekdays and all day Saturday at 5031 North Broadway. No alcoholic beverages. Private party facilities available weeknights for 25 or more people. Troubleshooter: Nancy Orchid Tran (owner). Inexpensive.

Hue is one of several restaurants on Chicago's Far North Side serving the city's burgeoning Vietnamese community, as well as the rest of us fascinated by this still-exotic cuisine. The menu offers concise explanations of some truly striking preparations that illustrate the Asian concern for balance in all things. Thus, smooth textures contrast with coarse, and cool temperatures are accented with hot seasonings. For example, the spring rolls, which come three to the order, are circles of translucent rice paper wrapped around a filling of cold meat and vegetables, served with a spicy peanut sauce. There are some enchanting soups, the asparagus crab among them.

Unusual combinations are part of the Vietnamese table. You can order chao tom, coarsely ground shrimp pressed tubelike around a length of sugarcane and then grilled. The idea is to remove slices of the shrimp from the sugarcane bit by bit, and wrap them in rice paper with some sauce to taste. (The chao tom is served only on weekends.) Although stir-fried chicken with walnuts and snow peas may sound like what you'd find in a Chinese restaurant, it is far from that. The walnuts have a depth seldom found in the Chinese style of cooking. For a more tropical accent, try spicy chicken with lemongrass and peppers.

K/Rating of 16/20: Decor 2/4, Service 5/5, Food 7/9, Value 2/2

Chicago Hwe Kwon

Korean

4918 North Lincoln, Chicago
Telephone: (312) 878-0999

Hours: Monday–Saturday 11:30–midnight, Sunday 11:30–10:30. Reservations unnecessary. No cards. Private party room for up to 50 people. No alcoholic beverages. Troubleshooter: Chang Sung Song (owner). Inexpensive.

One of the biggest pleasures available in Chicago is the search for storefront ethnic restaurants. So, when I saw a place with a sign in large Korean script with "Korean Restaurant" the only English translation, I could hardly wait to try it. A bright, fairly large dining room welcomes diners. Most tables have a gas-fired burner for preparation of grilled meats or other specialties that are hallmarks of Korean food. As with other Asian dining experiences, going with a party of six or eight people will enable you to order a greater variety of tastes.

The menu makes no distinction between appetizers and entrées, but no matter what you order, several small saucers will be the first things delivered. They will contain the pickled, peppery cabbage called kimchi, which is virtually a Korean national passion, several kinds of pickled or even candied radishes, spinach, seaweed, dried fish, tofu, and other nibbles.

You should order pajun, a Korean-style pancake in which the batter has been mixed with green onions. The texture is much like cornbread, the flavor delicious and well suited to a few sprinkles of ginger soy sauce. Try the meat-filled fried dumplings called duk mandoo kuk, or any of a trio of noodle dishes.

Then move onto the meats and fish. Chicken bokem is a delicious platter of small pieces in a spicy sauce. Monkfish, served in deep-fried chunks, lives up to its nickname "mock lobster." Grilled marinated beef is exceptional, whether as short ribs or in slices.

K/Rating 18/20: Decor 3/4, Service 4/5, Food 9/9, Value 2/2

Ron of Japan

Japanese

230 East Ontario, Chicago
Telephone: (312) 644-6500
Other location is listed opposite.

Dinner: Monday–Thursday 5–10, Friday–Saturday 5–11, Sunday 4:30–10. Cards: AE, CB, DC, MC, V. Reservations suggested. No-smoking section. Valet parking. Full bar service. Troubleshooter: Rieko Shito and Tom Aoyama (managers). Expensive.

Among Chicago's Japanese teppan restaurants, Ron of Japan is about the best. Teppan refers to the flat griddle around which diners sit and observe a chef work his magic. You can get a feel for the samurailike precision with which vegetables are diced, shrimp are flayed, and meats cut and cooked. It is a real treat to watch a master and at the same time enjoy the wonderful mingling of aromas rising from the griddle.

Japan is famous for its Kobe beef, and while it is not available here, you can be sure that all the beef served at Ron's is prime. Dinners include a small salad with soy-based dressing, a clear chicken soup, grilled vegetables and rice, plus dessert and tea. You can go all out and order the shogun dinner, which adds a lobster tail appetizer, but I frankly don't think a lobster tail is worth the extra $13 or so charged. The same steak dinner without the lobster can be ordered from the imperial dinners list. These begin at $9.95 for an all-vegetable selection and go up to nearly $17 for sirloin steak. For those who prefer something other than the beef dinners, teppan shrimp, sautéed on the grill and topped with an egg batter, is a delicious alternative.

Ron of Japan is an excellent way to introduce children to a different experience. They, like you, will be fascinated with the beautiful Japanese decor and with the colorful way in which the cooking is done right at your table.

Ron of Japan has a second location at 633 Skokie Boulevard (312-564-5900), Northbrook.

K/Rating of 18.5/20: Decor 4/4, Service 4.5/5, Food 8.5/9, Value 1.5/2

CHICAGO: NORTH

NEAR NORTH
MIDNORTH
NORTH
FAR NORTH

NEAR NORTH

THE PUMP ROOM

American

1301 North State Parkway, in the Hotel Omni, Ambassador East, Chicago
Telephone: (312) 266-0360

Hours: Monday–Thursday 7 am–11 pm, Friday–Saturday 7 am–midnight. Sunday brunch: 10:30–2:30. Sunday dinner: 5–10. Cards: AE, CB, DC, MC, V, LEYE. Reservations mandatory. Jackets required for gentlemen in evening. No-smoking section. Valet parking. Full bar service. Private party facilities in hotel. Troubleshooter: Rich Melman (owner). Expensive.

The Pump Room has just observed its fiftieth anniversary, and the world is far different from those days in 1938 when the doors first opened under the guidance of legendary Chicago restaurateur Ernie Byfield.

The restaurant long ago shed the formality that made it a place for movie stars and political elites. Now most of the stars are of the TV and rock-music variety and booth one still remains as good a place as any in town to spot a luminary. As for the food, it continues to be handsomely served with as much attention to detail as is possible in a kitchen geared to turning out some two hundred dinners at a crack. Desserts are top-notch, as is the wine list. All in all, The Pump Room has matured considerably since those days of The Twentieth Century Limited when Milton Berle would quip, "Everything comes served on a flaming sword, except the check!"

K/Rating 17/20: Decor 4/4, Service 5/5, Food 7/9, Value 1/2

THE BUTCHER SHOP

American

358 West Ontario, Chicago
Telephone: (312) 440-4900

Dinner: Sunday–Thursday, 5–10, Friday–Saturday 5–11. Cards: AE, MC, V. Reservations accepted. No-smoking section. Valet parking. Full bar service; wine list heavy on California bottlings. Private party room for 30–400 people. Troubleshooter: Dennis Day (manager). Moderate.

You can't complain about your steak being overcooked or undercooked at The Butcher Shop, since you probably will be doing the grilling yourself. The Butcher Shop is the Chicago edition of a growing chain of steak restaurants around the country. The steaks are all choice grade and priced at $15.95, no matter what the cut. You pay $2.00 more if the restaurant's chefs do the cooking for you.

But going to the grill yourself here is half the fun. Chances are you'll strike up a conversation with other people who have the same thing on their minds as do you . . . namely, how good that steak is going to taste after it has been treated to some seasonings and about twenty minutes over the coals. And if you should have a problem, your waiter or one of the grillmen will help.

The steaks run from a fourteen-ounce bacon-wrapped filet mignon to a giant twenty-eight-ounce porterhouse. All come with a handsome salad and baked potato. If that sounds like too much to eat, diners can opt to split any of the steaks and each pay $10.95 to cover the setup, extra salad, and potato. It may be the best steak dinner deal in town.

As for quality, the twenty-ounce rib eye is fine. The beef is tender and without any rough spots. Since diners can go up to the large cooler cabinets and pick out individual cuts, it is unlikely that anything could go wrong. Plus, my waiter gave the impression that the people running The Butcher Shop will do all they can to make sure every diner leaves satisfied.

There are a couple of choices other than steak on the menu, including marinated chicken breasts ($11.95), two boneless breasts grilled over charcoal.

K/Rating 18/20: Decor 4/4, Service 5/5, Food 7/9, Value 2/2

LAWRY'S THE PRIME RIB

American

100 East Ontario, Chicago
Telephone: (312) 787-5000

Lunch: Monday–Friday 11:30–2. Dinner: Monday–Thursday 5–10:30, Friday–Saturday 5–11:30, Sunday 3–9:30. Cards: AE, CB, DC, MC, V. Reservations suggested. Jackets and ties requested for gentlemen. No-smoking section. Full bar service. Extensive private party and banquet facilities, including separate cocktail lounge; controlled lighting and stage area for audio-visual presentations. Troubleshooter: Thomas McHugh (general manager). Moderate.

Since it first opened, Lawry's has run into stiff competition from such beef specialty houses as Morton's (page 37) and The Palm (page 39), but the prime rib served here remains the house specialty and is a definite attraction for beef eaters. In fact, prime rib is the only thing served at dinner. It is carved from a rolling silver cart in one of three thicknesses ($16.95–$22.95) and served with a sometimes overly dry Yorkshire pudding, mashed potatoes, and a house salad. At lunch, Lawry's offers a variety of entrées, including lighter fare such as salads, fish, and omelets, as well as a variety of beef choices. Desserts are sweet and grandiose. An excellent selection of wines is cellared.

K/Rating of 17.5/20: Decor 3/4, Service 5/5, Food 8/9, Value 1.5/2

THAT STEAK JOYNT

American

1610 North Wells, Chicago
Telephone: (312) 943-5091

Hours: Sunday 4–2 am, Monday–Thursday 5–2 am, Friday–Saturday 5–3 am. Cards: AE, CB, DC, DISC, JCB, MC, V. Reservations suggested. Discount parking in nearby garage. Full bar service; one of the most extensive wine collections in the city. Handicap accessible. Three private party rooms for 20–50 people, sit-down dinners for up to 300 people. Troubleshooter: Billy Siegel (owner).
Moderate.

That Steak Joynt serves up about as good a piece of beef as you'll find. And they do it with variety: broiled, charcoaled, sautéed, with or without onions and garlic. You name it, and they can do it. I've never been crazy about their bérnaise sauce, but at least it is different. The barbecued ribs continue to be among the most popular in the city. The atmosphere remains 1880s San Francisco bawdy house. Service is accomplished with courtesy and finesse. This is the kind of place that really knows how to pamper a guest. If you have a friend visiting Chicago for the first time, That Steak Joynt will give him or her a good feel for how the town and Wells Street's Olde Town used to be. The ornate antique bar may be the only one in existence with a built-in piano. Bruce Neils is at the keyboard; you've probably heard him playing the organ at Cubs home games.

K/Rating 18.5/20: Decor 4/4, Service 5/5, Food 7.5/9, Value 2/2

ED DEBEVIC'S

American

640 North Wells, Chicago
Telephone: (312) 664-1707
Other location is listed opposite.

Hours: Monday–Thursday 11–midnight, Friday–Saturday 11–1 am, Sunday 11–10. Cards: LEYE. No reservations. Dress code: angora sweaters, bowling shirts, saddle shoes, etc. Valet parking and street parking. Full bar service. Handicap accessible. Private party rooms for 25 and 35 people each. Troubleshooter: Here? You've got to be kidding! . . . but you could contact Lettuce Entertain You, Inc. if you have a problem.
Inexpensive.

Ed Debevic's is in a time warp. The goal was to re-create those diners that dotted America in the 1950s. They were all about the same. The food was secondary. Guys looking for girls, and vice versa, were not all that concerned with the haute cuisine of the local gathering spot. What was important was a jukebox with the latest by Elvis, The Everly Brothers, and Buddy Holly. That, by and large, is what Ed Debevic's is all about. There may not be carhops, but it's still a teenage hangout for grownups, and maybe for those among us who don't want to grow up.

The restaurant is probably larger than most hangouts of the fifties. But the seats are covered with that sickly blue plastic that was someone's idea of interior decoration in the days before golden arches and whoppers. The food is good enough for what it is. The meat is ground fresh for the hamburgers. And the chicken-fried steak tastes just as chicken-fried steak should taste. The fried chicken is like what we had in those good old days thirty years ago when pimples were of more concern than cholesterol. The malts are thick and flavorful; no, yummy would be a better word. Chances are you won't find a better malt or shake anywhere.

Ed Debevic's has a second location at 660 West Lake Cook Road (312-945-3242), Deerfield.

K/Rating of 16.5/20: Decor 4/4, Service 5/5, Food 5.5/9, Value 2/2

CHICAGO CHOP HOUSE

American

60 West Ontario, Chicago
Telephone: (312) 787-7100

Hours: Monday–Friday 11:30 am–2:30 am, Saturday–Sunday 5–2 am. Cards: AE, CB, DC, MC, V, house accounts. Reservations suggested. Casual dress. No-smoking section. Valet parking. Full bar service; handsome long bar reminiscent of nineteenth-century Chicago; extensive wine list; piano bar. Private party room for 10–90 people. Troubleshooter: Henry Norton (owner). Moderate.

Chicago Chop House is splashed with antique-style photographs and etchings of the city's history. The first floor is occupied by one of the best-looking bars in the city, a serpentine affair that wraps its way around in an invitation to conversation. The main dining room is up a flight of stairs.

The menu is straightforward, with little in the way of frills. Beef is the big item here. I use the word "big" with all deliberateness since the restaurant actually serves a sixty-four ounce porterhouse steak for $64 or a forty-eight-ounce version for $18 less. The still large, but by comparison more modest T-bone for $25, the still smaller filet mignon, and the tried-and-true New York strip are all featured, as are traditional roast prime rib and assorted chops. Seafood includes swordfish, Dover sole, and french-fried jumbo shrimp in a beer batter, as well as a few other choices.

There is time to linger between courses and even after dinner, which is a positive note about hospitality.

K/Rating of 18.5/20: Decor 3.5/4, Service 4.5/5, Food 8.5/9, Value 2/2

HARRY CARAY'S

American/Steaks

33 West Kinzie, Chicago
Telephone: (312) HOLYCOW

Lunch: daily 11:30–3. Dinner: Sunday–Thursday 5:30–10:30, Friday–Saturday 5–midnight. Bar hours: daily 11:30–1:30 am. Cards: AE, MC, V, house accounts. Reservations for lunch only (dinner waits substantial). Casual, but neat dress. No-smoking section. Valet parking, parking lot, and street parking. Full bar service; service bar is 50 feet long (the distance from pitcher's mound to home plate); excellent list of Italian and American wines and domestic and imported beers. Private party rooms for up to 250 people for sit-down banquet, 500 people for cocktails and hors d'oeuvres. Troubleshooter: Kenton C. Jenkins (manager). Expensive.

Just for the record, Harry is more inspiration than restaurateur. The place is owned and handled by restaurant professionals and must be judged on that basis.

The menu is a mix of meat, fish, and some Italian specialties. Service is cordial, with just the perfect amount of personality. Right out of the batter's box, try an excellent seafood salad. The portion, large enough to split for two, is loaded with cold squid, perhaps some cod, shrimp, and other seafood, all in an oil and vinegar dressing seasoned with herbs. A less successful choice from the appetizer list, which also includes carpaccio, shrimp cocktail, roasted peppers, and fresh or baked clams, is toasted ravioli. Toasting defeats the whole purpose of this pasta, which is meant to be tender, not crisp.

Things get back to high ground as you begin to round the bases of entrées. From a list of pastas and other Italian specialties, the spaghetti carbonara is a solid hit. The pasta is bathed in a full-flavored sharp cheese sauce that clings to each noodle. Bits of bacon are tossed into this classic recipe. A couple of turns of the pepper mill, and it's better than a seat in the bleachers. If you like lamb, you'll love a trio of lamb chops oreganato. These are simply broiled lean chops, meaty and with the kind of flavor you'd trade away your best shortstop for. Among other meat selections is veal piccante, a major leaguer on any team. This veal, however, can be a bit light on buttery sweetness, though tender enough easily to be a two bagger.

Batting cleanup at Harry Caray's are the steaks and other chops, a full lineup from porterhouse to peppered.

Rounding third and heading for home plate are desserts, piled high on a three-layer cart, just waiting to be picked for your All-Star Team. They range from apple tart to chocolate torte and pumpkin cheesecake.

Harry Caray's is in the World Series of sports restaurants.

K/Rating of 17.5/20: Decor 4/4, Service 4/5, Food 7.5/9, Value 2/2

MORTON'S

American/Steaks/Lobster

1050 North State, Chicago
Telephone: (312) 266-4820
Other locations are listed below.

Dinner: Monday–Friday 5:30–midnight, Saturday 5:30–1 am. Cards: AE, CB, DC, MC, V. Reservations taken only before 7 and after 10. Parking available in building. Full bar service and lounge. Troubleshooter: George Jimenez (manager). Expensive.

Tucked away in what used to be a basement storage area in posh Newberry Plaza, Morton's has become one of Chicago's most popular restaurants. Even though prices are up there ($40 per person is not uncommon), it's often hard to get a table without a wait. But if steak or lobster is your dish, the wait can be worthwhile. There is a chalkboard menu near the front of the spacious, stuccoed dining room. Specialties include a twenty-four-ounce T-bone or a slightly smaller sirloin, as well as excellent double-cut prime rib. Lobsters are hefty enough to feed two or more people. Appetizers, salads, and desserts are à la carte. Order the dessert soufflé when you place your main order since it takes time to bake.

Morton's has a second location at 22nd and Wolf Road (312-526-7000), Westchester, and a third at 9525 West Bryn Mawr (312-678-5155), Rosemont.

K/Rating 19/20: Decor 3.5/4, Service 5/5, Food 9/9, Value 1.5/2

DITKA'S

American/Steak/Chops

223 West Ontario, Chicago
Telephone: (312) 280-1790

Lunch: daily 11–3. Dinner: 5–midnight. City Lights: 9 pm–4 am. Cards: AE, CB, DC, MC, V. Reservations only for lunch. No-smoking section. Valet parking. Full bar service and lounge. Handicap accessible. Extensive private party facilities. Troubleshooter: Ed Minasian (Mike's busy with the Bears). Expensive.

Ditka's is the kind of place you would go to if rubbing shoulders with sports stars is especially important. That doesn't mean each time you visit you are going to run into a linebacker or nose guard, or even the coach himself. But presumably the possibility is there to bend elbows with the celebs.

And make no mistake about it, a lot of elbow bending goes on at Ditka's. At least half the floor space is given to a large rectangular bar, not to mention the vast, even cavernous City Lights Night Club in the same building.

It is perhaps fitting that Ditka's and City Lights are housed in a structure that once was home to a trucking company, because the food served here comes out in truck-sized portions. This is a meat-and-potatoes operation, with the kind of food the guys like, and if their wives or girlfriends do too, well that's all the better. The menu is short and to the point. All dinners come with your choice of a side potato, including mammoth baked or cottage fries, or sautéed onions. First out after you sit down is a basket of onion bread and butter. This is not the same onion bread Chicagoans might remember from Fritzel's a decade or more ago, but at least the memory is brought to mind. You could begin with an appetizer or salad; order both and you really won't need any dinner. At least one of the salads, the appropriately named Fridge, is a meal in itself and then some. You'll get a heaping bowl of greens mixed with other vegetables and large chunks of beef, ham, chicken, and just about anything else in the fridge. You'd need the appetite of number 72 just to finish the whole thing in one sitting. But not to worry; you can take leftovers home in what are called Grabowski Bags.

Chances are you'll end up taking home a portion of the twenty-four-ounce T-bone steak. Do people really eat that much steak these days? Well, if you do, it's at Ditka's. Not only is the steak large, but it is also tender, marbled but not gristled. Order it rare and that's how it comes; ask that it be rubbed with garlic or butter and you've got it. Incidentally, I think an à la carte Caesar salad is a good way to preface you steak. It's as tangy as they come.

Smaller steaks are also served, as is a single veal chop, a trio of pork chops, and lamb chops. A delicious calf's liver steak is sweet and flavorful, and yes it is buttery tender. For liver lovers, this one is a gem.

There are few seafood choices, but, like everything else on the menu, they tend to be hearty. A case in point is swordfish, crosshatched from the grill, served without any embellishments to mask the natural flavor of this meatlike fish. Except for a chocolate mousse cake (do real men eat mousse?), desserts stick to the basics—cheesecake, ice creams, fresh fruits. Bar drinks tend to be expensive, as are the wines from a not very impressive list. Service is friendly and always helpful.

Ditka's is crowded and boisterous, ideal for people whose good time includes more than just good food.

K/Rating of 17/20: Decor 3.5/4, Service 5/5, Food 7/9, Value 1.5/2

Carson's

American/Ribs

612 North Wells, Chicago
Telephone: (312) 280-9200
Other locations are listed below.

Hours: daily 11–midnight. Cards: AE, DC, MC, V. No reservations. Ample free parking. Full bar service. Moderate.

Ask most Chicagoans where the best ribs are, and chances are they will tell you Carson's. The reason these ribs get such accolades is the sauce, a pungent, spicy-sweet brew with just the right smoky aftertaste that rib lovers savor. The sauce's two-stage preparation is what makes it so special. In step one, a popular commercial base is doctored with as many as eight spices and seasonings, plus a liberal helping of brown sugar. Then this is slathered onto the ribs, which are slow baked in specially designed electric ovens. Now precooked, the ribs are ready for finishing beneath a gas broiler. Again they are hit with more sauce, this time without the brown sugar to avoid burning.

In addition to these outstanding ribs, Carson's also serves some of the best steaks around. They range from a giant twenty-four-ounce New York sirloin down to smaller cuts for just under $10. Considering the price (which includes an excellent salad of greens or tasty coleslaw, potatoes as you choose, and rolls with butter), this may be one of the most value-packed steak dinners in town. If you still crave the barbecue flavor, but your taste doesn't run to ribs, you should find ample pleasure in a whole barbecued chicken, with meat that virtually falls from the bones. There's only one fish choice: boneless fillets of breaded pike, panfried and served with tartar sauce—the next best thing to a shore dinner. Although Carson's fame for ribs rests largely on its take-out business, the dining rooms are handsomely appointed. Service is a bit rushed, however, apparently to turn tables quickly.

Carson's has more locations at 5970 North Ridge (312-271-4000), Chicago; 8617 Niles Center Road (312-675-6800), Skokie; 400 East Roosevelt Road (312-627-4300), Lombard; 5050 North Harlem (312-867-4200), Harwood Heights.

K/Rating 18/20: Decor 4/4, Service 4/5, Food 8/9, Value 2/2

THE PALM

American/Steaks/Lobster

181 East Lake Shore, Chicago
Telephone: (312) 944-0135

Hours: Monday–Friday 11:30–10:45, Saturday, 5–11:45. Cards: AE, CB, DC, MC, V. Reservations essential. Casual dress, but no shorts. No-smoking section. Valet parking. Full bar service. Handicap accessible. Private party room for up to 65 people. Troubleshooter: John Baldino (general manager). Expensive.

The traveling Chicagoan's favorite New York restaurant got off to a rocky start when it first opened a branch here in 1980. But despite the noise, the hustling and bustling activity, and the sawdust floor, The Palm is a first-class operation. The brassiness of the joint is regarded by some as part of its charm. The decor features bright cartoon murals of some of the city's toniest celebs, unsanded wood-paneled booths, brass railings, and comfortable seating. Even though the noise level may be akin to the back of a bus, it really is quite easy to carry on a fairly private business discussion or any other kind of rendezvous.

The Palm specializes in gigantic steaks, huge lobsters, and prices to match. The smallest lobster weighs in at three pounds, the largest is a monstrous ten, and these are priced by the pound at current market rates. A typical dinner including melon and prosciutto, steak, à la carte salad, a combo order of fried onions and cottage-fried potatoes, plus coffee and cheesecake brings the tab up to around $40 per person, not including cocktails, wine, and tip. Even though the prices may be high, the food is uniformly excellent. Veal piccata is a first-rate preparation, retaining the simplicity of the butter-lemon flavor, but served in a slightly roux-thickened sauce that binds it all together. Steak à la Stone consists of sliced sirloin served over sautéed peppers and thick slivers of onions.

For dessert, the specialty of the house is cheesecake; rich, heavy, and everything a New York-style cheesecake ought to be. And maybe that's symbolic of the restaurant itself. The Palm is everything a restaurant ought to be, even if prices are rather high.

K/Rating of 18.5/20: Decor 4/4, Service 4/5, Food 9/9, Value 1.5/2

ELI'S THE PLACE FOR STEAK

American/Steak House

215 East Chicago Avenue, Chicago
Telephone: (312) 642-1393

Lunch: Monday–Friday 11:30–2:30. Dinner: Monday–Friday 4–10, Saturday–Sunday 4–10:30. Cards: AE, MC, V. Reservations suggested. Jackets requested for gentlemen. No-smoking section. Discount parking in building garage. Full bar service; piano lounge. Troubleshooter: Marc Schulman (owner). Moderate.

Though one of Chicago's bright lights went out with the death of restaurateur Eli Schulman, his restaurant continues under the guidance of his family, who had been involved all along. And that's part of the secret to Eli's tremendous success; at a time when restaurants come and restaurants go, this place has always been a major draw on Chicago's northern flank. Sure, the interior is glitzy, even garish by today's modern restaurant standards. But the quality is enduring.

Despite the fact that "steak" is in the restaurant's name, my favorite dish has always been the calf's liver Eli. It's as sweet and tender as you can imagine, the kind of dining that could even make a liver lover out of someone who refuses to touch the stuff. Thin slices are sautéed with sliced onions, green peppers, and mushrooms. Yes, it's decidedly untrendy, but what a treat! Among steaks, you will find all the cuts, plus a delicious breaded boneless breast of chicken with sautéed mushrooms. All dinners include a lavish bread and matzoh basket, a relish tray, salad, and potato. Eli's is nationally famous for its cheesecake. Here's a chance to have a slice where it all began.

K/Rating of 17/20: Decor 3/4, Service 5/5, Food 7.5/9, Value 1.5/2

GENE & GEORGETTI

Steaks/Italian

590 North Franklin, Chicago
Telephone: (312) 527-3718

Hours: Monday–Saturday 11:30–12:30 am. Cards: AE, CB, DC, house accounts. Reservations mandatory. Casual dress. Valet parking. Full bar service. Private party room for up to 35 people. Troubleshooters: Gino Mori and Gene Michelotti (owners). Expensive.

Ask some folks where the best steak is served in Chicago and they will tell you at Gene & Georgetti. I am not quite ready to bestow that much of an accolade, but there is no question that this is one of the best steak houses of its kind. Served without embellishment, steaks come straight from broiler to table. Ask for a garlic rub, or salt and pepper to taste at your table, and you will get perfect satisfaction.

Gene & Georgetti does a commendable job with Italian specialties. I particularly like the linguine in white clam sauce. Meat sauces are thick, with any tomato harshness cooked away in the Tuscan manner. This place has always been popular not only with local Chicago types, but also with out-of-towners doing business at the nearby Merchandise Mart and the new Wolf Point Apparel Center.

K/Rating of 17/20: Decor 2.5/4, Service 5/5, Food 8/9, Value 1.5/2

RANDALL'S RIBHOUSE

Ribs/American

41 East Superior, Chicago
Telephone: (312) 280-2790

Lunch: Monday–Friday 11:30–3. Dinner: Monday–Thursday 5–11:00, Friday–Saturday 5–midnight, Sunday 4–10. Cards: AE, CB, DC, MC, V. Reservations suggested. No-smoking section. Valet parking. Full bar service. Private party room for up to 50 people. Outdoor café in warm weather months. Troubleshooter: Paul Turmberger (manager). Moderate.

You might be concerned about what to wear at Randall's Ribhouse considering it's just about the classiest rib joint you are likely to find. But not to worry about stains. They'll give you a cloth bib to protect your own bib and tucker. And that's just the start of being pampered, maybe entertained, and generally well fed. Although you will pay for it! The pick of the litter among rib dinners is the baby backs. The small, almost delicate bones are encased in ample, tender meat with no fat to be seen. The Provimi veal ribs also are not fatty, but they are short on meat. They are more for bone suckers than rib eaters. By some tastes, the beef ribs simply have too much fat to make them worth the effort.

Of course, ribs need a good sauce to really please. Randall's uses an assertive, spicy sauce, with an up-front sweet flavor on initial contact with the tongue, but more than a hint of pepper in its aftertaste. It's really not necessary to order appetizers, since all dinners include a crisp salad of mixed greens and assorted toppings, a large baked potato, and corn bread, plus a family-style platter of french-fried potatoes and onions.

K/Rating of 18/20: Decor 4/4, Service 5/5, Food 7/9, Value 2/2

D.B. KAPLAN'S

Delicatessen

845 North Michigan Avenue
(Seventh Level, Water Tower Place),
Chicago
Telephone: (312) 280-2700

Hours: Monday–Thursday 10–10, Friday–Saturday 10–midnight, Sunday 11–11. No cards or personal checks. Reservations only for parties of 8 or more. No-smoking section. Parking in building. Full bar service. Handicap accessible. Private party facilities for up to 50 people, with a minimum of 20. Troubleshooter: Sarah Wojcik (general manager). Inexpensive.

Where is it written that delicatessens always have to be dark, crowded, and smell of pickles? That is not the case with D. B. Kaplan's, a rather glitzy establishment with bright enameled walls and bold graphic designs. For the hungry Water Tower Place shopper who wants to refresh on Jewish K rations, this is the place. But it is also more than corned beef, pastrami, and pepper beef: some 150 things more. The menu may be the *War and Peace* of restaurant menus with its scores of sandwiches, omelets, fish platters, and ice cream desserts.

It is also a compendium of puns. For instance, there are the obvious ones like "Standout from the Kraut" (hot dog and sauerkraut), "Ike and Tina Tuna," or "Goldie Lox and the Three Eggs." If you crave pepper beef, Swiss cheese, chopped liver, and all the trimmings on egg challah, try "Live and Let Liver." "Studs Turkey" is not only the bird, but lots of tongue and Canadian bacon plus shredded lettuce and cranberry sauce. Despite the cutesy names, the sandwiches are all that you could expect between two slices of bread. There is lots more, including a six-foot triple-decker with Danish ham, salami, bologna, summer sausage, and all the trimmings, just the thing for a party of forty or so sandwich-starved friends. For $100 and three days' notice it's yours. If you are an ice cream freak you will find all you could ever want, including more outrageous puns like the "Yalta Malta."

K/Rating of 17/20: Decor 3/4, Service 4/5, Food 8/9, Value 2/2

ARNIE'S

American/Eclectic

1030 North State, Chicago
Telephone: (312) 266-4800

Lunch: Monday–Friday 11:30–2. Dinner: Monday–Friday 5:30–midnight. Sunday brunch: 10:30–2:30. Cards: AE, CB, DC, MC, V. Reservations required. Jackets requested for gentlemen. No-smoking section. Full bar service; excellent wine list with many choices available by the glass; good stock of premium cognacs and other brandies. Handicap accessible. Private party rooms for groups of 35–125 people. Troubleshooter: Arnold J. Morton (owner). Expensive.

Arnie's is a place to see and be seen, but thanks to consistent upgrading, it is also a genuinely fine restaurant, and Arnold Morton has come a long way from the days when he would boast: "I'm a saloonkeeper, not a restaurateur!" Arnie's was the first to bring pasta primavera to Chicago; the tableside preparation is a joy to watch, as seasonal vegetables are quickly sautéed in butter, coated with parmesan cheese, then deftly mixed with al dente linguine. This makes a great appetizer when split between two or more diners. For main-course choices, pepper steak is as robust as you will find it anywhere. Rack of lamb is usually available from a rolling cart, although not on the printed menu; your waiter will remind you of its presence. Fresh seafood generally gets an elegant French touch in presentation and saucing. Desserts are rich and lavish.

K/Rating 19/20: Decor 4/4, Service 5/5, Food 8/9, Value 2/2

METROPOLIS

American/Eclectic

163 West North, Chicago
Telephone: (312) 642-2130

Hours: Monday–Thursday 11–9:30, Friday–Saturday 11–10:30. Cards: AE, MC, V, house accounts. No reservations. Casual dress. Parking lot or street parking. Wine and beer. Handicap accessible. Troubleshooters: Cathy and Erwin Drechsler (owners). Moderate.

The atmosphere is strictly 1940s dinette city, but the food is 100 percent new wave. There is no printed menu; in fact, items change regularly. For an appetizer try ceviche of Alaskan baby halibut, or a simple rice salad with smoked mussels and cashews. The hot-appetizer choices might include a fascinating crêpes gateau. The crêpes are flavored with ginger and stacked with a filling of wild mushrooms and goat cheese that serves as a light binder.

Dinner entrées show a broad range of style and influence. Tagliatelle with bay scallops, roasted eggplant, leeks, yellow tomatoes, garlic, and olive oil will likely share the menu with a dish showing an Asian touch, such as sautéed baby coho salmon served with a wasabi (Japanese green horseradish) mayonnaise. The mayonnaise lessened the sharp impact of the fiery hot wasabi. For something more substantial, there might be roasted game hens stuffed with boudin sausage.

Desserts run the gamut from French-style fruit tarts and pastries to good old-fashioned American bread pudding. The kitchen staff at Metropolis has a talent for taking simple ingredients and presenting them in a fresh, imaginative way.

K/Rating of 16/20: Decor 3/4, Service 3.5/5, Food 7.5/9, Value 2/2

NINETY FIFTH

American Contemporary

875 North Michigan
(John Hancock Center), Chicago
Telephone: (312) 787-9596

Lunch: Monday–Friday 11:30–2:30. Dinner: Monday–Thursday 5:30–10:30, Friday 5:30–11:30, Saturday 6–11:30. Cards: AE, CB, DC, MC, V. Reservations mandatory. Full bar service. No-smoking section. Handicap accessible. Private party facilities for up to 200 people. Troubleshooter: Christian De Vos (general manager). Expensive.

Despite its empyrean setting high atop the John Hancock Center, the Ninety Fifth has only recently come back to the culinary heights it once maintained. After a period of time in which the restaurant seemed geared only to tourists in polyester sport shirts, a new direction is now firmly in place. With seasonal menus that change quarterly, the Ninety Fifth is offering some marvelous examples of the new American cuisine. Most, if not all, is without contrivance or artifice. Selections can be as basic as grilled smoked bratwurst for an appetizer, but with the addition of cabbage and apples it becomes something a bit more special. Other choices might include a duck confit with mushrooms, spinach, and polenta in an imaginative combination of flavors.

In addition to the excellent à la carte selections, diners can choose the prix-fixe menu, which offers an exceptional dining value. The Ninety Fifth wine list is one of the best in the city, reflecting an interest not only in the fine French vintages, but those of America's West Coast wineries that deserve special attention. It's a joy to welcome back this handsome and, once again, exceptional restaurant into the list of Chicago's finest.

K/Rating: 18.5/20: Decor 4/4, Service 3.5/5, Food 9/9, Value 2/2

LA TOUR

American/Nouvelle

800 North Michigan, Chicago
Telephone: (312) 280-2222

Breakfast: daily 7–10:30. Lunch: daily 11:30–2:30. Dinner: daily 6–11. Cards: AE, CB, DC, MC, V, house accounts. Reservations required. Jackets required for gentlemen. Valet parking. Full-bar service; sophisticated, extensive wine list. Private dining room for parties up to 12 people. Handicap accessible. Expensive.

This is one of the prettiest restaurants in Chicago. The floor is imported rose marble; the color theme is picked up in the furnishings and upholstery. And the view gives La Tour its name, with floor-to-ceiling windows offering diners a life-sized look at Chicago's most famous landmark, the Old Water Tower. Of course, each table has fresh flowers. Platters are ringed with floral decoration. The food is uniformly excellent, executed with a finesse well matched to the elegance of the dining room. Prepared in the style of the new American cuisine, each dish is a visual attraction as well. Desserts come from kitchen and pastry cart; among recent choices was a raisin tart with pine nuts. While food is next to perfect, service can be a little ragged. On one visit, no one was ready to pour coffee refills until asked; nor was there anyone to assist diners trying to get out from banquette seating by sliding their table out of the way. But such lapses are fairly minor and easily corrected considering the other overall attractions.

K/Rating 17.5/20: Decor 4/4, Service 4/5, Food 8/9, Value 1.5/2

THE WATERFRONT

Seafood

16 West Maple, Chicago
Telephone: (312) 943-7494

Hours: Sunday–Thursday 11:30–midnight, Friday–Saturday 11:30–1:00 am, Saturday and Sunday brunch 11–3. Cards: AE, DC, MC, V. Reservations recommended. Casual dress. No-smoking section. Valet parking ($5). Private party facilities for 12–50 people. Troubleshooters: Basil Georgeson and Larry Gray (owners). Moderate.

Batten down the hatches, hoist the mainsail, and steer a course for West Maple Street. The decor of weathered wood, bare brick, and fixtures normally seen aboard a brigantine sailing the seven seas leaves little to the imagination. You'll sit in captain's chairs or church pews at copper-topped tables. All that's missing is the gentle motion of waves and the salt smell of the sea. The Waterfront is the only place in town that I know of for cioppino. Despite its foreign-sounding name, cioppino traces its origin to San Francisco, where Italian fishermen created a waterfront dinner composed of delicacies from their catch. At The Waterfront, cioppino includes shrimp, oysters, clams, and crabmeat in a Tabasco-like hot sauce seasoned with bay leaves and spices. Served piping hot in a cast-iron skillet, it is highly seasoned and not for the timid. Milder are such entrées as sole almondine, trout, or red snapper. Sole en sacque, not often found on local menus, is a beautiful preparation as pleasing to the eye as it is to the palate. All dinners include access to the salad bar. In addition to the regular dinner menu, there is a lower-priced selection of snacks for lunch or weeknight after-theater crowds.

K/Rating of 18/20: Decor 4/4, Service 4/5, Food 8/9, Value 2/2

GEJA'S CAFE

Fondue

340 West Armitage, Chicago
Telephone: (312) 281-9101

Dinner: Monday–Thursday 5–10, Friday 5–midnight, Saturday 5–12:30 am, Sunday 4:30–10. Cards: AE, CB, DC, MC, V. Reservations only on weeknights. Ample parking in lot north of restaurant; street parking difficult. Wine and beer; wine list features excellent selections from California boutique wineries. Nightly entertainment. Troubleshooter: John Davis (owner). Expensive.

Tables are covered with muted tartan cloths, bottles of wine line shelves in almost every nook and cranny, lights are kept low as conversation murmurs and laughter ripples from a table here or there. The atmosphere at Geja's is conducive to fondue, for this type of cooking is as much a social activity as anything else; it seems to stimulate good conversation. There is a camaraderie that grows in the simple act of preparing and eating foods together, and that, of course, is what civilized dining is all about.

Fondue cooking here is sometimes done in a pot of hot peanut oil. The various ingredients are speared with a slender small-tined fork and cooked in the bubbling oil to individual preference. The method works well with meat, firm-fleshed fish, and vegetables. Another branch of fondue cooking is cheese fondue. In this, melted cheeses are blended with kirsch, wine, and seasonings. The satisfaction comes in dipping chunks of crusty bread and tart apple wedges into the cauldron of smoothly melted cheese, covering your food with the warm bubbly sauce and enjoying the complex tastes and textures. By dinner's end, if you are up to dessert, the traditional way to go is chocolate fondue. Thick melted chocolate and kirsch are blended together and served with a selection of fruits and poundcake.

Geja's has a definite following among wine lovers. Owner John Davis is a dedicated purveyor of better wines at reasonable cost; wine goes hand-in-hand with the fondue experience at Geja's.

K/Rating of 16/20: Decor 4/4, Service 3.5/5, Food 7.5/9, Value 1/2

MIAMI BAR & GRILL

American/Caribbean

535 North Wells, Chicago
Telephone: (312) 644-1397
Lunch: Monday–Friday 11–2:30. Dinner: 5:30–10, Saturday 5:30–11, Sunday 3–9. Cards: AE, MC, V. Reservations suggested. Casual dress. Valet parking. Full bar service. Troubleshooter: Richard Gollinger (chef-owner). Moderate.

Miami Bar & Grill is a medley of aquamarine, flamingo pink, pale yellows. Diners sit on bamboo straight-backed chairs, which are surprisingly comfortable, amidst a sea of aquaria filled with gorgeous tropical fish. The decor seems to be not so much reality as it is a stylish takeoff on southern Florida and The Keys.

The menu is rich with Caribbean and Southern cookery. Barbecued baby back ribs, offered as an appetizer or dinner portion, are actually smoked before grilling. The rib sauce is thick, tomatoey, and sweet, with perhaps just a hint of vinegar and spices. Drums of heaven Jamacian style is a chicken drumstick appetizer that is rather underseasoned and therefore somewhat boring. But conch chowder is not to be missed, thick with vegetables, conch meat, and distinctive flavorings.

Diners can choose from salads that run the gamut from a fruit platter to smoked turkey on a bed of greens with chopped pecans, avocado, and tomato. The parmesan-brie dressing is rather unusual, and a good match for most any of the salads.

Among dinner entrées are some splended fish choices, though some fish seems a bit overdone; not dry, mind you, but just a bit less juicy than most fish lovers prefer. Otherwise, mahimahi with a unique and delicious smoked shrimp sauce is fine. Tuna steak, a recent fresh fish of the day, is simply grilled and garnished with capers. The menu offers swordfish, a couple of shrimp dishes, deep-fried conch steak, and a seafood stew in a tasty fish-based stock. Among meat choices, a filet mignon is basic fare, tender, properly cooked, handsomely served. Veal chop Key Largo promises a double-cut chop, but I think the portion is rather skimpy. Nonetheless, it is nicely trimmed and comes on a veal stock reduction enhanced with fresh orange segments and zest.

Desserts include Key lime pie, a bit on the sweet side, luscious turtle pie, and fresh kiwi sorbet. For warm summer evenings, there are drinks at the outdoor sidewalk cafe.

K/Rating of 17.5/20: Decor 4/4, Service 4.5/5, Food 7.5/9, Value 1.5/2

HAT DANCE

Mexican

325 West Huron, Chicago
Telephone: (312) 649-0961

Hours: Monday–Thursday 5–10:30, Friday–Saturday 5–1:30 am. Cards: AE, CB, DC, MC, V, LEYE. Reservations only between 5 and 7. Casual, "funky" dress. No-smoking section. Valet parking. Full bar service. Troubleshooter: Rich Melman (owner). Moderate.

If it's burritos, tacos, and enchiladas you crave, look elsewhere. But if it is some of the most inspired Mexican and Mexican-influenced cooking to be found north of the Rio Grande, Hat Dance is a must.

The restaurant is one of the newest creations of Rich Melman and The Lettuce Entertain You group. That immediately suggests the cutting edge of fashion and restaurant as theater. That's largely what Hat Dance is all about. The handsome high-ceilinged dining room is done up in a white-on-white or white-on-silver motif suggestive of Mexican or Aztec designs. There is a great deal of bustle and hardly any effort to cut down on the conversational noise of a busy restaurant that seats more than 200 people (and that doesn't include the bar with room for another 150 or so).

Of course, it is the food that sets Hat Dance apart. Try queso fundido, not made with Chihuahua cheese as is the custom, but with velvety smooth goat cheese. The cheese and a tingling, but not burning hot pepper sauce arrive in the small skillet in which they were warmed. Spread on a bit of tortilla, it is fantastic. The restaurant offers several different ceviches, and even some sashimi and steak or salmon tartare. The tartare dishes are a bit on the bland side and therefore not especially interesting.

That's hardly the case with some of the entrées. Tuna asada is unforgettable. A good-sized cut of tuna steak is grilled but left rare in the center, then napped with a chili sauce and papaya relish. The fish is as mild and as clean as can be. Had I been blindfolded, I might have thought I was eating rare beefsteak. For anyone who loves seafood, this is not to be missed.

Other outstanding entrées include carne asada, a tender strip steak in a mole-style sauce, or wood-roasted whole chicken with a trimming of assorted vegetables and a rubbing of ground chilies and other seasonings for flavor accent. Back on the seafood side, a sopa de marisco, the Mexican version of cioppino, is satisfactory but not as distinctive as many of Hat Dance's other choices.

Do not ignore dessert. Cinnamon pudding has a light citrus-flavored underpinning. And, if offered, the chocolate tostada should not be missed. Two granolalike cookies simulate the tostadas; they are filled with white chocolate mousse and rest in a pool of mango sauce.

Hat Dance is usually very busy, but if you come for dinner before 6:30, you should be able to waltz right in. Otherwise, prepare for a long wait.

K/Rating of 18.5/20: Decor 3.5/4, Service 5/5, Food 8.5/9, Value 1.5/2

FRONTERA GRILL

Mexican

445 North Clark, Chicago
Telephone: (312) 661-1434

Lunch: Tuesday–Friday 11:30–2:30, Saturday 10:30–2:30. Dinner: Tuesday–Thursday 5:20–10, Friday–Saturday 5:20–11. Cards: AE, CB, DC, MC, V. Reservations only for parties of 5–10 people. No-smoking section. Valet parking on weekends; public lot across the street. Full bar service. Private party facilities for 45–65 people on Sunday–Monday only. Troubleshooters: Rick and Deann Bayless (owners). Moderate.

Frontera Grill is like no other Mexican restaurant in Chicago. Forget about border food. Chef-owner Rick Bayless and his wife Deann have chosen to explore the diversity of Mexican cuisine.

The restaurant is crowded, noisy, and on the cutting edge of contemporary dining fashion. You might even say the place is boisterous without being rowdy—just lively enough to suggest the popular imagery of a cantina.

Diners will see some familiar items on the Frontera Grill menu, but any similarity with conventional Mexican cooking stops there. The guacamole is thick, chunky, with the full flavor of the avocado and a hint of seasonings. Chicken taquitos are thin fingers of crisp dough around a filling of seasoned minced chicken; the tasty cylinders are topped with dollops of a fresh sour cream unlike any I've tasted before, and frankly I'm no sour cream lover. Try the appetizer platter that brings the taquitos and guacamole, plus some small quesadillas and ceviche tostadas. For me, the tostadas are the hit of the list. The ceviche is cooling, laced with the raw bite of lime juice. A bit of cilantro and other herbs makes this a distinct winner.

You might also want to sample a platter of assorted sopes, cornmeal tarts, if your party numbers four or six. Frontera Grill serves them filled with plantain and sour cream, guacamole, chorizo, and chicken in mole.

Recently, Frontera Grill has been serving duck breast in a green pumpkin-seed mole. As in fashionable French restaurants, the duck breast slices are still slightly pink, bathed in a thick but not heavy sauce that complements the flavor of the poultry. The platter also comes with Mexican rice, rings of zucchini, and chayote.

Among other entrées are split game hens. The small birds are grilled over charcoal to seal in a marinade of garlic and spices. Dinner choices also include an unusual turkey breast steak with a red mole, fresh fish, chiles rellenos, and specials of the evening. The dessert list replaces familiar flan with a fruit custard, fresh ice creams, and other sweets.

Service is cordial and well informed, but since Frontera Grill takes no reservations except for parties of five or more, waits for a table can be an hour or longer.

K/Rating 18.5/20: Decor 3.5/4, Service 4.5/5, Food 9/9, Value 1.5/2

Su Casa

Mexican

49 East Ontario, Chicago
Telephone: (312) 943-4041

Hours: Monday–Friday 11:30–12:30 am, 5–12:30 am. Cards: AE, CB, DC, MC, V. Reservations required. Casual dress, but no T-shirts, haltertops, shorts. Valet parking. Full bar service. Private party room for up to 25 people. Troubleshooter: Charles Tatson (manager). Inexpensive.

While nothing in the universe is unchanging, and, as the philosopher Lucretius tells us, "even stones are conquered by time . . . high towers fall and rocks moulder away," it is comforting to report that Su Casa goes on serving consistently delicious Mexican fare. Here is an antique-filled white brick-walled restaurant with the feel of a Spanish colonial hacienda in Old Mexico. There are heavy carved doors, large metal ornaments, and ornate wood statues.

Su Casa proves that Mexican cuisine need not be unbearably spicy. To be sure, red pepper sauce and other condiments are placed on your table. But the food here is milder than what you find at many Mexican restaurants, though no less authentic. The combination dinner offers the most varied tastes, including Mexican-style grilled steak, stuffed peppers, delicious chicken enchiladas, cheese tacos, and creamy, cool guacamole. Chicken mole is a special treat; the sauce of unsweetened chocolate and a complex bouquet of spices is an altogether wonderful way to prepare chicken. Seafood lovers should try the trout with coriander for an unusual preparation. Desserts include flan, the classic Mexican custard in caramel sauce.

K/Rating of 17.5/20: Decor 4/4, Service 4/5, Food 7.5/9, Value 2/2

Toulouse

French

51 West Division Street, Chicago
Telephone: (312) 944-2606

Hours: Monday–Thursday 5:30–midnight, Friday–Saturday 5:30–1 am (lounge open until 4 am Friday and Saturday). Cards: AE, CB, DC, MC, V. Jackets required for gentlemen. Valet parking. Full bar service; excellent list of brandies. Handicap accessible. Troubleshooter: Bob Djahanguiri (owner). Expensive.

Toulouse may be the city's most romantic restaurant. Large booths enwrap couples who are looking for a little hideaway just off the busy glitter of Division and State. The piano bar adds just another touch of intimacy, while fresh-cut flowers bring their perfume indoors. Lovely seafood presentations are a highlight of the menu, which changes daily. The Norwegian salmon is about as good as it gets in Chicago. Among appetizers, sautéed sweetbreads are positively sexy. The onion soup speaks of earthy traditions. If you like dining in the classic tradition, the rack of lamb with rosemary sauce is a lovely presentation. Desserts are sensual in textures and creaminess.

K/Rating of 18/20: Decor 4/4, Service 5/5, Food 7.5/9, Value 1.5/2

THE DINING ROOM AT THE RITZ-CARLTON

French

160 East Pearson, Chicago
Telephone: (312) 227-5866

Dinner: Monday–Saturday 6–11, Sunday 6–10. Sunday brunch: 10:30–1. Cards: AE, CB, DC, MC, V. Reservations required. Jackets and ties required for gentlemen. Valet parking. Full bar service; excellent wine list with 500 bottlings. Handicap accessible. Troubleshooter: Toni Tontini (maître d'). Expensive.

What's in a name? A lot of reputation when the name is Ritz, as in Ritz-Carlton Hotel and its humbly dubbed restaurant, The Dining Room. Since its opening more than a decade ago, The Dining Room has had its culinary ups and downs. There are still some inconsistencies, but the restaurant nevertheless deserves some attention. The dinner menu offers two approaches to dining: an à la carte section and what is called "Alternative Cuisine." The latter is meant for dieters whose fear of caloric sauces outweighs their desire. With a change of selections regularly, the Alternative Cuisine menu was recently offering an appetizer of a collage of sliced lobster and mango or a pot-au-feu of red snapper in saffron broth; a handsome salad with several different greens, delicate beans, and wild mushrooms; and a main-course choice of veal-and-seafood raviolis on a nap of wild mushroom sauce or a seafood selection in lobster-vinegar sauce. All the Alternative Cuisine choices total fewer than 650 calories and are low in cholesterol and sodium.

The regular menu is fleshed out with appetizers including salmon tartare with chives, baked crab cakes with a scent of tarragon, and a duck liver, avocado, and herb salad, among several selections. Entrées, which are accompanied by an appropriate salad and fresh vegetables, number less than a dozen choices. Recent selections have included rack of lamb with a garlic mousse and ratatouille terrine, lobster and spinach lasagne, and honey-glazed squab in ginger sauce.

The Dining Room has been one of the city's more elegant restaurants since it opened. Its wood-paneled walls are highlighted by selective lighting. Service is generally impeccable. The wine list is as extensive as almost any diner could demand and includes a wide range of prices, some bottles as low as $17. Considering the diversity that is being attempted at The Dining Room at the Ritz-Carlton, the effort deserves its share of recognition.

K/Rating 17/20: Decor 4/4, Service 4.5/5, Food 6.5/9, Value 2/2

L'ESCARGOT ON MICHIGAN

French

701 North Michigan, in the Allerton Hotel, Chicago
Telephone: (312) 337-1717

Breakfast: daily 7–11. Lunch: daily 11:30–2:30. Dinner: 5–10:30. Cards: AE, CB, DC, DISC, MC, V. Reservations required. Dress from casual to suits and ties. Validated parking in 150 East Huron garage. Intimate French-style Le Bar Americaine serves wide variety of French wines, cognacs, and aperitifs; wines by the glass. Handicap accessible. Private parties in restaurant for up to 75 people; in Allerton Hotel for up to 200 people. Troubleshooter: Alan Tutzer (owner). Expensive.

Although founding chef Lucian Verge died in 1986, the legacy of his cooking and charm survives. Housed in an older hotel, the restaurant conveys the best of modern French cookery. The style is French provincial, but there are some contemporary influences that tend to lighten the cuisine. The freshest seafood is always a highlight. Roast leg of lamb, cassoulet, and roast duck are classically French. L'Escargot not only pleases for lunch and dinner, but is also open for breakfast and serves one of the better Sunday brunches in town. A petite four-course fixed-price dinner is served evenings from 5:00 to 6:15 and from 9:30–10:30; it is one of the better dining bargains around town.

K/Rating 19/20: Decor 4/4, Service 5/5, Food 8/9, Value 2/2

L'ESCARGOT ON HALSTED

French

2525 North Halsted, Chicago
Telephone: (312) 525-5522

Dinner: Monday–Saturday 5–10:30. Cards: AE, CB, DC, DISC, MC, V. Reservations suggested. Free parking in St. Sebastian School lot one block north at Wellington and Halsted. Full bar service with lounge. Troubleshooter: Alan Tutzer (owner). Expensive.

Risen from the ashes of a disastrous fire, L'Escargot is again offering patrons its country French menu. The restaurant shares common ownership with its sibling in The Allerton Hotel (see preceding listing). A minimum of seven different sauces and stocks are blended and simmered each day. Choosing the prix-fixe dinner offers a choice from among ten hors d'oeuvres. Nightly choices might include cold lobster parisienne, venison pâté, or mousse of scallops. Following a fresh soup course, entrées could range from roast rib eye of veal with green peppercorn sauce to roast rack of lamb or lightly poached fresh seafood in a complementary sauce. The house salad precedes dessert and coffee. The restaurant also offers service from its à la carte menu and has been featuring pretheater dining at substantially reduced cost ($14.50) for a three-course dinner.

K/Rating 18/20: Decor 4/4, Service 4/5, Food 8/9, Value 2/2

THE WHITEHALL CLUB

French

105 East Delaware, Chicago
Telephone: (312) 280-3085

Lunch: daily noon–2. Dinner: daily 6–10. Cards: AE, CB, DC, MC, V, house accounts. Reservations required. Jackets and ties required for gentlemen. No-smoking section. Valet parking. Full service bar; wine list won 1987 Wine Spectator Award. Private club room seats up to 40 people; 5 banquet rooms served by the restaurant kitchen are available in the Hotel Whitehall. Troubleshooter: Driss Idrissi (maître d'). Expensive.

After thirty-one years as a private dining room, The Whitehall Club is now open to the public. But for all practical purposes it is likely to remain a domain for the wealthy. Despite the change to public status, one still pays for a kind of clubby exclusivity, which may make The Whitehall Club Chicago's most expensive restaurant.

Is the experience worth the money? Chef Charles William Hayes is bringing the best cooking to The Whitehall Club I have ever tasted on the several occasions I have dined there over the years. His style is largely French, with some contemporary American overtones.

Pheasant Souvarov comes sliced, resting in a rich demi-glace of its own juices fortified perhaps with cognac. The cooking technique yields one of the most intensely flavored pheasants I have tasted. The pheasant is served with a lovely woven potato basket filled with egg-shaped roasted potatoes. Roast rack of lamb gets the same elegant treatment. The large portion of chops is roasted with a coating of bread crumbs and herbs. Underneath the rack is an exquisite pasta with the combined flavor of black pepper and mint, an unusual pairing, to say the least.

When it comes to fish, there is hardly another as satisfying as Chef Haynes's Dover sole. Recognizing its special qualities, he prepares it in a simple meunière sauce, without further embellishment. Hardly any traces of butter are to be found, leaving the essential goodness of the fish itself.

On the à la carte appetizer list are snails (out of the shell) baked beneath a deeply flavored herb-cheese blanket infused with wine. For dessert, the double chocolate cake with burnt caramel sauce is exquisite.

The Whitehall Club is in the big leagues of Chicago fine dining.

K/Rating of 18/20: Decor 4/4, Service 4/5, Food 8.5/9, Value 1.5/2

Monique's Cafe

213 West Institute Place, Chicago
Telephone: (312) 642-2210

Lunch: Monday–Saturday 11:30–3. Dinner: Tuesday–Thursday 5:30–9:30, Friday–Saturday 5:30–10:30. Sunday classical music brunch: 11–3 (plate service). Cards: AE, CB, DC, MC, V. Reservations suggested. No-smoking section. Valet parking. Casual, but neat dress. Full bar service; wine by the glass plus espresso and cappuccino service. Facilities for private parties of up to 90 people. Troubleshooter: Monique Hooker (owner). Moderate.

French

Monique's Cafe is in Chicago's River North, a part of the city that is to Chicago what SoHo is to New York. The food is strictly French, contemporary to a point, studded with regional accents and Monique Hooker's personal touch. The menu changes seasonally and often includes items Monique has brought back from her frequent trips to France. After one such trip, she served breast of duck with a cassis wine sauce. The sauce was made from black currants Monique harvested over the summer at her family's farm in Brittany. That's about as personal and involved as one can get in one's own cooking. Unwilling to follow a trend that Monique cannot justify in terms of her vision of cuisine, she serves duck breast grilled medium-well, rather than the pink, even bloody manner that is considered fashionable.

Or try some other selections from her ever-changing menu. Old-style Lyonnaise sausage and lobster sausage demonstrate the variety to be found in this restaurant, which began as a charcuterie. Monique often cooks game; roulade of rabbit and sweetbreads with prunes illustrates an inventiveness based on the logic of French cuisine, rather than the trendiness of the moment.

K/Rating 17.5/20: Decor 3.5/4, Service 4/5, Food 8/9, Value 2/2

Biggs

1150 North Dearborn, Chicago
Telephone: (312) 787-0900

Dinner: daily from 5. Cards: AE, CB, DC, MC, V. Reservations required. Jackets required for gentlemen. No-smoking section. Valet parking ($4). Full bar service; good wine selection. Troubleshooters: Peter H. Salchow (owner) and Larry Peters (maître d'). Expensive.

French

The mid seventies saw this restaurant floundering. New ownership and management have turned things around quite nicely, thanks especially to the hiring of a chef who knows how to mix the satisfying richness of classic preparation with the light touches demanded by today's diners. Housed in an elegant nineteenth-century mansion, Biggs is as handsome a setting for dining as you are likely to find. In addition to the à la carte menu, several table d'hôte dinners are offered each evening, generally $20 to $25 for five courses.

Roast rack of lamb, almost always offered, gets marvelous treatment with just a hint of garlic. Sometimes there is grilled salmon in a preparation that would make Marco Polo happy. The salmon is served in an oriental-style sauce of scallions, ginger, and red pepper, with a side of the seldom seen Italian ricelike pasta called orzo. Grilled swordfish, on the other hand, seems more New World, with a tomato-pineapple salsa given a bit of fruitiness with the addition of balsamic vinegar. Steamed salmon in ginger-champagne sauce, roasted breast of duckling in pinot noir sauce, and veal with sauces that vary from day to day also show up on the menu.

Biggs is one of the few restaurants around that still serves a classic beef Wellington; beef wrapped in a delicate pastry is brought to your table on a rolling cart, then sliced, sauced, and plated before you.

K/Rating of 18.5/20: Decor 4/4, Service 4.5/5, Food 8/9, Value 2/2

LE PERROQUET

70 East Walton, Chicago
Telephone: (312) 944-7990

Lunch: Monday–Friday 11:45–3. Dinner: Monday–Saturday 5:45–10. Cards: AE, CB, DC, MC, V, house accounts. Reservations required; no reservations for tables of more than 6 people. Jackets and ties required for gentlemen. Parking in adjacent garage. Full bar service. Handicap accessible. Troubleshooters: Jean Pierre and Gerard Nespaux (owners). Expensive.

French

The testament to Le Perroquet's genuine greatness lies not only in its success as a commercial venture, but in the tremendous influence it has had on dining in Chicago. No other restaurateur has specifically tried to imitate the understated sophistication that has prevailed at Le Perroquet for nearly a decade. But its influence on the acceptance of nouvelle cuisine in Chicago cannot be ignored. Its kitchen was the first to emphasize lighter sauces and pastel presentations. The standard for excellence was unquestionably set here. The fixed-price menu ($46.50) still proffers what are now Le Perroquet standards. Diners will find a succulent mushroom tart among the appetizers, as well as escargots, oysters, and assorted pâtés. Entrées include tantalizing sweetbreads in a beurre blanc enhanced with tarragon, pigeon stuffed with forcemeat, and tender tournedos with shallots in a wine demi-glace.

The evening specials even rise a cut above the regular selections. An intensely rich tomato mousse is encircled by scallops in a light sauce; the color, flavor, and texture contrasts are perfect. Many restaurants serve swordfish, but not like that found at Le Perroquet. Thin slices of fish, resting in a greatly reduced fish stock, are topped with a sprinkling of the tiny, delicate sea snails called periwinkles. Another variation has the fish in a mild vinaigrette flavored with thyme and lemon. For meat eaters, leg of lamb is sliced almost paper thin and served with an herb sauce so subtle that it does not overwhelm the naturalness of the lamb's own flavor. Naturalness is also the key to a recent rendition of duck; by roasting the meat in its own fat the chef achieves a rich, but not intensely oily flavor. Slices from the breast come served with the leg prepared as a confit. Desserts include classic soufflés (at an additional charge), as well as table d'hôte sweets such as chocolate torte, fruit tarts, and incomparably delicious sherbets and ice creams. Le Perroquet remains the rare jewel in Chicago's dining crown it has always been.

K/Rating 20/20: Decor 4/4, Service 5/5, Food 9/9, Value 2/2

BISTRO 110

French/Eclectic

110 East Pearson, Chicago
Telephone: (312) 266-3110

Hours: Monday–Thursday 11:30–11, Friday–Saturday 11:30–midnight, Sunday 11:30–10; bistro closes one hour earlier during winter. Cards: AE, CB, DC, MC, V. Reservations at lunch for any-size party, at dinner only for parties of 6 or more. No-smoking section. Full bar service. Handicap accessible.
Troubleshooter: Cynthia Lanuti (manager).
Moderate.

Want to try French-bistro foods in an American setting, within the shadow of the Water Tower? Bistro 110, comfortably decorated in pastels and rich green upholstered seating, is large, noisy. The bar is usually crowded, as is an enclosed cafe that gives diners a near-outdoor feeling, even in the dead of winter.

The menu features roasted meats, fish, and even vegetables from a wood-burning oven that one waiter claimed could reach temperatures as high as 900 degrees. Well, I just wanted dinner, not my car painted and baked.

Once seated, diners are brought warm crusty bread, butter, and a whole head of roasted garlic. Some restaurants will charge as much as $7 for what Bistro 110 offers as standard equipage. If you have never enjoyed warm, creamy garlic on fresh bread, you are in for a treat.

Appetizers range from roasted mushrooms and a potato basket with three caviars to foie gras, oysters, and escargots in herb butter with a crown of puff pastry. A crock of classic French onion soup, baked with a cap of Gruyère cheese, is wonderfully satisfying, almost the proverbial meal in itself.

Entrées include such classics as cassoulet and steak and pommes frites, plus assorted pastas, fish, and some house specialties. Poussin, young, free-range chicken, is tender, well roasted, nicely seasoned, and, like many entrées, served with an accompaniment of roasted vegetables. Bistro 110 also serves calf's liver steak in a gargantuan portion. Do not order this any way but medium well or you will run the risk of a raw center. The liver, tender despite its girth, is served with a flavorful balsamic vinegar and crispy little fried onions.

Fruit tart for dessert can leave much to be desired. One I tasted came on a tired crust, with little in the way of syrupy sweetness. The addition of a scoop of ice cream or some crème fraîche helps.

K/Rating of 17.5/20: Decor 3.5/4, Service 4.5/5, Food 7.5/9, Value 2/2

CHARLIE TROTTER'S

French/Eclectic

851 West Armitage, Chicago
Telephone: (312) 248-6228

Dinner: daily from 5:30. Cards: AE, CB, DC, MC, V. Reservations required. Jackets and ties required for gentlemen. No-smoking section. Valet parking and street parking (difficult). Full bar service; small service bar seats 10 only; diverse wine selection. Second-floor dining room available for private parties of up to 36 people. Troubleshooters: Charlie and Lisa Trotter (owners). Expensive.

When talk among food mavens turns to fine dining, the name Charlie Trotter invariably comes up. Trotter is the young chef who, along with his wife, runs the restaurant that bears his name.

Trotter is not quite an iconoclast when it comes to food, but he is willing to experiment with traditional conceptions. For example, his ever-changing menu might feature an unusual smoked quail creation for an appetizer. The bird is fashionably underroasted, still somewhat pink. Its pieces are set among slices of yellow papaya, pale litchis, and hazelnuts. Drizzled on top is bittersweet Gianduia, that delectable blend of chocolate and hazelnut. Somewhat contrived, yes, but the conception works, if only because of its very boldness.

You may also find a carpaccio of red snapper instead of tenderloin, a takeoff on sashimi that adds a mix of Asian noodles for texture and a mayonnaise flavored with sesame oil. Or consider Trotter's use of wild mushrooms in a stylized ragout that serves as binder for diced sweetbreads in a leafy spinach wrap. Intensely flavored, the concept is marred only by an oiliness that very well could be drained away.

A trio of salads is regularly offered. One of Belgian endive, arugula, roasted cashews, and warm chèvre cheese is large enough to be easily shared by two. Entrées at Charlie Trotter's are a confluence of tradition and that spark of ingenuity that marks the chef and his kitchen staff with more than commonplace ability. Though he calls it lasagne, what Trotter does with his ingredients is hardly related to the standard Italian recipe. In this case, black squid-ink pasta serves as sheeting between levels of sea scallops and little else. As the waiter described it, the lasagne is held together by nothing more than gravity.

The pasta and scallops are napped in an intense saffron sauce that speaks volumes about why in the past whole armies were sent around the globe in search of this treasured herb.

There is another sort of creativity in the preparation of seared tuna and lobster in an olive sauce known as tapenade, served with a couscous galette. A galette usually refers to a cake or a shredded-potato patty not dissimilar from American hashbrowns. In this case, couscous, a North African grain specialty, is shaped into a patty that balances the sharp taste of the tapenade with the fresh flavor of the tuna and the two whole lobster claws.

Desserts are not to be overlooked. Blueberries may be showcased on a fresh tart dough, held in place by amaretto sabayon. But it is the baked chocolate mousse that is truly unforgettable. Baking gives the mousse a heavier character than normal. It comes with a chocolate wafer that stands high over the platter much like a goosenecked tuille. The finishing touch is an intense burnt caramel sauce that simply could not be better.

Exquisite is a word that comes to mind when thinking about Charlie Trotter's. Expensive is another one. Dinner for two will easily cost more than $100, plus tax, tip, and drinks.

K/Rating 19.75/20: Decor 4/4, Service 5/5, Food 9/9, Value 1.75/2

AVANZARE

Northern Italian

161 Huron, Chicago
Telephone: (312) 337-8056

Lunch: Monday–Friday 11:30–2. Dinner: Sunday–Thursday 5:30–9:30, Friday–Saturday 5:30–10:30. Cards: AE, CB, DC, MC, V, LEYE. Reservations suggested. Chic dress. Discount parking at nearby lot. Full bar service; good selection of Italian aperitifs and grappas, digestifs, etc.; wine list includes over 100 bottlings, most Italian, some Californian. Handicap accessible. Troubleshooter: Rich Melman (owner). Expensive.

Avanzare is one of the hottest Near North dining spots with both the expense-account crowd and seekers of good food. The kitchen often makes use of trendy ingredients such as the radicchio or porcini mushroom components of an antipasto. Carpaccio comes lightly oiled, with a minimum of seasoning. The pasta choices go far beyond marinara and bolognese, which are the limits at less-ambitious restaurants. Pine nuts and smoked goose may show up in one preparation, bound in virgin olive oil and a deeply flavored goose broth. Another good choice, when available, is the Avanzare version of linguine with clam sauce. I hesitate to use the word "sauce," because this is more like seasoned chopped clams served over pasta.

For the pork tenderloin on turnip purée, four pieces of tenderloin are sliced into petals and arranged handsomely on a squared-off nap of the purée. A scattering of pomegranate seeds gives seasonal coloring. Seafood specials change daily. Sea bass may be grilled and served with a delicious pesto hollandaise. Sometimes veal scallopini is sautéed and served with a counterpoint of matchstick-cut carrots and zucchini. Desserts include delicious kitchen-made ice creams and ices, as well as ricotta cheesecake.

K/Rating of 19.5/20: Decor 3.5/4, Service 5/5, Food 9/9, Value 2/2

CAFE SPIAGGIA

Northern Italian

One Magnificent Mile, 980 North Michigan, Chicago
Telephone: (312) 280-2764

Hours: Monday–Thursday 11:30–10:30, Friday–Saturday 11:30–11:30, Sunday noon–9. Cards: AE, CB, DC, MC, V. Reservations suggested. Casual dress. No-smoking section. Parking in building. Full bar service. Handicap accessible. Moderate.

Located right next to its more posh and expensive sibling Spiaggia (see below), the Cafe shares the same kitchen and some of the same menu items at substantially less cost. This is a casual, romantic European-style cafe set up like a galleria overlooking the Michigan Avenue side of One Magnificent Mile. The emphasis is on northern Italian food, although other regional Italian cooking is not ignored. Signature items include elaborate antipasti, gourmet pizzas from a wood-burning oven, and rotating specials that complement the printed menu. Not as pricy or formal as its namesake, this is a captivating alternative when one is not on an expense account.

K/Rating 19.5/20: Decor 3.5/4, Service 5/5, Food 9/9, Value 2/2

SPIAGGIA

Northern Italian

One Magnificent Mile, 980 North Michigan, Chicago
Telephone: (312) 280-2750

Lunch: Monday–Saturday 11:30–2:30. Dinner: Monday–Thursday 5:30–9:30, Friday–Saturday 5:30–10:30, Sunday 5:30–9. Cards: AE, CB, DC, MC, V. Reservations required. Jackets and ties required for gentlemen. No-smoking section. Parking available in building. Full bar service; extensive selection of premium Italian wines. Handicap accessible. Private party rooms. Troubleshooter: Marty Fosse (general manager). Expensive.

Spiaggia means "beach" in Italian, and that's part of the view diners get when they look out the floor-to-ceiling windows here. This is the most exciting vista in the city for people watching. You can look out onto the intersection of Michigan Avenue, Oak Street, and Lake Shore Drive, the most prime real estate in the city, with the stretch of Oak Street Beach in the near distance. Not only is the view the best, but so too is the interior decor. The restaurant is all marble and brass, with accents of greenery to soften the effect.

Chef Anthony Mantuano prepares stylized northern Italian food to fit his magnificent setting. The restaurant was among the first in Chicago to introduce gourmet pizzas baked in a wood-burning oven. They, along with all courses, share a certain elegance of preparation and style. Flavors are in balance. This is the kind of Italian dining that makes it easy to comprehend how this world-class cuisine gave inspiration, if not birth, to classic French cookery. Expensive, yes, but certainly an experience if sybaritic dining is your pleasure.

K/Rating of 19.5/20: Decor 4/4, Service 5/5, Food 9/9, Value 1.5/2

CARLOS & CARLOS

Italian

1540 West North, Chicago
Telephone: (312) 384-1300

Lunch: Monday–Friday 11:30–2:30. Dinner: Monday–Friday 5–10:30, Saturday 5:30–11:30, Sunday 5–10. Cards: AE, MC, V. No-smoking section. Valet parking. Full bar service. Handicap accessible. Troubleshooter: Don Evans (manager). Moderate.

One of the constants in the Chicago restaurant picture is how often unusually good restaurants pop up in the most unusual locations. One example is Carlos & Carlos. Though the name and even the location might suggest a Spanish or Mexican menu, Carlos & Carlos is northern Italian, but with a decided personal flair present in the kitchen.

The menu is not strictly Italian. Oysters Rockefeller appear along with minestrone and fettuccine. The cooking leans toward richness, with cream sauces bathing several of the entrées. Thus, it is probably best to begin with a simple appetizer such as carpaccio. The paper-thin slices of beef come handsomely fanned out on a large platter, accompanied by a mild mustard-mayonnaise sauce. The oysters Rockefeller are done in classic fashion, the baked shellfish cloaked in a hollandaise sauce flavored with just enough Pernod to remain true to tradition. Other appetizers include deep-fried calamari, the wide slivers of squid breaded and accompanied by a smattering of capers. Carlos & Carlos also seems to have taken a tip from newer cuisines, with a smoked duck salad in vinaigrette. The duck has been fully cooked, however, and does not come out blood rare as in some of the trendier establishments.

The printed menu is supplemented by daily specials announced by the waiter. There has been black linguine, which is darkened by octopus ink. The ink is turned into the pasta along with chunks of fresh cooked seafood, resulting in a marvelous mix of nautical flavors. Among other pasta selections is fettuccine verdi, green noodles with mushrooms. I found the cream sauce that binds everything together too rich for the delicate flavor of the Italian mushrooms. Similarly served in a cream sauce is the house namesake, veal Carlos. Three large veal scallops are floured and then sautéed in butter to a golden goodness. Shallots and cream are added to the pan to form what is described on the menu as a champagne sauce. Here again, however, such richness may be a blessing or not, depending upon your taste and appetite.

Carlos & Carlos does not ignore some of the basics of Italian cuisine. Consider Italian sausage with just a hint of fennel, served with a smooth marinara sauce and fresh spinach. This is the kind of Italian eating that goes right to the roots of the cuisine.

Service is a bit slow and without the finesse that shows real professionalism. But waiters are pleasant and helpful within the limits of their training. The restaurant decor creates an ambience more casual than the food being served suggests. Bare brick walls contrast with the white linen napery. The kitchen is open on three sides, in full view of diners.

K/Rating 16/20: Decor 3.5/4, Service 3.5/5, Food 7/9, Value 2/2

GEORGE'S

Italian

230 West Kinzie, Chicago
Telephone: (312) 644-2290

Hours: Tuesday–Sunday 11:30–10:30. Cards: AE, DISC, MC, V. Reservations suggested. Casual dress, but no shorts, no jeans. Valet parking. Full bar service; good selection of Italian wines Troubleshooter: George Badonsky (owner). Moderate.

To someone who thinks of Italian food only in terms of pizza, garlic, and red tomato sauce on top of overcooked spaghetti, George's will come as a revelation. I think of George's as neo-northern Italian because of the strong handprint of imaginative presentation on the basic principles that guide the traditional northern Italian cook. The à la carte menu allows the diner to experiment through the various courses. Begin with delicious fried calamari as a hot appetizer, or try carpaccio, the Italian version of steak tartare: almost transparent strips of beef accompanied by a mild pepper sauce.

George's more imaginative pastas include penne with four contrasting cheeses forming the sauce. Linguine with white clam sauce is redolent with garlic and bits of clam. The tortellini in cream sauce offers a quiet study in texture, contrast, and mildness. Daily entrée specials feature fresh fish; when soft-shell crabs are available in summer months, snap them up. Listen to your serving person's advice. I'll readily pass on a suggestion I heeded to order scampi in a hot pepper sauce. For dessert the fresh tarts are beautifully colored circles of fruit and custard on flaky crusts. Or try one of Chicago's best chocolate tortes, filled and frosted with white chocolate mousse.

K/Rating 18.5/20: Decor 4/4, Service 5/5, Food 8/9, Value 1.5/2

SCOOZI

Italian

410 West Huron, Chicago
Telephone: (312) 943-5900

Lunch: Monday–Friday 11:30–2. Dinner: Monday–Thursday 5:30–10:30, Friday–Saturday 5:30–11:30, Sunday 5–9. Cards: AE, DC, MC, V, LEYE. Reservations at lunch only. Casual to high-fashion dress. No-smoking section. Valet parking. Full bar service in 80-seat area. Handicap accessible. Troubleshooter: Rich Melman (owner). Moderate.

Scoozi is a restaurant popular with people in their mid-twenties, reviewed by a man in his mid-forties with the appetite of a man in his mid-thirties and the digestion sometimes of a man in his sixties. This place is generally acknowledged to be the hottest thing in the Chicago restaurant industry today. What that means is that you will wait for about an hour or more for your table unless you get there before five or after nine. This is the kind of restaurant where people waiting for tables spend the time watching other people waiting for tables.

Scoozi is also restaurant as theater to the *ne plus ultra*. But as it turns out, it serves some uncommonly, even surprisingly good food. The menu is quite detailed without being exhaustive in its exploration of northern Italian cookery. Dining is à la carte, but portions are generally large and foods are reasonably priced. The best way to begin is by ordering a large pizza from the list of about half a dozen specialties. My favorite is the finanziera, which the menu describes as caramelized onions, gorgonzola cheese, and escarole. When the waiter brought out two large tomato cans that he said would be a platform for the pizza, I thought this was just the affectation of a trendy restaurant. Then he brought the pizza, and I realized it did need a platform. It came out on a large, board about eighteen inches long. The pizza, instead of the nine- or ten-inch circle I expected, was gargantuan, a large ellipse of flavor on a thin, crisp crust. Flavors were absolutely sensational. Scoozi could earn its reputation just on its pizza.

But there was much more to be ordered. Not only are there some unusual pasta choices, but the kitchen produces fresh risotto every half hour. Properly made it is a soft blend of rice and light seasonings, especially saffron, butter, and cheese. Although risotto alla milanese may be the most well-known, there are any number of recipes, and each evening at Scoozi brings a different one. As for the pastas, a delicate flavor marks fusilli della valtellina. Fusilli are small ringlets, or twists, of pasta, designed so that the varied surfaces of the noodle will pick up and hold the sauce. In this case, the sauce is little more than romano cheese, lots of garlic, some roasted peppers, and pieces of arugula. The bite of the arugula contrasts nicely with the other flavors. Another pasta choice, really ample enough for a main course, is linguine el golfo. The linguine is mixed with clams, mussels, calamari, and shrimp, making it somewhat akin to a zuppa di pesce. The dish is given a bouquet of seasonings, the most pronounced of which seems to be mild fennel.

Fennel, by the way, is featured as a vegetable side dish. It is roasted and served cold in an oil bath, for a good palate refresher. Among meat choices, osso buco, classic veal shanks from Milan, come in a syrupy rich gravy with roasted potatoes, mushrooms, and pearl onions. The flavor is full and hearty. Among other choices I tried was a fine veal chop, breaded and sautéed, then served with a roasted pepper relish.

The restaurant is noisy and crowded, but it is fun.

K/Rating of 18/20: Decor 3/4, Service 4.5/5, Food 8.5/9, Value 2/2

CLUB LAGO

Italian

331 West Superior (at Orleans), Chicago
Telephone: (312) 951-2849

Hours: Monday–Friday 11–8, Saturday 11–3. No cards. Reservations accepted. Street parking. Full bar service; limited wine list. No party room as such, but entire restaurant can be taken by up to 100 people if planned far enough ahead. Troubleshooter: Francesco Nardini (owner). Inexpensive.

Long before the north river area was discovered by yuppies, gallery owners, and other entrepreneurs, Club Lago was going strong. Without knowing what's going on inside, you are likely to take a look at the corner tavern exterior and just keep on going. The truth is that Club Lago is a small and casual Italian restaurant where dinners need not be much more than $5 or $6. The menu changes from day to day, featuring ubiquitous Italian fare sauced more in the northern than the southern or Sicilian manner; tomato acidity is muted. For example, lasagne, which shows up Monday and Thursday, is so subtle in its flavors that the sweet bite of basil can easily be detected among its seasonings.

Among other treats I enjoy here is the green spinach noodles al forno, which like most of the pastas is served every day. Although this is featured as a lunch or dinner entrée, I think it is best enjoyed as a pasta course split among others at your table. Then you can choose one of the veal dishes for a main course, perhaps veal limone with a light citrus bite in its butter-herb sauce. Or try the traditional veal parmigiana (a Wednesday special) smothered in a thick blanket of cheese and tomato sauce. Other rotating veal choices include rusticana with eggplant, saltimbocca with cheese and Italian ham, piccata, Marsala, and cacciatore. Club Lago also serves a selection of sandwiches and omelets at lunch, as well as steak and fish. And be sure to order the fried zucchini sticks, juicy mushrooms, and garlic pizza bread.

K/Rating 16.5/20: Decor 2/4, Service 5/5, Food 7.5/9, Value 2/2

GINO'S EAST

Italian/Pizza

160 East Superior, Chicago
Telephone: (312) 943-1124
Other location is listed below.

Hours: Monday–Thursday 11–11, Friday–Saturday 11–midnight, Sunday 2–10. Cards: AE, CB, DC, MC, V, LEYE. Reservations taken Monday–Thursday for lunch or dinner, Friday for lunch only. No-smoking section. Semiprivate party facilities for up to 100 people. Troubleshooter: Rich Melman (owner). Inexpensive.

A place popular with college kids, hospital technicians, and secretaries, Gino's East just happens to have some of the best pizza around. It is Chicago-style pizza, deep dish with a thick, almost cake-crumb crust, rich sauce, and gobs of toppings over cheese. If something other than pizza is your choice, pasta dishes are most satisfying here; I particularly enjoy the green noodles with meatballs. There are two dining rooms served by the same kitchen. One is downstairs, a grottolike affair with wooden tables and bench seating. The upstairs dining room has a gracious white-tablecloth setting. Take your pick, depending on how you are dressed and what mood suits you. By the way, you can stick with the house wines by C-K Mondavi and not go wrong.

Gino's East has a second location at 1321 West Golf Road (312-364-6648), Rolling Meadows.

K/Rating 18.5/20: Decor 3.5/4, Service 4/5, Food 9/9, Value 2/2

SAYAT NOVA

Armenian

157 East Ohio, Chicago
Telephone: (312) 644-9159
Other locationis listed opposite.

Hours: Monday–Thursday 11:30–11. Friday–Saturday 11:30–midnight, Sunday 3–10. Cards: AE, CB, DC, MC, V. Reservations suggested. Casual dress. Full bar service; extensive wine list. Troubleshooter: Leon Demerdjian (owner). Moderate.

You will want to taste a variety of dishes here, so be sure to come with a group; six is an ideal number. Start with a selection of appetizers that includes cold eggplant, tomatoes, and onions sautéed in olive oil, and phyllo pastries stuffed with spinach or ground meat and pine nuts. Another choice is borek; imagine mild brick cheese lightly seasoned with green onion and the yolk of an egg, then baked in an airy pastry. Or try sarma, stuffed grape leaves, slightly sweet on the tongue.

For dinner you may choose from several options. There is a combination platter that offers a balance of tastes and textures. Shish kebab, lamb or beef skewered with tomato and green pepper, is slowly roasted over charcoal and served with rice pilaf on the side. Entirely different is lula kebab, ground beef or lamb formed into a shape much like a sausage without a casing. Sautéed lamb is another excellent choice. My favorite dessert is atayef with cream, a half-moon of puff pastry filled with a delicate sweet cream curd and topped with warm honey. It is somewhere between a pudding and a chiffon.

Sayat Nova has a second location at 20 West Golf Road (312-296-1776), Des Plaines.

K/Rating of 20/20: Decor 4/4, Service 5/5, Food 9/9, Value 2/2

BOMBAY PALACE

Indian

50 East Walton Chicago
Telephone: (312)664-9323

Lunch: daily 11:30–2:30. Dinner: 5:30–10:30. Cards: AE, CB, DC, MC, V. Reservations suggested. Casual dress, but no shorts. Valet parking. Full bar service; small cocktail lounge; small wine list. Private party area for up to 60 people. Troubleshooter: Ravi N. Sahni (manager). Moderate.

Bombay Palace is a handsome, open double dining area with a marble floor. An illuminated stained-glass ceiling represents modern Indian abstract art. The food, however, is as traditional as that found at any of the several Indian restaurants that dot the Chicago area.

Initiates might want to order a set dinner, which includes several of the basics, but ordering à la carte is far more rewarding. Though going this route can get rather expensive, you will have the opportunity to sample a wider range of tastes.

Begin with a platter of the dough puffs called pakoras, which are fried fritters of a sort, and samosas, deep-fried, vegetable-filled triangles. Taste some grilled chicken tikka, boned bite-sized pieces hot from a deep charcoal-fired clay urn that serves as an oven. Next might come soup. The Bombay Palace version of mulligatawny is creamier than many, but is still an amalgam of the spices and seasonings that characterize Indian cookery.

This is one of the most aromatic, most delicately perfumed cuisines. Coriander and cardamom, turmeric, cinnamon, and cloves are part and parcel of the Indian bouquet of flavors. The framework for some of this culinary tradition is the unique method of cooking in the tandoor, the clay urn used for grilling meats and fish, or as an oven for baking some of the most delicious breads to pass from platter to lips.

In addition to the bright red tandoori chicken, diners might try the exceptional rogan josh, an incredible casserole of cubed lamb in a mildly seasoned yogurt-based gravy, or another casserole-style recipe, such as chicken Vindaloo, with a spicier sauce.

Vegetables are an important part of the Indian diet. Thus, lentils, peas, cauliflower, potatoes, spinach, onions, and chick-peas come in various cream sauces that add their own special flavor. It is, in short, a complex and infinitely rewarding way of dining.

Desserts are in a class of their own, quite unlike most sweets to which you may be accustomed. Sweetened cheese, mango ice cream, and small candies are all points of interest.

As fine as the food is at Bombay Palace, the service unfortunately borders on the indifferent. There needs to be greater attention to this important aspect of every restaurant experience.

K/Rating of 16/20: Decor 4/4, Service 3/5, Food 8/9, Value 1/2

GAYLORD INDIA RESTAURANT

Indian

678 North Clark, Chicago
Telephone: (312) 664-1700

Lunch: Monday–Friday 11:30–2:30, Saturday–Sunday noon–3. Dinner: daily 5:30–10:30. Cards: AE, CB, DC, MC, V. Reservations suggested. No-smoking section. Free parking lot. Full bar service. Private party facilities for up to 60 people. Troubleshooters: Mr. Soni (manager) and Mr. Puri (maître d'). Moderate.

Gaylord India Restaurant offers some of the best Indian cooking available in Chicago. Though far from what you may usually think of as a chain restaurant, it is part of an international network with branches in India, London, New York, and San Francisco. There are scores of cooking styles in the large and populous Indian subcontinent. Gaylord offers a taste of northern cuisine, characterized by cooking in tandoors, deep clay-lined pits embedded in a tile-covered counter. Each holds a bed of white-hot charcoal over which long-marinated meats are quickly cooked to seal in flavor and juices. When roasted in the tandoor, chicken or lamb, covered with a red-colored, yogurt-based marinade, takes on a complex charcoal taste that you just can't capture in your backyard barbecue.

No beef is served here because of the Hindu taboo, but delicious chicken, lamb, prawns, and vegetarian dishes are regular menu items. Naturally, vegetables are handled in an outstanding way, some spicy, others mild. Combination platters offer beginners a good assortment of textures and tastes. At the end of your meal take hot tea and any of the refreshingly sweet desserts. Wines are available, but beer is preferable with curries.

K/Rating of 19/20: Decor 4/4, Service 5/5, Food 8/9, Value 2/2

SZECHWAN HOUSE

Chinese (Szechwan)

600 North Michigan, Chicago
Telephone: (312) 642-3900

Hours: Sunday–Thursday 11:30–10:30, Friday–Saturday 11:30–11:00. Cards: AE, CB, DC, MC, V, house accounts. Reservations suggested. Valet parking after 6. Full bar service. Private party room for up to 60 people. Troubleshooters: Austin Koo and Charles Lin (owners). Moderate.

Szechwan cooking is characterized by a liberal use of hot peppers. Keep that in mind when dining at Szechwan House, which serves a wide variety of genuinely interesting and well-prepared foods that demonstrate the Chinese predilection for contrasts in taste and texture. Flavorful appetizers include ground shrimp wrapped in seaweed and deep fried, and steamed dumplings presented in a woven basket steamer—hot and plump with a mild ground-meat filling. Eat these little delights with a bit of vinegar and soy sauce and a dab of fiery-hot red pepper sauce. An order of snails is another recommended choice. The little morsels come in a spicy sauce radically different from the garlicked French snails with which many diners are familiar. From the cold appetizer selection, hacked chicken is the best of the lot: narrow strips of white meat are served in a peppery peanut sauce with shredded lettuce. Now jellyfish may sound like a turn-off, but the thin, transparent, noodlelike pieces are rather easy to enjoy.

Among entrées I like is ma la frog legs in a hot garlic sauce with just a hint of ginger. One of the most unusual choices is beef with strips of orange peel and vegetables in a complex hot pepper sauce. The tart orange flavor coupled with the vegetables and the juicy beef sets taste buds tingling. Order some à la carte vegetables such as broccoli or spinach to balance flavors. For stylish and delicious Chinese dining, Szechwan House is hard to beat.

K/Rating of 19/20: Decor 3.5/4, Service 4.5/5, Food 9/9, Value 2/2

HOUSE OF HUNAN

Chinese (Mandarin)

535 North Michigan, Chicago
Telephone: (312) 329-9494

Hours: daily 11:30–10:30. Cards: AE, CB, DC, MC, V. Reservations recommended. Casual, but neat dress. No-smoking section. Discount parking at 158 East Grand garage. Full bar service. Handicap accessible. Private party facilities for up to 60 people. Troubleshooter: George Kwan (owner). Moderate.

Chinese cuisine may be the world's oldest and most diversified: it can be dark and subtle, hot and fiery, light and almost playful. Drawing from the cooking of all the major regions of China, the food at the House of Hunan on Michigan Avenue can be all this and perhaps more. Shrimp toast practically bursts with succulence. Among other appetizers, barbecued beef is a delicious blend of seasonings that leaves a semisweet aftertaste on the tongue. The Chinese do not ignore cold appetizers, nor should you. Marinated beef is tantalizing with the complex flavor of five-spice powder. Bean curd, almost like cold chicken, tendrils of jellyfish much like transparent starch noodles, drunken chicken chilled in wine sauce—all give display to the Chinese penchant for pleasurable tastes and textures.

With nineteen separate appetizer selections, the temptation is to stay with the tidbits, but leaf through the detailed menu and savor more. You may rave about sliced leg of lamb Hunan. The tender meat is served in a sauce that teases with Oriental peppers and scallions. Yet seasonings are held in check without destroying a complex balance. Shrimp Hunan is another recommended choice. Milder is Shanghai pike, bits of fish fillets prepared with egg whites for a silken texture, then served with vegetables in a delicate white wine sauce. Beef with broccoli is a pleasure, too. Vegetarians should enjoy any of several mixed-vegetable preparations.

Note: House of Hunan on Michigan Avenue has no connection with the House of Hunan on Lincoln Avenue.

K/Rating 19/20: Decor 4/4, Service 5/5, Food 8/9, Value 2/2

MEMORIES OF CHINA

Chinese

1150 North State (Newberry Plaza), Chicago
Telephone: (312) 642-1800

Lunch: daily 11:30–2:30. Dinner: daily 5–10. Cards: AE, CB, DC, MC, V. Reservations required. No-smoking section. Discount parking in building garage. Full bar service. Handicap accessible. Large party room for 100-plus people; two smaller rooms for more intimate groups. Troubleshooters: Alfred Hsu (maître d') and Martin Binder (owner). Moderate.

Memories of China is unforgettable. This is easily the finest Chinese restaurant Chicago has seen in years; certainly it is the best I have come across.

The menu takes up more than a dozen pages. The food is flawless. Presentations are exquisite. Many selections are brought to the table with elaborate figurines handcarved from vegetables. In one case, two figures were bearing a closed carriage, a scene right out of old Cathay. The workmanship of the carvings is exceptional.

This same attention to detail is present in all the dishes served at Memories of China. Among appetizers, pot stickers are more delicate than any I have eaten. The dough is light, the filling smooth, and with a balance of seasonings. Or consider scallion pancakes. Diners are served wedges of quick-fried pancakes with just a hint of spicy sharpness in the flavoring. A little soy-ginger sauce is the ideal accompaniment. Among other choices is a delightful cold salad of pickled turnips and carrots. The taste is sweet but not cloying.

Every entrée I have tasted here has been perfect. Among fish choices are at least half a dozen species that can be prepared in any of seven different ways. Stir-fried orange roughy brings the delicately cooked fish tossed with a mix of oriental vegetables and mushrooms. I can only think of two or three other occasions when I have enjoyed fish as much. For a meat course, I ordered an exotic treatment of barbecued lamb. The meat has a sweet flavor, almost fermented, a flavor that comes from being marinated in miso bean sauce. The lamb chunks are quickly seared and then wrapped in leaf lettuce so that they can be eaten out of hand. Another inventive selection is haw gee kaye chicken. The cut-up white meat is cooked in a mild brown sauce with snow peas for flashes of color and texture, chewy mushrooms, and other vegetables. If you love noodles, be sure to get double fried noodles, at once both soft and crispy.

K/Rating 20/20: Decor 4/4, Service 5/5, Food 9/9, Value 2/2

STAR OF SIAM

Thai

11 East Illinois, Chicago
Telephone: (312) 670-0100

Hours: Sunday–Thursday, 11–9:30, Friday–Saturday 11–10:30. Cards: AE, CB, DC, DISC, MC, V, house accounts. Reservations accepted. Casual, but neat dress. No-smoking section. Ample parking on street or in lots. Full bar service; extensive selections of wines and beers. Private party room for up to 100 people. Troubleshooter: Adirek Dulyapaibul (owner). Moderate.

Star of Siam, located on the first floor of a renovated loft building, looks different than most other Thai restaurants. Its food, however, is among the best. The restaurant has a modish decor of bare brick walls and bench-type seating that gives a feeling of spaciousness. In a sense, Star of Siam is "yuppie Thai," with an appeal that seems as much urban as ethnic.

The menu offers the traditional balance between sweet and hot, although even the spiciest recipes are reserved enough so that the complexity of seasonings is not overwhelming. Appetizer choices include spring rolls with a honeylike plum-sauce glaze and cool filling of vegetables, tofu, and minced scrambled eggs. An order of satay brings lightly grilled chicken or beef marinated in a bath of sweet coconut milk and accompanied with a spicy peanut sauce that sets off the flavors of the meat. Fried tofu, another appetizer, comes in deep-fried thick wedges that taste best when dipped into a tangy plum sauce.

Thai dining is not complete without a soup course, and a large bowl here is sufficient for four people. Thai soups are built on a clear chicken broth accented with a complexity of peppers and seasonings, especially lemongrass and coriander. The tom yom, a shrimp soup that has been my benchmark for testing Thai foods over the years, is first rate at Star of Siam.

The menu designates several main-course selections as specialties of the house, but I have found that even the regular entrée list offers delightful dining. For example, roast duck brings slices from the breast in a sauce of honey and soy. The meat is tender, rich, and relatively lean, as good as duckling can be. If you "like it hot," try the fried spicy basil leaves with meat. You can have shrimp, chicken, or beef in a sauce that is certainly spicy, though not as perfumed with the basil as I expected. Star of Siam features several curries and a number of noodle dishes. Pad Thai is a classic noodle dish in my book. Cool, almost soothing rice vermicelli noodles are served with crushed peanuts, eggs, bean sprouts, and tofu. Entirely different is lard nar, broad, flat wheat noodles in a thickened gravy with collard greens and shrimp. This is a dish in which the texture of the noodles is all important, and when done right, as at Star of Siam, is completely satisfying.

Although Asian restaurants are not particularly known for desserts, Star of Siam does have some genuine treats. One favorite is Thai Star custard, a near cakelike preparation rich with the sweet flavor of coconut.

K/Rating of 18/20: Decor, 3.5/4, Service, 4.5/5, Food 8/9, Value 2/2

ANANDA

Thai

941 North State, Chicago
Telephone: (312) 944-7440

Lunch: Tuesday–Saturday 11:30–2:30. Dinner: Tuesday–Thursday, Sunday 5–10, Friday–Saturday 5–10:30. Cards: MC, V. Casual dress. Street parking and nearby parking lot. Full bar service. Handicap accessible. Private party facilities for up to 75 people. Troubleshooters: Ananda and Marzina Seetapun (owners). Moderate.

For occasions when you have a taste for Thai food in a somewhat more handsome setting than basic storefront and you are willing to spend more for the experience, there is Ananda. A dinner of appetizer, soup, and entrée can cost as much as $30 per couple, which may not seem like a lot of money by today's restaurant standards, but is actually about double what you might spend in more simple surroundings. There is no question that the food served at Ananda seems to be more refined in both its presentation and tastes. I was told that this is a style of seasoning found in the larger cities of Thailand. Thus, a shrimp soup called tom yum goong (or a similar appellation, depending upon the transliteration used) is somewhat timid, without the sharp bite of red chili peppers and pronounced lemongrass that makes it so appealing in other restaurants. Similarly, a Thai chicken curry with ginger in a coconut sauce was not hot and spicy, proving that there are many roads to curry nirvana.

Other dishes are temperate, but enjoyable in their own way. Thai spring rolls, a pleasant contrast to traditional egg rolls, are a cool, refreshing palate cleanser; they come stuffed with pieces of sausage and coarsely chopped firm vegetables in sweetened syrup sauce. The best of the appetizer selections are the fried fish cakes, double-bite-sized fritters with a crisp breaded coating, delicious eaten in the company of the tangy sauce with which they are served. For those who cannot tolerate truly hot seasonings and spices, plus want Thai food in a more sumptuous atmosphere than the usual plain storefront, Ananda is the answer.

K/Rating 15.5/20: Decor 4/4, Service 4/5, Food 6.5/9, Value 1/2

HATSUHANA

Japanese

160 East Ontario, Chicago
Telephone: (312) 280-8287

Lunch: Monday–Friday noon–2. Dinner: 5:45–10, Saturday 5:30–10. Cards: AE, CB, DC, MC, V. Reservations suggested. No-smoking section. Full bar service; sake and Japanese beers. Private party facilities for up to 50 people. Troubleshooter: Nick Nakamura (manager). Expensive.

Hatsuhana was the first restaurant I know of to serve sushi and sashimi in Chicago. In spite of its popularity, the restaurant manages to offer a serenity that exists in only one or two other Japanese restaurants in the city. The dining area has white walls accented with blond wood. Individual tables accommodate small groups, and a twenty-five-seat sushi bar lets diners watch the sushi masters perform their culinary artistry.

Sushi can be ordered à la carte or in fixed-price portions that offer samples of several different styles. Should you find the idea of eating plain raw seafood unpleasant, start with something such as chopped tuna and scallions, much like a seafood version of steak tartare but with mild oriental seasonings. Then work up to bite-sized pieces of raw fish on a wedge of vinegared rice wrapped in a sheet of dried seaweed. Or you might try the raw fish open-faced, seasoned with a dab of hot green wasabi (horseradish) and a bit of thinly sliced pickled ginger.

In addition to the selections of sushi and sashimi, Hatsuhana serves complete lunches and dinners with soup, pickled vegetables, rice, and tea. À la carte selections will raise your tab, but they will also give you the chance to work through the menu and try some of the more exotic fare. More conservative diners may want to stay with tempura, lobster, or steak. But whatever you choose, Hatsuhana is the best of its kind in Chicago.

K/Rating 20/20: Decor 4/4, Service 5/5, Food 9/9, Value 2/2

YANASE

Japanese

818 North State, Chicago
Telephone: (312) 664-1371

Lunch: Monday–Friday 11:30–2:30. Dinner: Monday–Saturday 5–10. Cards: AE, CB, DC, MC, V. Reservations accepted. Casual dress. Street parking can be difficult. Wine and beer. Troubleshooter: Kenju Horiboshi (owner). Inexpensive.

While you can find Japanese food prepared and served with more finesse, there's no room to quibble about a product as tasty as what you will find at Yanase. The restaurant forgoes some of the elaborate carved vegetable garnishes that add a gorgeous visual touch to Japanese place settings. But one can do without such frills if the goal is good budget dining.

Sushi, which is uniformly fresh and ample here, may tack on a few dollars to the bill. A combination platter usually includes tuna, octopus, and yellowtail, along with various other sea-fresh items. An excellent grilled salmon entrée is often offered as the fresh fish of the day. Chicken teriyaki and beef teriyaki are enhanced with the traditional sweetened soy sauce characteristic of Japanese cuisine. Equally commendable is the sukiyaki. Served in the cast-iron skillet in which it has been cooked, a generous portion of thinly sliced beef is bathed in a mild broth, along with squares of bean curd, sliced onions, shredded cabbage, and hearty noodles.

K/Rating of 16/20: Decor, 2.5/4, Service 4/5, Food 7.5/9, Value 2/2

> MIDNORTH

STAR TOP CAFE

2748 North Lincoln, Chicago
Telephone: (312) 281-0997

Hours: Tuesday–Thursday 5:30–10, Friday–Saturday 5:30–11. Cards: AE, CB, DC, MC, V. Reservations suggested. Ample street parking. Full bar service; fine wine list. Private party facilities available Sunday–Monday for up to 50 people. Troubleshooter: Michael Short (chef). Moderate.

American/Eclectic

Though the name and location are the same, this is not the same Star Top Cafe listed in previous editions of this book. New ownership has brought in a new chef and a new way of doing things. But some things remain. The sign out front is marred by peeling paint. The front door and window trim are scuffed. Your table centerpiece might be an old bowling trophy. And the food is inspired madness! As much as I liked Star Top Cafe when I first reviewed it a few years back, the cooking is even better today, thanks to the capable and eclectic work of chef Michael Short. His kitchen looks like a scene from the 1960s counterculture. Short says if he can't have fun, he won't do it. Fortunately for Chicago diners, he is apparently having a ball!

Short says he was classically trained as a cook and has spent the last ten years unlearning all of that. His style is hardly classic, yet there are hints of an order in his sauces, which run all over the map from Chinese, to Mexican, and yes, even to French.

The Star Top Cafe menu changes nightly, but my recent dinner is typical of what to expect from the unexpected. An appetizer of pasta estiva brings linguine in a sauce of cooked vegetables and peppers that leaves a slight tingle in its wake. Grilled shrimp with avocado and a pumpkin-seed salsa is served with a bit of Chihuahua cheese. The blend hardly leaves the shrimp to their own devices, but the other elements are not so powerful as to overwhelm the shellfish. A bit of Continental influence creeps in with a duck confit, mushrooms, and polenta with a garlic cream sauce. The fact is that there is very little one can do with polenta, no matter the best of intentions. But the effort proved interesting, if not exceptional. Best of the appetizers I tasted was a small platter of bay scallops with cappellini pasta, fresh mint, and montrachet cheese sauce. This was an imaginative treatment, a truly unusual combination of tastes.

Were the cooking not so good, chef Short could be accused of contrivance. But his imagination runs within logical limits. A duck breast sauté comes with a Szechwan peppercorn sauce, marrying two cultures in a defined balance of flavors. Less successful is grilled chicken breast in a beurre blanc adapted with pistachios, lemon, and whole cranberries for color and flavor accent. Short undercooks his chicken and makes no excuses for it. Frankly, I'm a little gun-shy of rare chicken these days. More on the mark is an almost conventional entrée-portion steak salad that combines radicchio, roasted peppers, mushrooms, and a sun-dried-tomato vinaigrette with slices of rare beef. Yet another unusual product of the Star Top Cafe kitchen is duck confit with caponata and a combination of Italian cheeses, all served with a copious portion of broad noodles. The result is like a noodle stew except for the eccentricity of ingredients.

The desserts served at Star Top Cafe are somewhat less unusual than other courses.

K/Rating 16.5/20: Decor 2.5/4, Service 4/5, Food 8/9, Value 2/2

JEROME'S

American/Eclectic

2450 North Clark, Chicago
Telephone: (312) 327-2207

Hours: Tuesday–Thursday 11:30–10:30, Friday 11:30–11:30, Saturday 8 am–11:30 pm, Sunday 10–10. Cards: AE, MC, V. Reservations suggested. No-smoking section. Discount parking at Columbus Hospital lot one block north on Clark. Full bar service. Troubleshooter: Jerome Kliejunas (owner). Moderate.

Certainly Jerome's cannot be called a budget restaurant, but considering that the dinner menu starts as low as $8.95 (including soup or salad, vegetables, and potato), it's far from exorbitant. Like other quality restaurants, Jerome's features some daily specials. For instance, I enjoyed an excellent baked grouper one evening. The fish came with a stuffing generously accented with oysters, shrimp, green pepper, celery, and onion. Another recent special was roast chicken served in a cucumber sauce with garlic and paprika; each flavor was distinct, yet all worked well with the poultry. Jerome's is a favorite spot in summer months because of its outdoor patio fronting busy Clark Street—one of the town's better spots to see and be seen. The restaurant bills itself as a "fresh food restaurant" and from all I can determine that claim is true. For one thing, there are delicious baked goods in addition to fresh soups, salads, and desserts. If you're not a big spender, you can order by the glass from the wine bar.

K/Rating 17/20: Decor 4/4, Service 4/5, Food 7/9, Value 2/2

KING CRAB

Seafood

1816 North Halsted, Chicago
Telephone: (312) 280-8990

Hours: Monday–Thursday 11:30–11, Friday 11:30–midnight, Saturday 5–midnight, Sunday 12:30–10:30. Cards: AE, CB, DC, MC, V. Reservations only for parties of 6 or more. Valet parking. Full bar service; good selection of beers and wines. Troubleshooter: Koorosh Sadeghi (owner). Moderate.

To keep up with freshness, there are no printed menus here. Everything is listed on blackboards with prices and descriptions. Those prices are generally low enough, and since several items are available as main course or appetizer, you might just want to put together your own buffet of sorts and graze. But before anything else, order a bowl of seafood chowder, laden with mushrooms, water chestnuts, ample seafood, celery, and seasoning in a cream-based soup so thick you could almost use a fork.

Among appetizers, don't ignore mussels in vermouth and garlic butter. The namesake crab is featured among shellfish. Lobsters tend to be a pound to a pound and a half and are priced according to market. Other specialties often include Mexican grilled prawns, Pacific Dungeness crab, grilled salmon steaks, as well as some chicken, steaks, and burgers for nonnautical diners. For dessert there is a quartet of cheesecakes. The restaurant is casual and comfortable, well worth a trip from your neighborhood.

K/Rating 18/20: Decor 3.5/4, Service 5/5, Food 7.5/9, Value 2/2

RAGIN' CAJUN

Cajun/Creole

3048 West Diversey, Chicago
Telephone: (312) 342-6427

Lunch: Sunday–Thursday 11–3. Dinner: Sunday–Thursday 5–10, Friday–Saturday 4–1 am. Cards: AE, MC, V, house accounts. Reservations suggested. Casual, but neat dress. No-smoking section. Street parking. Full bar service. Small lounge and dining areas for private groups. Troubleshooter: Harvey Durrson (chef-owner). Moderate.

From outside, Ragin' Cajun looks run-down in an almost primeval sort of way, as if it were built out in a bayou instead of in the middle of Chicago. A similar mood pervades inside. After all these years, the restaurant has begun to show its age. This down-at-the-heels atmosphere in no way affects the greeting of diners, who are treated with courtesy and even familiarity. The cooking may be Cajun, but is definitely not trendy. This is the kind of kitchen that outlives fads.

Ragin' Cajun serves five-course table d'hôte dinners that range in price from about $14 to $20. Meals begin with a small scoop of shrimp pâté so lightly flavored it doesn't need any accompaniment. Cajun-style remoulade or cocktail sauce is offered if you want that little extra jolt. Next comes soup. Peanut is thick and creamy; gumbo is loaded with bits of okra, vegetables, meat, and rice in a tangy blend of seasonings. There is a version of onion soup, and a Creole oyster and artichoke, its oyster and chicken stock evident beneath the complexity of herbs and spices that give the broth depth. Salad is a mix of greens in a mustard vinaigrette, a welcome prelude to the entrées. There are a dozen choices, including catfish in several preparations, chicken, prawns, a chef's evening special, and a blackened sirloin, which seems to be the only nod to culinary fashion on the Ragin' Cajun menu.

Of course there is jambalaya, that deliciously flavored rice casserole awash with ham, shrimp, peppers, herbs, and, as the menu puts it, "whatever Harvey sees fit to add . . . ," meaning chef Harvey Durrson. Among fish dinners, red snapper comes smothered in a tomato-based Creole sauce; snapper is sometimes a bit too strongly flavored for my taste, but real seafood lovers will enjoy the version at Ragin' Cajun. And there are étouffées, either chicken or catfish. The deboned chunks of fried fish come in a thick gravy of Cajun seasonings, not the least of which are peppers. The fish is smothered in its gravy, befitting the traditional service of an étouffée. Then, all of this is ladled out onto a mound of fresh steaming rice. A cold bottle of Dixie beer goes down mighty nice with this dish. If you insist, you could order a plain baked or deep-fried catfish and still enjoy the fish without all the other fuss.

Desserts at Ragin' Cajun are good, not great; sweet potato pie may be the best of the lot. In addition to the set dinner, you can order some à la carte appetizers or menu lagniappes such as hush puppies or rice fritters.

K/Rating 16/20: Decor 2.5/4, Service 4/5, Food 7.5/9, Value 2/2

BLUE MESA

American Southwest

1729 North Halsted, Chicago
Telephone: (312) 944-5990

Lunch: Monday–Friday 11:30–2:30. Dinner: Monday–Thursday 4–11, Friday–Saturday 4–midnight. Cards: AE, MC, V, house accounts with prior approval. Reservations only for parties of 8 or more. Valet parking. Full bar service; excellent margaritas; good wine list. Handicap accessible. Private party room for up to 45 people. Troubleshooters: Phil Marienthal and David G. Marienthal (owners). Moderate.

The restaurant is a picture of New Mexican design, with its pueblo-inspired interiors, whitewashed walls, low-key art, cacti, and blooming desert greens. For warm-weather dining there is also the patio. The menu stresses the lighter style of cooking that is characteristic of today's tastes. Still, there is that peppery Mexican influence found in such appetizers as frito pie, which, with its studied blend of corn chips, beans, cheese, and sauce, seems as if it were developed by a gringo. Fried cheese fingers are lightly breaded and served with a tasty salsa. Other choices are smoked trout, Blue Mesa fritters, and grilled cubed sirloin.

Dinner specialties include an unusual presentation of chicken or cheese enchiladas, layered much like a Mexican-style lasagne. Honey-lime chicken is also an enjoyable choice; the two flavors work beautifully to create a sweet-tart glaze that's just right for the chicken. For beef eaters, there is carne asada in a gloriously delicious sauce of mixed peppers, onions, tomatoes, and sautéed cactus. One of the tastiest dinners is veal Southwest in a sauté of chewy mushrooms and a garnish of pine nuts. For smaller appetites there are some à la carte choices, including an absolutely delicious chili loaded with shredded beef and pinto beans, lavishly topped with melted cheddar and a dollop of sour cream. You can get it with a red chili sauce or the milder green sauce. This chili is so good I suggest you order some for an appetizer and split it among your party. Then again, you might just want a bowl all to yourself.

K/Rating 17.5/20, Decor 4/4, Service 4/5, Food 8/9, Value 1.5/2

AQUI MI TIERRA

Mexican

1039 West Belmont, Chicago
Telephone: (312) 929-7955
Other location is listed below.

Hours: daily 11–4. Cards: AE, MC, V. Reservations accepted. Street parking can be difficult. Full bar service; limited wine list; good selection of beers. Troubleshooter: Louis Nunez (owner). Moderate.

My friend Bob has an interesting theory about restaurants. It has to do with tablecloths. Those that have them, he believes, serve smaller portions; those without them will feed you until you can hardly walk. At Aqui Mi Tierra, Bob's tablecloth theory proves true. Neat as a pin, the restaurant has a homey feel to it, shutting out the urban bustle beyond its front door.

The menu says its charcoal steaks are specialties; the carne asada, prepared Tampico style, comes with a cheese enchilada and some guacamole on the side. That guacamole, by the way, is top-notch—rich with the flavor of fresh avocado. The meat is a cut of skirt steak, charcoal grilled as the menu advertises. Other grilled meats, none more costly than $9, include a boneless rib eye, small fillet, or T-bone, as well as Mexican-style shish kebab. The shish kebab ($5.95) mixes thin slices of beef with equally thin rounds of bacon. It's a handsome and tasty combination. The steak Milanesa is less satisfactory. The breading is almost nonexistent, and though the meat is tender, it is without much flavor. All of the special dinner platters are served with delicious fried potato wedges, beans, salad, and tortillas, either wheat or corn.

Aqui Mi Tierra offers tacos, burritos, and enchiladas found on the menus of most Mexican restaurants. The chiles rellenos are the kind to write home about. The deep-fried pepper is sweet, filled to near bursting with melted Mexican white cheese; if the seasoning is not quite to your taste, you can always zip things up with the salsa, a house condiment that is found on every table.

Aqui Mi Tierra has a second location, called Nanci's Restaurant Mexicano, at 7134 West Cermak (312-795-1460), Berwyn.

K/Rating 16/20: Decor 3/4, Service 4/5, Food 7/9, Value 2/2

EL JARDIN

Mexican

3335 North Clark, Chicago
Telephone: (312) 528-6775

Hours: Monday–Thursday 11–11, Friday–Sunday 11–midnight. Cards: AE, CB, DC, MC, V. Parking lot and street parking. Full bar service; specialty drinks include margaritas, piña coladas, sangría; California wines. Handicap accessible. Banquet hall available for private parties. Troubleshooters: Elizabeth Ortiz and Maria Quinones (owners). Inexpensive.

Probably due to our unpredictable weather, Chicago restaurants have been slow to adopt the trend of outdoor garden dining. One restaurant that has featured an al fresco setting for years is El Jardin, even incorporating the concept in its name. When weather permits, the graveled, enclosed courtyard is indeed a fine place for sipping margaritas and whiling away a star-filled evening. Unfortunately, the margaritas are one of the weak points at El Jardin.

The menu presents the typical Mexican selections, with some hits and misses. Among the choices I can recommend is lengua en salsa, a robust tongue stew. Or try the enchiladas a la potosina, stuffed with chili and cheese. Though the menu makes no mention of this, you can ask that the enchiladas be sauced with mole for a deeper flavor accent. I have had problems with some dinner choices, but the dessert offering of flan is not only great, it may be the best flan I've ever had—chewy, almost like cheesecake in its richness. Despite the hits and misses, El Jardin on balance is still a pleasant way to go Mexican, particularly when the garden is open.

K/Rating of 15.5/20: Decor 3.5/4, Service 3.5/5, Food 6.5/9, Value 2/2

PABLO'S CAFE

Mexican

3056 North Oakley at Clybourn, Chicago
Telephone: (312) 477-0505

Hours: Monday–Thursday 10–10, Friday–Saturday 10–midnight, Sunday 3–10. Cards: MC, V. Reservations accepted. No-smoking section. Street parking. Full bar service; Mexican and American beers, mixed Mexican drinks, sangría. Private party facilities for up to 35 people. Troubleshooters: Paul and Mary Ann Garza (owners). Inexpensive.

Little more than two or three years ago, Pablo's Cafe was just another neighborhood tavern. There was nothing wrong with that, if all you were looking for was a comfortable place for conversation, a few drinks, maybe a hamburger or a slab of ribs.

But the owners wanted to do something more. Slowly but surely, and without losing that neighborhood tavern appeal, they have transformed Pablo's Cafe into a top-notch, low-priced Mexican restaurant. The restaurant shows its Mexican character with serape wall hangings, some extruded metal Mexican artwork, posters, and the like. Nothing is overdone, and just to let its regulars know it is still the same old place for them, burgers, ribs, and perch remain on the menu.

There are also chimichangas, burritos, and enchiladas, the chiles rellenos and guacamole, the carne asada and flan. In terms of food, the word "terrific" would be a good place to start! For an appetizer, one of the world's truly large burritos makes great nibbling when split among a table of four. Add queso fundido, melted Chihuahua cheese lightly seasoned but not spicy. Take the cheese while it is hot and runny and scoop it onto a taco chip or wrap a warm tortilla around some. Other appetizers include the ubiquitous nachos and guacamole for tasty nibbling.

Getting down to the brass tacks of a main course, the choices may be the same old Mexican foods you have seen elsewhere, but preparation is uniformly excellent. Chiles rellenos, which can be sodden and uninteresting unless perfectly prepared, are indeed perfect at Pablo's Cafe. The mild green pepper is stuffed with cheese, lightly seasoned and breaded, and then deep fried to a golden puffiness. A chile relleno should be tender enough to cut without a knife, and this one is. For folks who cannot make up their minds, Pablo's Cafe offers a variety of combination platters.

Desserts usually include homemade flan served with a lightly sweetened caramel syrup. The pace is slow and should stay that way. So if you go, don't rush things.

K/Rating 19/20: Decor 3.5/4, Service 4.5/5, Food 9/9, Value 2/2

TANIA'S

Cuban

2659 North Milwaukee, Chicago
Telephone: (312) 235-7120 or 235-6797

Hours: Monday–Saturday 11 am–3 am, Sunday 1 pm–2 am. Cards: AE, CB, DC, MC, V. Reservations suggested. Casual dress, but no jeans or sneakers. Valet parking and parking lot. Full bar service; cocktail lounge and dance floor. Handicap accessible. Private party rooms. Troubleshooter: Ellen Sanchez (owner).
Moderate.

Lumping all the foods of Latin America into one big pot is a mistake; to think that all the people south of the border cook like they do in Mexico compounds the error. Cuba's own distinct cuisine has a more tropical character than that of Mexico. A typical meal will include meat, often pork, rice, beans, and usually a cooked starch such as fried plantain (banana).

Naturally, since Cuba is an island, seafood gets prominent billing at Tania's. The paella is excellent, served in a portion for two in a large cast-iron pot. The creamy rice has been slowly steeped in a mild broth with various seafoods, chicken, and ham. In a dish called seafood and rice for two, diners will find a couple of large lobster tails, whole shrimp, clams in the shell, and a piece or two of finned fish. Saffron adds its light yellow color and distinctive flavor to the mix. Desserts include several kinds of puddings, flan, and various fruits. Tania's also serves a variety of Mexican entrées.

K/Rating 18/20: Decor 4/4, Service 5/5, Food 7/9, Value 2/2

THE BAKERY

Continental

2218 North Lincoln, Chicago
Telephone: (312) 472-6942

Hours: Tuesday–Friday 5–11, Saturday 5–midnight. Cards: AE, CB, DC, MC, V. Reservations required. Casual dress. Full bar service; diners may bring their own wines for modest corkage or order from the well-organized, well-selected wine list; name brand spirits and cordials. Handicap accessible. Troubleshooter: Louis Szathmary (chef-owner).
Expensive.

The Bakery restaurant has now passed the quarter-century mark and remains as controversial as ever. People either love it or hate it. The fact is that while the restaurant does not challenge today's really sophisticated diners, owner-chef Louis Szathmary was instrumental in making Chicagoans aware that there is more to dining than basic meat and potatoes. Now, just as in those first days a quarter century ago, the planked flooring is highly polished but otherwise bare, the bentwood-backed chairs seem unforgiving of a spine made of anything but solid steel, and the tables are set with white, crisply neat cloths and a single rose in a bulbous green vase. Actually, Louis was using empty Perrier bottles for his rosebuds before anyone ever dreamed that Perrier would become so famous. For most of that twenty-five years, the restaurant has been in a time warp. Chef Louis and his staff were doing what they had always done, while the rest of us moved ahead in search of ever more sophisticated dining experiences.

The five-course dinner now costs $23. The basic core menu remains, including beef Wellington, pork tenderloin with Hungarian sausage, beef Stroganoff, and duckling with Michigan cherries. And there is the bouillabaisse on Friday and Saturday nights. But there are also some new touches that meet today's demands for original combinations and lighter fare. For instance, pan-sautéed walleyed pike was served recently with sliced mangoes in an orange liqueur sauce. The flavors were softened; it may not have been nouvelle, but it was novel. Other recent menu additions have included baby pheasant with fresh rhubarb sauce, spring lamb and turnips in white wine sauce, roast quail with stuffed kohlrabi, and Black Angus steaks with assorted sautéed fresh vegetables. The listing changes seasonally.

What it all boils down to is that The Bakery is very much like it always was, for those people who are looking for nostalgia in dining. But at the same time, there is a lighter touch in the preparation of foods and some new recipes, too, that go far beyond the basic five or six listings on the core menu. And The Bakery still represents one of Chicago's better dining buys, if not the city's most tony. By the way, the desserts are as sweet and luscious as ever. But would you want it any other way?

K/Rating of 18.5/20: Decor 3.5/4, Service 5/5, Food 8/9, Value 2/2

THE RED LION PUB

British

2446 North Lincoln, Chicago
Telephone: (312) 348-2695

Hours: Monday 4:30–midnight, Tuesday–Friday 11:30–midnight, Saturday 11:30–1 am, Sunday noon–10. Cards: AE, CB, DC, MC, V. Reservations accepted. No-smoking section. Street parking can be difficult. Full bar service. Handicap accessible. Private party facilities for 75–100 people (beer garden in summer). Troubleshooter: Collin Cordwell (owner). Inexpensive.

There are two common aphorisms about the gastronomy of Great Britain. One saying has it that "the British know how to eat well, they just don't know how to cook well." The other epigram declares that "in Britain the beer is too warm, and the bath water too cold."

The publican at The Red Lion Pub happens to be from merry old England, and I suppose he has done about as good a job of re-creating something from his homeland as a slim few Chicago restaurateurs have done in bringing burgers and pizza to London. The result tends to be perceptions of reality as much as the genuine goods.

There is a certain coziness to The Red Lion Pub, a warmth that goes beyond seasonal weather. The menu is rather concise and offers things like steak and kidney pie, fish (in beer batter) and chips, sausage rolls, and shepherd's pie. As you can see, the British like to wrap their meats in some sort of pastry or another.

The bangers are served with a touch of chutney. The fish is best when liberally moistened with malt vinegar, though you might have to ask for a bottle. The shepherd's pie comes in a baking crock, topped with mounds of browned mashed potatoes that cover a larder of meat and a liberal supply of flavorful cooked vegetables. It puts to rest the notion that British foods are as bleak as the moors on a dark winter's afternoon. In addition to the short printed menu card, a blackboard lists a few additional daily items.

The British have a talent for making a wide variety of sausages and an interest in eating same. A shire platter brings a slice or two of a course terrine punctuated with hazelnut slivers; a bland brick cheese and chutney are served alongside. There are a few sandwiches, including the un-British American hamburger with your choice of toppings.

Like any decent establishment of its type, The Red Lion Pub has a wide selection of lagers and ales. Desserts can be exceptional if the delicious trifle mounded in a round bottomed schooner and the open-faced blueberry tart are examples of the typical handiwork. Service is as convivial as the atmosphere, with no effort to rush patrons and turn tables, even on a busy night.

K/Rating 16.5/20: Decor 3.5/4, Service 4/5, Food 7/9, Value 2/2

ANN SATHER'S

Swedish/American

925 West Belmont, Chicago
Telephone: (312) 348-2378
Other location is listed opposite.

Hours: Sunday–Thursday 7 am–11 pm, Friday–Sunday 7 am–midnight. Cards: MC, V. No reservations. No-smoking section. Full bar service; wine by the glass. Handicap accessible. Private party facilities for 10–200 people. Troubleshooter: Thomas Tunney (owner). Moderate.

This bright, high-ceilinged, cheerily decorated restaurant serves a varied menu at prices that might make an accountant wonder how it stays in business! The dinner price includes everything from freshly baked rolls and muffins to beverage, soup, salad, vegetables, and your choice of marvelous homemade desserts. The menu states that Ann Sather's serves "Just Good Food," and no truer statement is likely to be heralded anywhere in the world of advertising. Among specialties great for any time of day or evening are Swedish pancakes, wispy thin, but as large as dinner napkins, folded and deliciously sweetened with lingonberry syrup.

Most other fare is more substantial. Baked chicken almond loaf is stuffed with shredded chicken and breading; the almonds add texture to the stuffing, and candied sweet potatoes and cranberry sauce add an almost festive note to the platter. Beef liver, only $6.25 at dinner, comes with fried onions plus all the other courses that accompany meals here. As for service, your waitress is likely to do everything to make you feel at home short of urging you to eat more. In a sense she will even do that by keeping your bread basket supplied with delicious freshly baked muffins, breads, and cinnamon rolls. The dining room is usually packed with people, but turnover is quick. If there is a wait it shouldn't be too long, and it will definitely be well worth it.

Ann Sather's has a second location at 5207 North Clark Street (312-271-6677), Chicago.

K/Rating of 20/20: Decor 4/4, Service 5/5, Food 9/9, Value 2/2

THE CHARDONNAY

French

2635 North Halsted, Chicago
Telephone: (312) 477-5130

Hours: Tuesday–Thursday 5–9, Friday–Saturday 5–10:30, Sunday 5:30–8:30. Cards: MC, V. Reservations suggested. Street parking is difficult. Full bar service with excellent wine list. Handicap accessible. Troubleshooter: Mitch Dulin (owner). Expensive.

At first blush, The Chardonnay seems like more of a wine bar than a restaurant. The menu is short, as if the food were merely an afterthought to the imbibing. But such an impression is deceptive, because The Chardonnay offers first-class dining.

The menu changes every two weeks. From a short list of appetizers, the house pâtés offer a trio that might include a chicken liver mousse, smooth venison, and a coarse-cut country blend. The pâtés are handsomely presented with a garnish, as is every platter. A pasta came with whole shrimp, small calamari, and scallops in a sauce punctuated with black olive slices and redolent with fresh rosemary and lemongrass. The combination proves that lemongrass can be used as a significant flavoring outside of Asian cuisines.

Consider the special entrée I tried one night at The Chardonnay. Slices of lamb were wrapped in fresh spinach leaf and a spread of creamy goat's cheese, encased in a light pastry dough, and then served in sweet red pepper sauce. The wrapped lamb was arranged along the edges of the platter, centered around an eye of scalloped potatoes. Included in the circular vegetable garnish were beautifully cooked fresh brussels sprouts, blanched so that they held their crunchy texture. Particularly notable is that the lamb had none of that unctuous quality that sometimes intrudes upon its delicate flavor.

Duck à la Chardonnay came with sautéed breast and leg; the leg had been crowned with red pepper flakes, offering an accent not usually found in poultry, especially duck. Twin fillets of beef were served in a pinot noir and shallot sauce.

Seafood lovers usually get a choice of two offerings. Grilled amberjack came in a red wine sauce with just the slightest hint of ginger and sautéed fresh cranberries. A garnish of matchstick carrots and zucchini served as vegetable accompaniment.

The desserts are as tempting as the entrées. Tarte tatin comes with a broiled caramel glaze; chocolate cake is like fudge. A simple lemon tart is the ideal palate refresher.

K/Rating 19/20: Decor 3.5/4, Service 4.5/5, Food 9/9, Value 2/2

ST. TROPEZ

French

3170 North Sheridan, in the Hotel Belmont, Chicago
Telephone: (312) 327-1100

Hours: Tuesday–Friday, Sunday 5–10, Saturday 5–11. Sunday brunch: 11–2:30. Cards: AE, CB, DC, MC, V. Reservations required. No-smoking section. Valet parking. Full bar service; good wine list. Handicap accessible. Private party room for up to 40 people. Troubleshooter: Kim Erickson (manager). Expensive.

St. Tropez is a restaurant where the fashion range runs from sweats to business suits to, at least in the case of the maître d', tuxedoes. The interior color scheme is dominated by mint green and pinkish beige, with gold-leaf ceiling accents.

Chef Guy Petit's style of cooking is not as light nor as pastel as the decor suggests. Portions are large, and foods tend to be imaginative and always well prepared. When soft-shell crabs are in season, those at St. Tropez are not to be missed. The crabs are sautéed in butter with the unusual addition of mixed nuts; the latter contribute not only texture to the dish, but also enhance the flavor of the shellfish. Linguine with seafood and a calamari ragout are also offered as appetizers. The ragout has a light, delicate sauce that leaves no doubt of its nautical origins. Diners may try ceviche with sun-dried tomato and avocado, or a salad of periwinkles and mussels in a tantalizing Asian-inspired dressing flavored with ginger and soy sauce.

Entrées are similarly exciting. Recently, a veal chop stuffed with veal mousse came in a woodsy morel mushroom sauce. The mousse was as light as a classic quenelle de brochet, but with a mild meaty flavor infused with herbs. It is an imaginative creation. Another dish that goes well beyond the ordinary is braised sweetbreads in a truffle sauce with lightly blanched spinach leaves on the side. Sweetbreads are a benchmark by which I think it valuable to judge a restaurant kitchen. These at St. Tropez were perfect, firm on the surface, yet with that silken center that makes them the most sensual of all foods. Shrimp in a red pepper coulis served with ratatouille is a well thought out combination of flavors and texture. Entrées come with a crunchy vegetable bouquet with definite Oriental influence.

Desserts are faultless, ranging from classic crème brûlée to light mousses and an unsampled but marvelous sounding hot apple tart with caramel sauce.

K/Rating 19.5/20: Decor 4/4, Service 4.5/5, Food 9/9, Value 2/2

AMBRIA

French

2300 North Lincoln Park West, Chicago
Telephone: (312) 472-0076

Hours: Monday–Thursday 6–9:30, Friday–Saturday 6–10 30. Cards: AE, CB, DC, MC, V, LEYE. Reservations required. Jackets and ties required for gentlemen. No-smoking section. Valet parking. Full bar service. Troubleshooter: Gabino Sotelino (chef). Expensive.

Ambria is firmly among The Big Five of local eateries (Carlos, Le Francais, The Everest Room, and Le Perroquet are the others). Diners are not pampered so much as respected. Waiters know their foods and wines and will offer more than superficial knowledge when asked for a suggestion. There is a stylish wit about the service that keeps things from becoming pretentious.

The menu changes from time to time. Among recent first-course selections were raviolis stuffed with lobster and garnished with generous slices of black truffle in a nap of sauce nantua, or lobster, this time in strudel dough with a julienne of red and green sweet peppers. Other selections might be a wild mushroom terrine, nearly as smooth as mousse, with a decidedly unusual cranberry sauce.

À la carte entrées have included several imaginative seafood presentations, such as John Dory in a pale butter sauce, or charcoal-grilled sea bass served on a tomato coulis and framed by sautéed thinly sliced new potatoes. Sweetbreads sometimes appear sautéed in a pistachio-nut breading; all buttery rich, the sweetbreads are creamy and silky in texture. They come, as do many other entrées, with a collection of hand-carved baby vegetables that add color to the platter and texture the centerpiece.

Desserts are magnificent, ranging from the signature white chocolate mousse bathed in dark chocolate fudge sauce to creamy smooth crème brûlée, coconut glacé, fruit tarts, and a full-flavored chocolate torte stuffed with whole pitted cherries and served with a caramel sauce.

Ambria features a five-course degustation for $35 that, like the menu, changes regularly.

K/Rating of 20/20: Decor 4/4, Service 5/5, Food 9/9, Value 2/2

YOSHI'S CAFE

French

3257 North Halsted, Chicago
Telephone: (312) 248-6160

Dinner: Tuesday–Thursday 5:30–10, Friday–Saturday 5:30–10:30, Sunday 5–9. Cards: AE, MC, V. Reservations mandatory. Jackets required for gentlemen. Free parking lot or street parking. Full bar service; excellent list of domestic wines and champagnes. Handicap accessible. Troubleshooter: Nobuko Katsumura (chef-owner). Expensive.

The cafe atmosphere at Yoshi's may prompt you to expect bifteck et pommes frites, but that's not the style of chef Yoshi Katsumura's cooking. Schooled in the classic techniques, Yoshi blends that experience with a sense of Japanese balance. His platters are mini sculptures of delight, prisms of flavor. One recent entrée was a trio of veal medallions in a Madeira wine sauce accented with candied lemon zest and ginger. The veal surrounded a nest of fresh pasta. A seafood of the day might be Scottish sole bedded on daikon radish with a mustard-seed cream sauce and garniture of shrimp. Or consider tiny roasted quail stuffed with foie gras in a port wine sauce that naps the quail and an accompanying fresh fig. On the other half of the platter rests a boned chicken breast in a reduced pink-peppercorn cream sauce.

Yoshi's Cafe probably serves the best bouillabaisse to be found in Chicago, a pungent stock served traditionally with rouille on the side and thick-crusted toast. Among appetizers, diners will find California goat cheese baked en croute, served in a red bell pepper cream sauce. Not to be missed is a timbale of foie gras encased in aspic, flavored ever so lightly with cognac and Madeira; you are offered a glass of vintage port with this dish. Desserts, including tortes, tarts, and ice creams, are as lavish as the preceding courses.

K/Rating 20/20: Decor 4/4, Service 5/5, Food 9/9, Value 2/2

JEAN CLAUDE'S CAFE DU PARC

French

2442 North Clark, Chicago
Telephone: (312) 525-1800

Lunch: daily (except Tuesday) 11–4. Dinner: Monday, Wednesday–Sunday 4–11. Cards: AE, CB, DC, MC, V, house accounts. Reservations suggested. No-smoking section. Private party rooms for up to 75 people. Full bar service. Troubleshooter: Jean Claude Poilevey (chef-owner). Expensive.

Jean Claude's menu changes regularly with "the whim of the chef." Dining here brings some fresh approaches to some old ideas. Among appetizers, ratatouille is not the same tired combination of eggplant, onions, and peppers. This time out, the ratatouille is served with a garnish of grilled eggplant slices, which gives a visual balance to the platter. Or consider tuna ceviche, accented with coarsely chopped mild peppers for color and texture. Surprisingly, the restaurant's version of gazpacho eschews that same coarse cut, which to my taste is the heart and soul of this famed Spanish soup. More successful is an excellent seafood terrine of salmon and avocado, with tomato for color, a delicate spinach-leaf wrap, and a light soy-based dressing.

Entrées are generally well conceived. They include the bistro staple, grilled steak and fried shoestring potatoes, as well more ambitious choices. Grilled mahimahi does justice to this Pacific fish, which comes with a tomato coulis and fresh cilantro. Garlic lovers can revel in roast chicken flavored with whole roasted garlic cloves and thyme leaves, though the sweetness of the thyme is almost lost in the other flavors. Breast of duck is served with a conventional but tasty green peppercorn sauce, while rack of lamb gets a now-standard treatment of rosemary.

Desserts include a too-sweet crème brûlée, an excellent chestnut Charlotte, and good versions of chocolate torte and mousse.

The à la carte menu can make things expensive here, and the service sometimes lacks the precision one expects at such a price level. Put simply, Jean Claude's Cafe du Parc would be better were it not so pricy. These days, when cafes abound, it seems like too much to have to spend $60 or more per couple for three courses, plus wine.

K/Rating 15.5/20: Decor 3.5/4, Service 3.5/5, Food 7.5/9, Value 1/2

CAFE BA-BA-REEBA

Spanish Tapas

2024 North Halsted, Chicago
Telephone: (312) 935-5000

Lunch: Tuesday–Saturday 11:30–2. Dinner: Monday–Thursday 5:30–11, Friday 5:30–midnight, Saturday 5–midnight, Sunday 5–10:30. Bar: Daily from 5. Cards: AE, CB, DC, MC, V, LEYE. No reservations. No-smoking section. Valet parking for dinner. Full bar service; features over 50 wines, with special emphasis on Spanish varietals. Semiprivate party facilities for 50–200 people. Troubleshooter: Gabino Sotelino (owner). Moderate.

Tapas are Spanish appetizers, but there is no way to describe their variety until you taste them. Perfect for grazing, they are the hot trend among those contemporary dining circles that emphasize eating smaller portions of several foods.

Among several tapas that really impress me here is squid stuffed with squid forcemeat and ground pistachio nuts, all in a light, chunky tomato sauce. Since tapas are not restricted by style, or even ethnic chauvinism, I found a trio of mushrooms, including Japanese shiitake and oyster, sautéed in garlic butter.

Although the idea behind tapas dining involves small tastes of many different foods, you still might want to try an entrée at Cafe Ba-Ba-Reeba. The winner, as far as I'm concerned, is the paella, a classic Spanish casserole that combines chicken, Spanish sausage, mussels, and shrimp with saffron-tinged rice. It's a splendid treat!

Desserts range from homemade ice creams and chocolate hazelnut cake to baked bananas in a thick caramel sauce. In addition, fresh fruit tarts and puddings are often featured.

K/Rating of 20/20: Decor 4/4, Service 5/5, Food 9/9, Value 2/2

ZUM DEUTSCHEN ECK

German

2924 North Southport, Chicago
Telephone: (312) 525-8121

Hours: Monday–Thursday 11:30–10:30, Friday 11:30–2 am, Saturday noon–3 am, Sunday noon–midnight. Cards: AE, DC, MC, V. Reservations suggested. Street parking. Full bar service with imported German beers on tap. Live entertainment and sing-along Friday, Saturday, and Sunday nights. Three private party rooms for groups of 25–400 people. Troubleshooter: Al Wirth (owner). Moderate.

Its name means "The German Corner," but over the years the restaurant has grown to encompass virtually a full block. Its newest remodeling has been achieved without losing the Old World flavor that has characterized Zum Deutschen Eck for years. For example, The Bavarian Room (one of several dining areas) features an authentic *Kachelofen*, a Bavarian fireplace built with imported ceramic tiles. On weekends, at its most crowded, the place is loud and boisterous with peels of laughter and German music. A couple of times during the evening, sing-alongs help whet the appetite for large steins of foamy beer. On weeknights, things settle down to a quieter pace.

Food is consistently good. Sauerbraten, a house specialty, is marinated a good two weeks in red wine, vinegar, and spices. Then, just before the beef is about ready to get up and walk away, it is cooked in its own juices and served up hot and spicy with spaetzle. Braised beef tenderloin à la Deutsch is another fine choice; the meat is baked in a red wine sauce and served with cooked fresh mushrooms, green peppers, onions, tomatoes, and seasonings. It may sound spicy but it is not; it's just a good example of basic Central European cooking. When available, the veal in a white cream sauce is excellent. Lots of lemon juice helps perk up the Wiener schnitzel. Hasenpfeffer is a seasonal favorite. Traditional German cold meat salads and homemade headcheese are among featured appetizers. The wine list includes some rarely seen German reds; one taste indicates why they are rarely seen. Stick to the whites or a mugful of frosty beer. Homemade dessert pastries include a flaky apple strudel.

K/Rating of 17/20: Decor 4/4, Service 4/5, Food 7/9, Value 2/2

THE GOLDEN OX

1578 Clybourn, Chicago
Telephone: (312) 664-0780

Hours: daily 11–11; closed Sunday July–August. Cards: AE, CB, DC, DISC, MC, V, house accounts. Reservations preferred. No-smoking section. Valet parking. Full bar service; excellent choice of wines and beers. Handicap accessible. Private party rooms for up to 80 people. Troubleshooter: Fred J. Grief (owner). Moderate.

German

Several years ago, when I first reviewed The Golden Ox, I called it the best German restaurant in Chicago. I still keep that opinion of this restaurant, which only seems to improve with the passage of time. Visually, The Golden Ox is stunning. This is not just some Black Forest kitsch. The Old World charm is refreshing at a time when newer restaurants are either fern bars or high-ceilinged warehouses where industrial-tech passes for atmosphere.

Soup has always been one of my yardsticks for measuring a restaurant kitchen's abilities. The liver dumpling broth at The Golden Ox is ample testimony to the capabilities at work here. The dark golden broth is generous with dumplings. The dinner entrées are so numerous and tempting, it is difficult to single one out. But if you choose the delicious sauerbraten, with its tangy bite of vinegar marinade and gingersnaps, you can't miss. The restaurant wanders away from its German roots with several chop and seafood choices. Dover sole with almondine sauce on the side is as good as fish gets. It is a meaty, firm seafood, and when dipped in butter seems much like lobster.

Desserts tend to the rich side of the spectrum, and, of course, include fruit strudels and Black Forest cake drenched in kirschwasser. Service is efficient, but not overbearing.

K/Rating of 19/20: Decor 4/4, Service 4/5, Food 9/9, Value 2/2

MIRABELL RESTAURANT

3454 West Addison, Chicago
Telephone: (312) 463-1962

Lunch: Tuesday–Saturday 11:30–2:30. Dinner: Tuesday–Thursday 5–10, Friday–Saturday 5–11. Cards: AE, CB, DC, MC, V. Reservations suggested on weekends. Ample street parking. Full bar service; excellent selection of beers. Private party room for up to 35 people, or up to 50 people in main dining room. Troubleshooters: Werner and Anita Heil (owners). Moderate.

German/Austrian

If the mere thought of dumplings and spaetzle or schnitzel and sauerbraten sets your taste buds on edge with anticipation, a visit to Mirabell will bring satisfaction. Although the menu has more of a Rhenish than a Danubian turn, you will find a few Austrian classics, such as a quartet of excellent schnitzels. There is, of course, the classic Wiener schnitzel, a large thin slice of veal tenderloin breaded and panfried to a golden crispness; the veal is so tender it literally can be cut with a fork's edge. (In fact, all the meats used at Mirabell are cut, trimmed, and prepared to the specifications of owner and ex-butcher Werner Heil.) Parisian schnitzel offers the same fine quality, this time prepared in an egg batter with a golden, puffy crust. Mirabell is also one of the few restaurants to serve the authentically Austrian Zigeuner schnitzel, made with pork rather than veal, topped with sautéed peppers, mushrooms, and onions with paprika sauce. Goulash, heavily seasoned with cayenne pepper and paprika for added bite, is an impressive choice as either a small soup portion or as a main course. Yet another Austrian treat is Wiener rostbraten, a prime sirloin quickly sautéed in wine and its own juices, served with crisp double-fried onions and mushrooms.

This is hearty dining at its best. A number of German specialties—including sauerbraten and sausages—and some American-style steaks round out the menu. Desserts come from Lutz's, known throughout Chicagoland for their sweet deliciousness. Mirabell has two indoor dining rooms, plus a bar and an outdoor beer garden for warm-weather months.

K/Rating 19/20: Decor 3.5/4, Service 4.5/5, Food 9/9, Value 2/2

CAFFE PRANZO

Italian

4100 North Western, Chicago
Telephone: (312) 588-6181

Hours: Monday–Thursday 11–midnight, Friday 11–1 am, Saturday 4–midnight, Sunday 4–11. Cards: AE, MC, V. Reservations accepted. No-smoking section. Full bar service; good wine list. Handicap accessible. Private party facilities for up to 40 people. Troubleshooter: Tony Riggio (owner).
Moderate.

Caffè Pranzo reminds me of those Italian restaurants you have to travel to the western suburbs to find. A neighborhood fixture for years, the restaurant has been recently redecorated in handsome blond woods. It may look Swedish, but everything tastes Italian.

Although many dishes at Caffè Pranzo reflect a Sicilian influence, there are entrées and appetizers that come from all over Italy. They range from deliciously complex pasta with porcini mushrooms to the strong garlic flavor found in sautéed cheese argentera. In this appetizer, which comes served in a small cast-iron skillet, slightly sharp caciocavallo cheese is sautéed in hot olive oil liberally flavored with garlic. The idea is to scoop out the cheese with a small fork and then dredge chunks of crusty bread in the oil. Couple this with a reasonably priced Italian red wine such as a barbaresca, and your meal is off to a great start. Another appetizer option is small, thin-crust pizza. You can go the ordinary route with cheese, sausage, and the like, but pizza with pesto gets my vote. Fresh basil leaves, garlic, crushed pine nuts, and olive oil are married to whole plum tomatoes and mozzarella. The flavors are light and fresh.

Dinners come with a choice of soup or salad as well as a side of pasta. Of course, you can also order an à la carte pasta as your main course or to share as a separate course. The linguine in red or white clam sauce is a success here. The trick with this dish is to keep the pasta from becoming too oily; at Caffè Pranzo the sauce has just enough oil to bind the bits of clam and garlic to the noodles.

Speaking of garlic, it finds its way into several recipes with more than just a kiss. For example, the garlic in the veal Marsala carries a full-blown wallop. If you object to such a pronounced flavor, just ask that the seasoning be cut back.

Desserts include warm zabaglione, the inspiration for the French sabayon sauce, or freshly made cannoli. If you want something less rich, a dish of lemon ice is a fitting way to top off your meal.

K/Rating 18/20: Decor 3/4, Service 4.5/5, Food 8.5/9, Value 2/2

FRICANO'S

2512 North Halsted, Chicago
Telephone: (312) 929-7550

Dinner: Sunday–Thursday 4–10, Friday–Saturday 4–11. Cards: AE, CB, DC, MC, V. Reservations suggested. Street parking. Full bar service; modest wine list. Handicap accessible. Private party facilities for up to 50 people. Troubleshooter: Anthony Fricano (owner). Moderate.

Italian

On first impression you might think that Fricano's is just another trendy neighborhood saloon with a small kitchen incidental to the main job of serving booze. But attention to such detail as the sign posting daily seafood specialties is the tip-off that Fricano's is much more than a saloon. A walk beyond the front room reveals the larger main dining room, handsomely done up in shades of peach with dim lighting.

Dinners include a side of potato or pasta and, except for the daily seafood specials, are priced from around $5 for a platter of pasta to nearly $12 for a broiled fillet. That seafood might include Norwegian salmon, grouper, swordfish, or any of a number of other choices, depending on what's fresh at the market. As good as the grilled seafood might be, the Italian part of Fricano's culinary efforts is more interesting to me. The kitchen has perfected a delicious light tomato sauce for such items as mussels in red sauce or zuppa di pesce. For dessert, you might want to try the ricotta cheesecake and a cappuccino or espresso. This cheesecake is rather dense and reminds me more of a sweetened custard, but with a rougher texture.

K/Rating 19/20: Decor 3/4, Service 5/5, Food 9/9, Value 2/2

LITTLE BUCHAREST

Romanian

3001 North Ashland, Chicago
Telephone: (312) 929-8640

Hours: Monday–Thursday 11–10, Friday–Saturday 11–11. Cards: AE, CB, DC, MC, V. Reservations requested. Ample street parking. Full bar service; interesting list of Middle European wines. Private party facilities for up to 100 people. Troubleshooters: Alex Popa and Ilie V. Groza (owners). Inexpensive.

At first glance you might just drive by Little Bucharest taking no notice of its presence. But unless it is Sunday when the restaurant is closed, the place will be so busy you won't get in without a reservation. What draws people here is the excellent Romanian food served in heaping portions at budget cost. You won't find Gypsy violinists. Instead, a front bar room seems like any other neighborhood tap, except for the strong aromas of dillweed and other seasonings coming from the tiny kitchen. Farther back is the main dining room, brightly lit with chandeliers hanging from the wood-planked ceiling, the lights reflecting off gold-flocked wallpaper. A small cuckoo clock tolls the hours.

Dinners center around broiled, baked, and stewed meats, particularly veal in any of several recipes. If it is schnitzel you favor, the portion at Little Bucharest is golden brown with a rich egg batter and so large the chances are you may want to take half home for snacking the next day. A Romanian-style sauerbraten is without the gingersnap and brine bite of the German version. This is more like a pot roast with olives, onions, and tomatoes in a red wine sauce, accompanied by a fresh vegetable, red cabbage, and spaetzle. Similar but more flavorful is dry wine beef in a pleasantly pungent gravy.

A house special is stuffed chicken à la Bucharest. A liver dressing is stuffed between the meat and skin of a half chicken, which is then baked with white wine for moisture. It's a delicious dish. Be sure to order a bowl of one of the outstanding soups, such as veal meatball with vegetables and dumplings or ciorba, chicken soup with fresh-cut vegetables and small dumplings.

You cannot miss the desserts since the glass-door refrigerator that holds them is in plain sight of the dining room. The fridge is piled chock-full with a dozen or more tortes, crunchy with walnuts, creamy with chocolate or mocha, layered high with fillings.

K/Rating of 18.5/20: Decor 3.5/4, Service 4.5/5, Food 8.5/9, Value 2/2

UNCLE TANNOUS

Lebanese

2616 North Halsted, Chicago
Telephone: (312) 929-1333

Hours: Monday 5–midnight, Tuesday–Sunday noon–midnight. Cards: AE, MC, V. Reservations suggested. Casual dress. No-smoking section. Valet parking. Full bar service. Handicap accessible. Private party room for up to 60 people. Troubleshooter: Joseph Skaf (owner). Moderate.

Soft pastels, cloud murals, arabesque arches, and a graceful manner welcome diners to Uncle Tannous. Lebanese cuisine, like that of other Middle Eastern nations, is designed to be not only nourishing, but also the heart of an elaborate, often ritualized social encounter. It is the role of the host to offer his guests the best of whatever he has. This is the heart of dining at Uncle Tannous.

A waiter presents diners with a printed menu, but quickly adds that there is an evening special or two. And when fish is served, he may even invite you back into the kitchen to inspect the freshness of the seafood before it is cooked. The menu is enticing with its various grilled meats, fried or broiled seafoods, and the mildly seasoned vegetables characteristic of the Levant. Should you choose to be a bit adventurous, and should your appetite be up to the demands, order the mezza, at $25 for two people or $30 for three. A mezza is a selection of tastes, small portions of several foods spread across your table to pick and choose as you might in a Lebanese home. At Uncle Tannous, the assortment features at least twenty different foods, ranging from simple vegetables and sliced tomatoes to grilled liver and kidneys and such other classic Lebanese choices as falafel and hummus; baba ghannouj; spinach and meat pies; stuffed grape leaves; green beans in olive oil with herbs, spices, and light tomato sauce; fava beans and okra; tabbouleh salad; cucumber slices; seasoned onions in oil—a veritable cornucopia of foods.

Since most of these dishes can also be ordered à la carte, you might choose to stick to a few favored items. The falafel, crisp, lightly spiced ground chick-pea patties, are delicious. Tabbouleh, the traditional cracked wheat salad, is sharp with accents of lemon juice and spices, perfect as a palate refresher of sorts.

Should you choose to order à la carte, various kebabs and broiled cuts of lamb should please. Sometimes served as a special is kafta in the pan, ground beef patties coated with cracked wheat for texture, grilled, and served with potato slices in a tomato sauce.

Desserts include baklava, rice pudding, and crème caramel. The baklava is made without honey, the phyllo dough instead bound together with only finely ground nuts.

K/Rating 19/20: Decor 4/4, Service 5/5, Food 8/9, Value 2/2

New Taj Mahal

Pakistani/Indian

2614 West Devon, Chicago
Telephone: (312) 743-4545

Hours: Sunday–Thursday 11:30–10:30, Friday–Saturday 11:30–11. Cards: AE, CB, DC, MC, V. Reservations accepted. Street parking. No alcoholic beverages. Troubleshooter: Zeba N. Zaidi (owner). Inexpensive.

If you enjoy the discovery of new, small ethnic restaurants, then go and discover New Taj Mahal. It's a cultural odyssey merely to walk up and down Devon west of Western Avenue and inhale the aromas that pour out of the Indian and Oriental food markets. But that's just a bonus to the good foods one finds at the small restaurants along the way.

New Taj Mahal is a narrow storefront with one interior brick wall faced with stuccolike arches to give a feeling of gracefulness. Diners who know Indian restaurants will recognize the murghs and tikkas and masalas and goshts. Newcomers to the cuisine may find the foods spicier than that to which they are accustomed. Seasonings are generally well balanced, however, and it is not difficult to sense the essence of cloves, cinnamon, cardamom, and coriander among the blend of spices and herbs characteristic of the cooking. Begin with some of the finger-food appetizers such as samosas, which are large triangular dumplings filled with potato and other vegetables; pakoras, which are deep-fried vegetables; and perhaps shami kabobs, two patties of spiced minced beef grilled over an open flame. You could continue grazing on a small order of bite-sized pieces of tandoori chicken or fish tikka, lightly seasoned but still identifiably exotic. There are a handful of namesake dishes at New Taj Mahal. I especially like the chicken New Taj Mahal, boned chunks of breast prepared in a sauce of coriander and puréed vegetables. Almonds and cashews are added for a bit of contrast in texture. Although the menu describes this dish as mild, in fact it has just enough of a kick to be interesting. Another house specialty is lamb gorma, boned lamb chunks in a dark and complexly spiced gravylike sauce. The flavor of clove is more assertive than it should be, but this is a difficult spice to work with because of its characteristic variance in intensity.

Unlike its neighboring Hindu-run Indian restaurants, New Taj Mahal's Moslem staff prepare several beef dishes, since Islam does not preclude eating that meat. The New Taj Mahal also has a number of vegetarian choices for those who prefer that diet for ethical or religious reasons.

There is one drawback to the cooking. Food suffers from an excessive oiliness that shows up in some specialty breads such as naans and paratha. But such a fault is minor when compared to the overall pleasant dining experience. Service is very friendly and informative, and portions are large enough so that you may have leftovers to take home.

K/Rating 17/20: Decor 3/4, Service 4.5/5, Food 7.5/9, Value 2/2

JOW KOON

Thai

3466 North Clark, Chicago
Telephone: (312) 348-2875

Dinner: Monday–Thursday, Sunday 4:30–11, Friday–Saturday 4:30–midnight. Cards: AE, DC, MC, V. Reservations accepted. Casual dress. Ample street parking. No alcoholic beverages. Private party facilities for 20–60 people. Troubleshooter: Pete and Bonnie Pradipdipasena (owners). Inexpensive.

Chicagoans are fortunate to have such a wide selection of Thai restaurants, and while most are very good, Jow Koon ranks among the best. The seasonings seem designed not so much to assault as to mingle. Familiar Thai flavors—coconut milk, lemongrass, red and green chilies, basil, coriander—weave a consistent thread through the many dishes.

The Jow Koon menu seems weighted toward gaengs, that food category that depends upon a soup broth or sauce. I like to take a gaeng and mix it with some rice in a separate bowl, allowing the rice to absorb the liquid and flavors. Gaengs can be curried dishes or not, depending upon whims of the chef and demands of a recipe. The intensity of a Thai curry can often be gauged by its color. Yellow or golden curries are generally mild, those that are red are a little hotter, while green curries are generally reserved for only the most daring.

But just as curries and spicy flavors fight for their share of attention in Thai dining, sweetness also has a prominent place in a meal. Begin with spring rolls, rice paper wrapped around a filling of bean sprouts, cooked egg, pork, and vegetables and served in a sticky tamarind syrup. A piece of spring roll can be taken in hand or picked up with chopsticks without fear of the whole affair falling apart. It is not surprising that Thailand, considering its geography at the nexus of Southeast Asia, has borrowed from other cuisines. Thus a chicken satay inspired by Indonesia and coated with the identifying yellow of Indian turmeric is but made distinctly Thai with a complex sauce of peanut butter, coconut cream, and peppers. Among other appetizer choices, do not miss the roast duck. This is again a somewhat sweet dish, but not so sweet as to interfere with the rich, almost unctuous pleasures of duck roasted to perfection. An appetizer portion only teases; this would make a delicious main course, too.

For my taste, no Thai dinner is complete without an order of pad Thai, a noodle dish with shrimps, tofu, ground peanuts, garlic, bean sprouts, and eggs. This dish offers the satisfaction of pasta combined with the tropical exotica of Southeast Asia.

Desserts include delicious coconut-taro custard, fresh coconut ice cream, and bananas cooked in coconut milk.

K/Rating of 18.5/20: Decor 4/4, Service 4/5, Food 8.5/9, Value 2/2

Matsuya

Japanese

3469 North Clark, Chicago
Telephone: (312) 248-2677

Dinner: Monday, Wednesday–Friday 5–midnight, Saturday–Sunday noon–midnight. Cards: MC, V. Reservations accepted. No-smoking section. Street parking. Wine, sake, and Japanese beers. Handicap accessible. Troubleshooter: Michie Yokomoni (owner). Inexpensive.

This is one of the dozens of little finds that dot Clark Street. There is nothing on Matsuya's menu I have not found at other Japanese restaurants, but everything I have tasted is exceptional. You can order à la carte or from special combinations. From the appetizer selection, choose spinach in a soy-based sesame sauce; the spinach is cold, the sauce delicately sweet and salty. Matsuya does a fine job with fish, charcoal broiled with crisp skin. Fish varies depending on what is fresh; pike and mackerel are common selections. Broiled eel is for adventurous diners; sashimi is another tempting offering. Combination dinners offer a taste of this and that, including delicate tempura shrimp and vegetables, beef teriyaki, and sashimi. All dinners include a small cabbage salad, excellent clear hot broth, rice, light green tea with a delicate woodlike fragrance, and dessert.

K/Rating of 18/20: Decor 3/4, Service 4/5, Food 9/9, Value 2/2

Itto Sushi

Japanese

2616 North Halsted, Chicago
Telephone: (312) 871-1800

Lunch: Monday–Saturday noon–2. Dinner: Monday–Saturday 5:30–midnight, Sunday 4:30–9:30. Cards: AE, CB, DC, MC, V. Reservations only for parties of 5 or more. Free parking lot. No alcoholic beverages. Handicap accessible. Private party room for up to 30 people. Troubleshooter: Juco S. Hattori (owner). Moderate.

The Japanese word *itto* refers to a religious or spiritual quorum, a gathering of like-minded souls for a common purpose. Thus, devoted sushi lovers and those who appreciate its fellow traveler, sashimi, can gather at Itto Sushi. Here you will find a dozen or more varieties, all clearly illustrated on wall charts as well as at smaller table displays. The restaurant is classic in its sushi bar design: light blond woods for the counter and below, smaller sloped platforms on which the sushi chef will set your choices, unless you prefer them served on a common platter.

The restaurant also serves several broiled meat and fish dinners. Teriyaki beef can be a bit tougher than you might prefer, but otherwise nicely flavored in its sweetened soy-based sauce. The Japanese have a pronounced liking for sweet flavors, so it is not uncommon to find that stimulus sensation in almost any course. Even something as simple as a spinach hors d'oeuvre called goma-ae is served in a sweetened sesame sauce. Tempura batter is light and airy. Dinners are never rushed, which is perfect for those who like to linger at the sushi bar and watch the chefs at work.

K/Rating 18.5/20: Decor 4/4, Service 4.5/5, Food 8/9, Value 2/2

SAI CAFE

Japanese

2010 North Sheffield, Chicago
Telephone: (312) 472-8080

Hours: Monday–Thursday 4:30–11, Friday–Saturday 4:30–11, Sunday 3:30–10. Cards: AE, MC, V. Reservations suggested. Valet parking. Full bar service. Private parties for up to 30 people Sunday–Thursday. Troubleshooter: Jim Bee (owner). Moderate.

If there is such a thing as a neighborhood sushi bar, then Sai Cafe is it. The sushi and sashimi may be ordered by the piece, or there are a couple of combination platters that offer variety at better value. Much of Japanese cookery strives to achieve eye appeal. Take a look at some of the beautifully wrapped and sculpted pieces of California maki. This particular creation is a variation on tradition: avocado is mated with crabmeat and cucumber and set off with an understated etching of fire-hot wasabi (horseradish) on the tongue.

Once past a choice of sushi, you can graze from one appetizer to another or choose a more conventional entrée-centered dinner. Among the twenty appetizer choices is goma-ae, an artful presentation of spinach leaf molded into twin peaks, glazed with a sesame paste. It's a different way of dealing with a conventional green vegetable. Don't miss panfried scallops in a slightly sweetened sauce with sesame seeds. The dish is imaginative, without being contrived. The ubiquitous dumpling shows up in almost every cuisine. In Japan it is called a gyoza, and it comes hot out of a sauté pan to your platter with a light soy-based sauce for dipping.

The sukiyaki here is less a soup than some versions I know, consisting of a mound of thinly sliced steamed beef on a bed of translucent noodles. Or you might want an order of soba (buckwheat noodles) prepared with vegetables, beef, or shrimp. Though soba is considered not especially elegant in Japan, at Sai Cafe the panfried noodles come in a mix of colorful julienned vegetables or meat.

K/Rating 18/20: Decor 4/4, Service 4/5, Food 8/9, Value 2/2

NORTH

Edwardo's Natural Pizza Restaurant

American/Pizza

937 West Howard, Chicago
Telephone: (312) 761-7040
Other locations are listed below.

Hours: Sunday–Thursday 11–11:30, Friday–Saturday 11 am–12:30 am. Cards: AE, MC, V. Reservations suggested. Casual, but neat dress. Street parking. Liquor policy varies at different locations. Handicap accessible. Private party facilities. Troubleshooter: Edward Jacobson (owner). Moderate.

When it comes to pizza, Edwardo's takes the cake—or the pie, as the case may be. Edwardo's stuffed pizza is a towering freestanding pie at least three inches tall and oozing with delicious flavors. Besides serving the standard repertoire of toppings found most everywhere, Edwardo's was first to introduce such vegetable versions as spinach pizza. Only fresh herbs are used for seasoning. Edwardo's may do only one thing, but they do it better than just about anybody in town.

Edwardo's Natural Pizza Restaurant has more locations at 1321 East 57th Street (312-241-7960), Chicago; 1212 North Dearborn (312-337-4490), Chicago; 521 South Dearborn (312-939-3366), Chicago; 6831 West North Avenue (312-524-2400), Oak Park; 1904 South Elmhurst Road (312-952-9393), Mt. Prospect; 5002 South Main (312-964-9700), Downer's Grove; 9300 Skokie Boulevard (312-674-0008), Skokie; 401 East Dundee Road (312-520-0666), Wheeling; 2120 North Alstead (312-871-3400), Chicago; 240 Skokie Boulevard (312-272-5222), Northbrook.

K/Rating 18/20: Decor 3/4, Service 4.5/5, Food 8.5/9, Value 2/2

Capt'n Nemo's

Submarine Sandwiches

7367 North Clark, Chicago
Telephone: (312) 973-0570
Other location is listed opposite.

Hours: Monday–Saturday 11–8:30. No cards. No-smoking section. No alcoholic beverages. Handicap accessible. Troubleshooter: Louis Ragusi (owner). Inexpensive.

This is the ultimate submarine sandwich shop. A large board behind the counter lists several sandwiches, most in the $3 range and all available in half-loaf form for about half the price. By the time you finish with a soft drink, a cup of soup, and a dessert, you will be hard-pressed to spend much more than $5 per person. Sandwiches are built before your eyes on foot-long French loaves. They start with a dressing, your choice of a mild mustard or mayonnaise. Then comes your selection of meats such as turkey, ham, bologna, or hot meat loaf, plus cheeses, seasoned oil and vinegar dressing, onion, eggs, radishes, tomatoes, pickles, shredded lettuce—a veritable garden of sandwich delights. If you really have an ambitious appetite, you can order the soup of the day for about half a buck. Often available is thick and steamy split pea in a broth that would make Julia Child take notice.

What more can you say about a sandwich shop? A great deal in this case because there is a moral to be learned here: No matter what you do in life, do it well and your effort will be appreciated. I have never been in a restaurant where customers are greeted with such genuine friendliness and regard and where more pride is taken in what is being prepared. And yes, there is a real Capt'n Nemo who makes sure that all comers are well fed and satisfied.

Capt'n Nemo's has a second location at 3311 North Marshfield (312-929-7687), Chicago.

No K/Rating since restaurant is self-service.

FERNANDO'S

Mexican

3450 North Lincoln, Chicago
Telephone: (312) 477-6930

Hours: Monday–Thursday 3:30–10:30, Friday–Saturday 3:30–11:30. Cards: AE, CB, DC, MC, V, house accounts. Reservations accepted. No-smoking section. Street parking. Full bar service; Spanish wines. Handicap accessible. Private party room and patio for up to 100 people. Troubleshooter: Carmen Gonzales (owner). Inexpensive.

It's refreshing to find a Mexican restaurant that breaks the bond of similarity that often makes it difficult to distinguish one from another. Fernando's menu carries many of the traditional dishes to be expected at any Mexican restaurant such as tacos and enchiladas, burritos, and chiles rellenos. There are, however, a few regional specialties and one or two recipes that seem to come more from kitchen inspiration than tradition. For example, while the Mexican seafood classic snapper Veracruz-style gets due attention, so does brook trout sautéed in butter and topped with fresh coriander leaves and sliced cucumbers. True, coriander is typically used in Mexican cooking, but brook trout is not usually found on the menu of a Mexican restaurant. As for that snapper Veracruz-style, it is one of the best I've ever tasted. The large serving platter on which the fish comes is laden with a virtual garden of rice, tomatoes, avocado slices, carrots, broccoli, and cauliflower in a mild cheese sauce. It is one of the most beautiful presentations I've ever seen in a Mexican restaurant.

A good selection of appetizers, soups, and desserts is offered to round out dinner, and for dessert don't miss flan and crisp, sugared sopapillas.

K/Rating 17.5/20: Decor 3.5/4, Service 4.5/5, Food 7.5/9, Value 2/2

JIMMY'S PLACE

3420 North Elston, Chicago
Telephone: (312) 539-2999

Lunch: Monday–Friday 11:30–2. Dinner: Monday–Saturday 5–9:30. Cards: CB, DC, MC, V. Reservations required. Casual dress, but jackets requested for gentlemen. Free parking in adjacent lot. Full bar service; extensive wine list. Small private party room seats up to 12 people; a second room (available only Monday–Friday) seats up to 40 people. Troubleshooter: Jimmy Rohr (owner). Expensive.

French

In an otherwise gray industrial neighborhood, here is a small café decorated with splashes of lime green and bright yellow, featuring food that epitomizes the principles of nouvelle cuisine. The menu changes monthly, with such daily selections routinely available as braised sweetbreads in tarragon sauce, braised fresh rabbit dijonnaise, and veal Orloff, almost overpowering in the richness of its cream sauce. Fresh sockeye salmon might be lightly bathed in a beurre blanc pinkened ever so slightly by a purée of salmon roe with more roe atop. Appetizers usually include a seafood pâté stuffed with a light scallop mousse and sauced with tarragon mayonnaise. Fresh sherbets and pastries are served for dessert. There is a full wine list to match the quality of the food.

K/Rating 18/20: Decor 4/4, Service 5/5, Food 7.5/9, Value 1.5/2

MAREVA'S

1250 North Milwaukee, Chicago
Telephone: (312) 227-4000

Hours: Monday–Friday 11:30–11, Friday–Saturday 4–11. Cards: AE, CB, DC, MC, V, house accounts. Reservations suggested. No-smoking section. Free valet parking. Full bar service; excellent list of imported and domestic wines, champagnes, beers. Private party facilities for up to 250 people. Troubleshooters: Irene and Stanley Idzik (owners). Expensive.

Eastern European

People usually do not think of Middle European cuisine as particularly elegant, in the same way they might consider French fare elegant. But Mareva's may change all those old conceptions. Walking inside Mareva's from dreary Milwaukee Avenue is like stepping into an Old World painting. Brass chandeliers, forest green velvet banquettes, starched tablecloths, and handsome artwork contribute to the setting in which tuxedoed waiters move quietly between tables and kitchens.

Though the roots of the cooking at Mareva's are Middle European, specifically Polish, the style is firmly rooted in French preparation. Certainly, among appetizers, you can order a trio of pierogis stuffed with a forcemeat of wild mushrooms. But you may also choose smoked salmon, domestic and imported caviars, luscious raw blue points, or oysters Rockefeller. This last dish brings out a half dozen oysters bedded in the traditional manner with spinach and a hollandaise-style sauce. The aftertaste of Pernod is less evident than in some versions.

Though dinners include a small house salad and fresh, lightly steamed vegetables, there is a wide choice for the à la carte diner. Soups run a gamut from borscht to vichyssoise. Dinner-sized portions of pierogi may be filled with lobster or swordfish and sole, as well as a traditional Polish stuffing of cabbage, mushrooms, and seasonings. Even those soft chewy dumplings called uszka are here for the ordering.

Sauces are full flavored and sometimes heavier than many diners are accustomed to in the light of "nouvelle" conventions. There is endless satisfaction on the menu, however. Calvados roasted duck, served with baked apple chunks and wild mushrooms, arrives in its own confit, with the skin stripped aside and crackling crisp. The venison stew, a traditional "bigos," is rich with a deep, dark mushroom sauce. Beef tenderloin comes stuffed with kasha, a veal forcemeat, onions, and mushrooms in a creamed mushroom sauce. Among more than a dozen other entrée choices is veal Mareva, thin cutlets on a bed of julienned leeks, zucchini, tomato, and mushrooms. The veal is sautéed in butter and finished with sherry.

Desserts are lavish, befitting what has come before.

K/Rating 19/20: Decor 4/4, Service 4.5/5, Food 8.5/9, Value 2/2

YUGO INN

Yugoslavian/Serbian

2824 North Ashland, Chicago
Telephone: (312) 348-6444

Hours: Monday–Saturday 5–11. No cards. Reservations suggested. Casual, but neat dress. No pipe or cigar smoking. Ample street parking. Full bar service; good selection of Yugoslavian wines. Private party accommodations available. Troubleshooter: Rada Stupar Kuka (owner). Inexpensive.

The atmosphere here is far removed from Chicago. The L-shaped dining room, up a short flight of steps from a front tap room, is rather small and seats not many more than forty people. Tables tend to be close together. Ornate carved sideboards hold utensils and glassware. Waitresses bustle back and forth to the tiny kitchen, where a profusion of scents pours forth each time the door opens. The menu offers few surprises to anyone familiar with Serbian food. The soup, a deeply flavored homemade stock with meat and coarsely cut vegetables, is served in a large tureen for individual ladling. After one cup, you are certain to ladle back in for more.

Entrées include a combination platter that gives a taste of three traditional meats. Among other generously portioned main courses is the wiener schnitzel, called becka snicla in Serbian. The tender veal is traditionally floured and sautéed. The resulting crust is not puffy as in classic schnitzel and the flavor is very mild. A squeeze or two of fresh lemon juice is appropriate. Desserts include palacinka, crêpes filled with fruit, and the very non-Serbian, but still delicious Eli's famous cheesecake.

K/Rating of 18.5/20: Decor 4/4, Service 4.5/5, Food 8/9, Value 2/2

MIOMIR'S SERBIAN CLUB

Serbian

2255 West Lawrence, Chicago
Telephone: (312) 784-2111

Dinner: daily 5-2 am. Cards: AE, V. Reservations required. No-smoking section. Parking lot nearby. Full bar service. Handicap accessible. Private party room for up to 100; semiprivate accommodations for larger gatherings. Troubleshooter: Miomir Radovanovic (owner). Moderate.

Miomir Radovanovic knows how to throw a party and you had better have a good time—or else. Miomir's ebullience practically fills the room as he stops to talk, kiss a hand, or twirl a female patron across the dance floor. Add to that good hearty Balkan food, wines, and an ethnic floor show with songs in every language from Russian and Hungarian to Yiddish and Hebrew.

Serbian food reflects the crosscurrents that over the centuries have passed through that beautiful but sometimes troubled land. Thus you will find influences from Asia Minor, such as sarma, stuffed cabbage leaves filled with veal, beef, and rice, served with sour cream. From Middle Europe comes chicken paprika, the Serbian version of Wiener schnitzel called becka snicla, and goulash, born in Hungary but cooked at Miomir's with a Serbian flourish. Among other dinner choices are traditional grilled meats; cevapcici, ground veal and beef in sausage-shaped cylinders; muckalica, a spicy casserole of meat and vegetables; and pleskavica, a braised ground round steak. Begin dinner with traditional appetizers such as the cheese spread called kajmak, or ajvar, a purée of eggplant, green pepper, and other ingredients sautéed in olive oil. Dessert treats include strudel, crêpes (palacinke), and baklava, an influence from the Levant.

K/Rating 18.5/20: Decor 3.5/4, Service 5/5, Food 8/9, Value 2/2

CASBAH ARMENIAN RESTAURANT

Armenian

514 West Diversey, Chicago
Telephone: (312) 935-7570

Hours: daily 5–midnight. Cards: AE, CB, DC, MC, V. Reservations suggested. Validated parking at nearby lot. Full bar service; limited wine list. Troubleshooters: Vartan and Juliette Vartanian (owners). Moderate.

When the talk among experienced Chicago foodies and diners turns to Middle Eastern cooking, the name Casbah always comes up. I can recall that after first moving to Chicago almost twenty years ago, this premier Middle Eastern restaurant was among my friends' first dining recommendations.

Casbah has not changed all that much in the intervening years. I still like the fact that as soon as you go through the narrow front doorway and leave Diversey Avenue's turmoil outside, there is the sense of entering a different world. The somewhat threadworn decor of a few years ago seems to have been refurbished, though the patina of age remains. The service is as good as ever. The food, though still good, does not seem as remarkable as in the past, but that may be because the cuisine of the Levant is no longer so exotic in Chicago.

All dinners come with a choice of soup, salad, and rice pilaf or vegetables, as may be appropriate. In addition, à la carte appetizers are fine for starters, though prices seem a bit high considering portion size. Certainly, you would want a platter of hummus, the chick-pea, sesame paste, and olive oil purée that is so good when dabbed on pieces of pita bread. Similarly, the baba ghannouj, a spread of eggplant and seasonings, is a must. As for other nibbles, small phyllo dough pastries stuffed with either spinach or a mild white cheese, grape leaves with a rice, nut, and currant stuffing, and the cracked wheat and parsley salad called tabbouleh are fine for creating your own mezza, or appetizer assortment.

Under the guidance of founding owner Vartan Vartanian, Casbah in the past concentrated on Armenian fare. His portrait still dominates the menu, though dinner choices now cover a wider array of Mediterranean foods. Thus, couscous, a Moroccan dish of cooked semolina and any number of meat or vegetable toppings, is a favorite choice. It is served with a hot pepper sauce called harissa. Used sparingly it's delicious; without restraint it can be an inferno.

Another Moroccan dish offered here is pastilla, shredded Cornish hen in an almond-egg sauce baked inside a flaky crust. The "pie," sprinkled with a little powdered sugar, is as tasty as it is unique. Any of the lamb dishes should also please even the pickiest eater. I was sorry to see on my latest visit that daily specials are no longer available. These were often very interesting choices and their absence is a loss. But when restaurants come and go with the whim of dining tastes, Casbah is one that weathers all changes and rightly so.

K/Rating 16/20: Decor 3.5/4, Service 4/5, Food 7/9, Value 1.5/2

GANDHI INDIA RESTAURANT

Indian

2601 West Devon, Chicago
Telephone: (312) 761-8714

Lunch: daily 11:30–3:30. Dinner: daily 5–10. Saturday 5–11. Cards: AE, CB, DC, MC, V. Reservations accepted. Street parking. Full service bar. Troubleshooter: Sham L. Hans. Inexpensive.

Gandhi looks more like a coffee shop than an exotic restaurant, but one sniff reveals the true delights that await the hungry diner. Indian cuisine is dependent upon a bouquet of herbs and spices for its unique complexity. The use of seasonings—turmeric, cardamom, saffron, and others—is what this restaurant is all about.

The Gandhi menu explains most of the dishes, which makes this a welcome stop for both the old-timer and the novice. Start with a combination platter of appetizers. Many Indian foods can be eaten out of hand if you choose. Try the deep-fried pakoras and samosas. Pakoras are spiced chick-pea flour encasing different sorts of vegetables. Samosas are deep-fried potato-filled savory pastry triangles. Then pick up a piece of chicken tikka, roasted in the tandoor oven that has become standard equipage for Indian restaurant kitchens. Similarly tasty are the Indian shish kebabs, cubes of lamb given a deep charcoal roasting. Diners can order a prearranged dinner, or they can select dishes from the à la carte list, letting their own tastes and instincts be their guide.

Curries can be mild or hot; those I tasted at Gandhi seem to be somewhere in between. When you have your table spread with a multitude of dishes, you will find that each preparation has its own distinct flavor. There is no paucity to seasonings here, nor is there a sameness.

K/Rating of 17/20: Decor 2.5/4, Service 4/5, Food 8.5/9, Value 2/2

TASTY EAT

Pakistani

1618 West Montrose, Chicago
Telephone: (312) 784-5973

Hours: daily 11:30 am–2 am. Cards: AE, MC, V. Reservations accepted. Casual dress. Street parking. No alcoholic beverages; diners may bring their own. Private party facilities for up to 50 people. Troubleshooter: Shazad A. Khan (owner). Inexpensive.

Pakistani food is often confused with that of India, which is not surprising since the one was once part of the other. But where Indian food is largely vegetarian and often hotly spiced, Pakistani cuisine is more subtle and relies to a greater extent on meat. That's understandable when you realize

Pakistani tradition is Moslem and much of the country's heritage came with the Arabian conquests of the eighth century.

When choosing entrées at Tasty Eat you'll want to look for a balance of flavors and ingredients. The cooked lentils in a creamy sauce heavily accented with a spice blend strong on turmeric is a real favorite. Aloo palak combines potatoes with spinach churned into a near purée. There is a curried vegetable dish on the menu, although it is nowhere near as fiery as its counterparts from India's tropical realms. Still, there is a place for hot peppers in Pakistani cooking, showing up in a stew called karahi gosht, lamb pieces in a spicy tomato-and-pepper-based sauce. Broiled and grilled meats also have their place on the Tasty Eat menu.

Desserts reflect the sweet taste of both the Middle East and the subcontinent. Kulfi, a homemade ice cream made from cheese, is not to be missed. Even sweeter are gulab jaman, deep-fried cheese balls bathed in a sugar syrup.

K/Rating 15/20: Decor 2/4, Service 4/5, Food 7/9, Value 2/2

THAI VILLA

Thai

3811 North Lincoln, Chicago
Telephone: (312) 281-2323

Hours: Tuesday–Thursday, Sunday 4–10, Friday–Saturday 4–10:30. Cards: AE, DC, MC, V. Street parking. No alcoholic beverages; diners may bring their own wine or beer. Handicap accessible. Private party room for 10–15 people. Troubleshooter: Verayuth Chaijenkit. Inexpensive.

Thai food continues to make its mark on Chicago's tastes. One of the better Thai restaurants is the Thai Villa, a storefront setting where imitation walnut paneling, a photograph of the king and queen of Thailand, and fresh herbs growing in windowsill flowerpots set a pleasant tone. In restaurants where the food is less than familiar to all but experienced diners, service is all the more important. Most of the preparations are briefly explained on the menu; those about which you need more information will be detailed by a helpful waiter or waitress.

As with other Asian cuisines, Thai food is best eaten course by course. You can order the standard dinners or choose à la carte and end up spending about the same. Thai Villa offers four different kinds of egg rolls from among fifteen appetizer choices. I tried the Thai rolls that are served cold: A filling of tiny shrimp and bean sprouts is stuffed inside edible rice paper and drizzled with a honeylike topping. Other appetizers include pork satay on a skewer, or pla koong, mixed oriental vegetables with whole shrimp in a sharp pepper seasoning. One of my favorite dishes here is hot-and-sour soup, but you can also try a Vietnamese, vegetable, or won ton soup. Noodles make up an important part of the Thai diet. After a spicy soup, an order of fried noodles with meat, chicken, or shrimp serves as a real palate refresher. Or sample the beef fried rice, just sweet enough to make you appreciate the change in tastes from course to course. Main-course selections include several fried-fish platters, duck, and chicken. Barbecued chicken, Thai style, is nothing short of delicious. Beef with peanuts and red peppers perks things up while a side vegetable such as fried broccoli helps calm down tastes. The Thai Villa draws a sizable number of Thai diners, a sure sign of its authenticity.

K/Rating of 16.5/20: Decor 3/4, Service 5/5, Food 7/9, Value 1.5/2

ROSDED

Thai

2308 West Leland, Chicago
Telephone: (312) 334-9055

Hours: Tuesday–Saturday 11:30–9, Sunday noon–8:30. Cards: MC, V. Reservations suggested. Parking in nearby city lots. No alcoholic beverages. Troubleshooter: Choosri Sudhichitt (owner). Inexpensive.

Not only is Rosded one of Chicago's oldest Thai restaurants, but it remains one of the best, if not the absolutely best Thai restaurant I have had the pleasure to enjoy over the years. The restaurant is housed in a small storefront, simply decorated with wood-paneled walls and photographs of the owner's homeland. The menu is rather straightforward in its listing of foods by ethnic name, followed by a limited description of what to expect.

I love Thai soups. My favorite, one that has become my benchmark for Thai restaurants, is one whose spelling may vary from menu to menu, but is marked by an assortment of shrimp, scallions, green hot chili peppers, and lemongrass. When I asked the waitress if the Rosded version of this soup contained lemongrass, she pointed behind where I was sitting to show the plant from which pieces are picked to give the soup its distinctively exotic flavor. As in other Asian cuisines, it is best to try and balance out main-course choices. I selected chicken with cashews, decidedly different from the Chinese version, but no less satisfying; curried beef, noted on the menu as Thai curry; and a delicious meatless noodle creation called pud Thai. This mix of sautéed noodles, ground peanuts, onions, and bean sprouts in a slightly sweet sauce turned out to be the hit of the evening, though each dish was a distinctive success in its own right. At Rosded the ethnic dining is as good as it can be in Chicago.

K/Rating 18.5/20: Decor 2.5/4, Service 5/5, Food 9/9, Value 2/2

KOTOBUKI

Japanese

5547 North Clark, Chicago
Telephone: (312) 275-6588

Lunch: Monday–Tuesday, Thursday–Friday 11:30–2. Dinner: Sunday 4–9, Monday–Tuesday, Thursday 5–10, Friday–Saturday 5–10:30. Cards: AE, CB, DC, MC, V. Reservations only for parties of 6 or more. Street parking and nearby parking lot. Full bar service; Japanese rice wines. Semiprivate party room for up to 30 people. Handicap accessible. Troubleshooters: Kiyoshi Ono and Mas Morimoto (owners). Moderate.

The decor is blond-wood simplicity. Seating is comfortable, service thoughtful. Because only the freshest of fish can be used for sushi, the cost in most Japanese restaurants that have sushi bars is usually rather high. But at Kotobuki, it is possible to get a ten-piece platter of sushi for only $10.95, or a smaller array of eight pieces for $8.25. Not only that, but you can snack on a smaller platter of half a dozen pieces of maki for as little as $1.60.

The Kotobuki menu also includes a standard selection of à la carte dinners, which come with rice, miso soup, sunomono salad, and pale green Japanese tea. The choices range in price from as little as $4.75 for vegetable tempura up to $17.90 for yosenabe, a meat, fish, and vegetable casserole for two. The tempura is light and delicate, although some of the vegetables are a little bit too bland for my taste. Of course, that's why they give diners tempura sauce! Classic sukiyaki is steaming hot and loaded with strips of beef, transparent noodles, and assorted vegetables. If an order of that is typical, cooked fish seems to be as much of a house specialty as sashimi is. The fish is sautéed in butter and comes to the table butterflied, flaky, and sweet tasting.

K/Rating 19/20: Decor 4/4, Service 5/5, Food 8/9, Value 2/2

FAR NORTH

The Bagel

Delicatessen

3000 West Devon, Chicago
Telephone: (312) 764-3377
Other location is listed below.

Hours: daily 6 am–10 pm, Friday–Saturday 6 am–11 pm. No cards. Reservations only for parties of 7 or more. No-smoking section. Street parking can be difficult. No alcoholic beverages. Handicap accessible. Troubleshooter: Danny Wolf (owner). Inexpensive.

This is Jewish cooking, but with a flair that broadens its appeal. Sure, you still can get great matzoh ball soup in a savory chicken broth with jewellike sparkles of fat floating on the top. And though the chopped liver may not have as much schmaltz as I remember from how things used to be, it still has enough to give a cardiac surgeon cause for alarm. The deli sandwiches are stacked high with layers of corned beef, pastrami, and other cold cuts, fattened with slices of cheese, mayo, horseradish, or sharp mustard as you prefer.

But there are more than sandwiches, much more. The full dinners (none for more than $12 and most priced less) bring an appetizer of chopped liver or soup, salad, and vegetables or potatoes. À la carte entrées, for a dollar less, omit the appetizer. Either way, it's a terrific bargain and a lot of food.

One of my favorites at The Bagel is tzimmes. This is a casserole of sweet potatoes, carrots, and prunes in a honeyed stew of juices. Other appetizers include what the late Sam Levinson used to call "the Jewish K rations: kasha, kugel, and knishes." And there is old-fashioned Romanian caviar, more descriptively known as puréed smoked eggplant with onions and seasonings; it's great spread across a thick slice of challah bread.

From among the dinner entrées, the stuffed veal breast is a must, with its rich seasonings bound into a large slice of pale meat. The Romanian skirt steak is charcoal grilled and loaded with a shimmering glaze of grilled onions that practically ooze flavor into the meat.

The Bagel is not without some modern flourishes. Try broiled boneless breast of chicken with a side of stir-fried vegetables. True, it's not exactly spa cuisine, but it is far different from chicken in the pot, which they also feature as a regular specialty. Desserts run from merely terrific to fabulous.

The Bagel has a second location at the Old Orchard Shopping Center (312-677-0100), Skokie.

Rating 18.5/20: Decor 3.5/4, Service 5/5, Food 8/9, Value 2/2

MY PLACE FOR?

Greek Seafood

7545 North Clark, Chicago
Telephone: (312) 262-5767

Dinner: Monday–Saturday 3:30–midnight, Sunday 3:30–9 30. Cards: AE, CB, DC, MC, V. Reservations suggested. Casual dress. No-smoking section. Valet parking and parking lot. Full bar service. Handicap accessible. Private party room for up to 100 people. Troubleshooter: Steve Dorizas (owner). Moderate.

Though the foundation is Greek, My Place For? is really a seafood restaurant and an excellent one at that. Yes, you will find saganaki, baklava, and taramasalata, all staples of the Chicago Greek dining repertoire. But the My Place For? menu focuses principally on nautical fare.

All dinners include a small platter of taramasalata, a salmon roe purée, designed to whet appetites with its mild, clean taste. A green salad with a bit of feta cheese also comes with dinner. Should you like something else, the à la carte Caesar salad is just about perfect. The romaine leaves are still crispy, well oiled but not too much so, full of the flavor of garlic and the bite of anchovy. Once past the nibbling, it is time to get on to more serious endeavors.

One big test of a fish restaurant's devotion to quality is the freshness of the raw bar. At My Place For?, oysters on the half shell and cherrystone clams pass with flying colors. Each little bivalve slips down the gullet leaving a trace of its liquor on the tongue; it is almost like being at the seaside, listening to the surf and gulls. The fried calamari, those delicious rings of deep-fried squid, are without any oiliness, just crispy batter and surprisingly tender squid.

What can you say about a restaurant that still features shrimp de jonghe on its menu and makes it seem almost like a brand new idea? This cliché of Chicago dining nonetheless works at My Place For?, perhaps because it is understated. Yes, the shrimp are bathed in buttered, garlicky bread crumbs, but somehow one forgets how tired this dish can be in ordinary hands. The restaurant also serves a variety of fish, depending upon availability. You can usually count on sea bass and red snapper, prepared Greek style with a light brushing of butter and lemon juice. I particularly like psarosoupa, a Greek seafood stew much like cioppino or bouillabaisse. The waitress brings a large cauldron filled with a tomato-based broth studded with cod, scallops, shrimp, some calamari, and an ample-sized lobster tail. Be sure to ask for extra bowls, because others with you will want a taste.

K/Rating of 19/20: Decor 4/4, Service 4.5/5, Food 8.5/9, Value 2/2

BEIRUT

Middle Eastern

5204 North Clark, Chicago
Telephone: (312) 769-1250
Other location is listed below.

Hours: Sunday–Thursday 11–midnight, Friday–Saturday 11–1 am. Cards: CB, DC, DISC, MC, V. Reservations accepted. No-smoking section. Parking lot and street parking. Full bar service; selection of Lebanese beers. Troubleshooter: Mike Faraj (owner). Inexpensive.

The unfortunate present in Lebanon is put aside at Beirut, which specializes in the fabled cuisine of what may now be little more than an ephemeral past. Dining here is to be enveloped in the hospitality of a people as it no longer can be expressed in a troubled land.

The cooking at Beirut has a definite style, more assertive and distinctive than what you find at most other Chicago area Middle Eastern restaurants, even those that specialize in Lebanese cuisine. Diners can solve the problem of deciding what to order by selecting the traditional mezza, a Levantine spread of some fifteen different foods priced at $21.95 for two people. But I think it is just as satisfying, if not as economical, to order à la carte, selecting a few appetizers and then a main course. All dinners include a spicy lentil soup and tossed salad with lettuce greens and tomato wedges.

Certainly, you should order hummus, the creamy chick-pea spread that is scooped from its shallow serving dish with a wedge of warm, flat pita bread. The other traditional spread is baba ghannouj, a purée of eggplant and sesame that is not as garlicky at Beirut as it sometimes is. Falafel, deep-fried balls of ground chick-peas, make up for any reduced seasoning elsewhere, however. They have a definite peppery taste, surprising in a snack food that is often noted for its blandness. Other appetizer choices include tabbouleh, a parsley and cracked-wheat salad spiced with fresh mint and lemon juice and nurtured in light olive oil. You could round out an evening of dining with a spread of more appetizers, such as the meat or spinach pies and the deep-fried cracked-wheat balls stuffed with ground lamb and nuts here called kibbe.

The dinner entrées include a couple of whole fish selections, meat or chicken kebabs, chicken and lamb stews, and some grilled meats. Shawarma, which is to the eastern Mediterranean what hot dogs are to Chicago, is the most basic, cooked on a vertical rotisserie much like Greek gyros. It can be ordered in a sandwich with pita or on a platter. The best of the grilled meats, though, is kefta kebab, sausage-shaped tubes of ground lamb treated to savory herbs and spices and grilled over open charcoal. You'll get a good taste of the kefta, plus shawarma, some falafel, cubes of shish kebab, and rice pilaf on a special combination platter for $8.95. Four dollars more brings the deluxe platter, which adds chicken kebabs and stuffed grape leaves.

Beirut has a second location at 4708 North Kedzie (312-509-1800).

K/Rating of 17/20: Decor 3/4, Service 5/5, Food 7/9, Value 2/2

ARBELA

Middle Eastern/Assyrian

6243 North Western, Chicago
Telephone: (312) 338-7200

Hours: Monday–Thursday, 11:30–midnight, Friday–Saturday 11:30–3 am, Sunday 5–11. Cards: AE, MC, V. Reservations accepted. No-smoking section. Street parking or at city lot at 6300 North Western Avenue (north of restaurant). Full bar service; good wine list. Private party facilities for up to 120 people. Troubleshooters: Hanny Baba and Edmond Michael (owners). Inexpensive.

Arbela is the best Middle Eastern restaurant I have been to in years. Its heritage is Assyrian, the dining rooms touched with influences of Mesopotamia. The service is friendly, informed, unrushed. The food is often heavily seasoned, complexly flavored, aromatic.

I don't think there is any way you can go wrong here. Dinners include rice or potatoes and Middle Eastern pita bread; for $1 more you get soup or salad. Begin with a selection of appetizers that can be ordered à la carte or on a combination platter. The platter comes with grilled chicken and beef shish kebabs; stuffed grape leaves; meat, spinach, and cheese pastry pies, feta cheese with salty black olives; a trio of spreads, including a chick-pea purée called hummus, an eggplant-and-sesame purée called baba ghannouj; seasoned yogurt; a type of Arabian pizza with a thin, crêpelike dough; deep-fried ground chick-pea balls called falafel; and assorted marinated vegetables. It's almost a meal in itself and an especially good way to become acquainted with a traditional array of appetizers, or mezza. Particularly outstanding is the baba ghannouj, in which the eggplant is roasted over a flame, its pulp taking on a dark smoky flavor that is haunting in its intensity. The meat, cheese, and spinach pies are the Middle Eastern version of filled dumplings; in this case, the pastry wraps are deep fried to a golden crispiness.

Entrées include beef, lamb, or chicken shish kebabs, several styles of lamb, roasted chicken, and some fish. A highlight is sautéed lamb, which is not on the printed menu but was a special the night I visited. The lamb chunks are sautéed in oil, with sweet red and green peppers, onions, and a bouquet of spices. Another special, simply named Middle Eastern chicken, brings grilled chunks lining a platter of steamed rice. The chicken has obviously been marinated, treated to a mix of seasonings whose spiciness underscores the meat. Diners with smaller appetites can order any of several sandwiches. Shawarma, which is the Arabian version of gyros, comes shredded with lettuce, tomatoes, and onions on a large French roll. Its flavors are well married and satisfying. I think the sandwich is nicely complemented by a side order of tabbouleh, a cracked wheat, parsley, and mint salad in a mild vinegar dressing.

K/Rating 19/20: Decor 3.5/4, Service 4.5/5, Food 9/9, Value 2/2

On the Tao

Chinese

1218 Morse, Chicago
Telephone: (312) 743-5955

Dinner: Tuesday–Sunday 5–11. Cards: MC, V. Reservations suggested. No-smoking section. Free parking lot. Full bar service; good wines available by the glass; good selection of beers. Handicap accessible. Private party room for up to 22 people with special menus available. Troubleshooter: Margie Chan (maître d'). Moderate.

The Tao is "The Way" for millions of Chinese. That concept provides more than a small clue to what this unique restaurant is all about. Chef G. K. Chan is a man who seeks not to re-create the classic recipes of his tradition, but rather to achieve a style of preparation marked by individual talent and personality. Like the decor, the food is understated; Chef Chan never uses MSG, and even eschews salt and other flavor additions. Thus, in a salad dressed with sesame oil, the flavor of the oil is evident. There are no intrusive seasonings in the egg rolls to block out the natural flavors of the complex vegetable filling. While regional influences may be apparent, it is also apparent the chef has gone his own way, cooking not by whim, but by applying his experience and taste to traditional concepts. If this were Western cuisine, the temptation would be to label it "nouvelle." There is a newness, a freshness about veal medallions in a mix of snow peas, Chinese bok choy, fresh spring ginger, and mushrooms. Lamb is given a zing of pepper, but not so intrusive as to betray the natural flavor of the meat.

K/Rating 16.5/20: Decor 4/4, Service 3.5/5, Food 8/9, Value 1/2

Dynasty

Chinese (Cantonese)

6031 North Cicero, Chicago
Telephone: (312) 685-8934

Hours: Monday–Friday 1:30–9:30, Saturday 6–9:30, Sunday 4–9. No cards. Reservations suggested. Ample street parking. No alcoholic beverages. Troubleshooter: Wilson Chan (owner). Inexpensive.

In recent years, Cantonese food has largely been forgotten in the rush to explore other regional Chinese cuisines. And Dynasty makes a quick bow to such tastes with a small listing headed Mandarin Dishes, which includes a pair of mu shu offerings, three kung pao preparations, and Mongolian beef. The mu shu plates here are also more highly seasoned than most I've tried. The Dynasty versions are also served with pancakes that are sturdier than the wispy crêpes most often provided. Although not as delicate, these pancakes are, however, more practical for holding in all the juices.

A look at the rest of the Dynasty menu is no tip-off to the fine culinary skills of the kitchen. The egg roll is one of the best I've had, with a delicious nutlike aftertaste. Fried won tons are a bit tough, but like most other dishes, they are delivered within seconds of cooking. Dynasty beef strips come four to the order; the grilled meat is infused with the flavor of a sharp marinade.

Like so many neighborhood Chinese restaurants, Americanized chow mein and chop suey are standard preparations. And there are the sweet-and-sour choices of pork, chicken, shrimp, and fish. The sauce at Dynasty is really not all that sweet; in fact, it shows a sense of balance, if not restraint. The chicken was nicely battered and fried, and surprisingly light. Similarly restrained was an order of shrimp with lobster sauce. The thick, meaty sauce was milder than most lobster sauce I've tasted; it bathed several large shrimp that had been steamed just short of toughness.

The Chinese do not make a big deal of dessert, and neither does Dynasty, except for a tasty almond cookie and the ever-present fortune cookie. No wine or liquor is served. Service is prompt and friendly. There are only seven tables in the whole place. Walls done in bright red and off-white handsomely show off what can be done with more imagination than money.

K/Rating 16/20: Decor 3/4, Service 4/5, Food 7/9, Value 2/2

Gin Go Gae

Korean

5433 North Lincoln, Chicago
Telephone: (312) 334-9235

Hours: Thursday–Tuesday 11–10:30. Cards: MC, V. Reservations accepted. Street parking. No alcoholic beverages. Handicap accessible. Private party facilities. Inexpensive.

If looks could tell, this restaurant would not tell much of a story. From outward appearances, Gin Go Gae looks like just another diner. But it happens to be one of the most popular restaurants among Chicago's large Korean-American community. Although the decor may be Western, the cooking is strictly "Seoul-food."

The Korean language menu appears to be more extensive than that given English-speaking customers, but once you convince your waiter or waitress you want to order more broadly, you probably will be well rewarded. Still, the basic selections are satisfying and reflect the Korean love of charcoal grilled beef in a barbecue-style sauce. Try the short ribs or strips of sirloin, each served in that semihot sauce common to Korean fare. Chop chae, as ubiquitous on Korean menus as steak and potatoes is on American, is a casserolelike dish of stir-fried vegetables and meat mixed with transparent noodles for bulk and texture. Of course, various fashions of Korean vegetable preparation are demonstrated, too. The kimchi (pepper-hot fermented cabbage) is one of the best to be found in the city.

K/Rating 16/20: Decor 2/4, Service 4/5, Food 8/9, Value 2/2

CHUN SOO CHANG

Korean

3534 West Lawrence, Chicago
Telephone: (312) 539-2444

Hours: Thursday–Tuesday 10:30–10:30. No cards. No reservations. Street parking. No alcoholic beverages. Handicap accessible. Inexpensive.

Chun Soo Chang is in the heart of Chicago's burgeoning Far North Korean community. The menu does not seem as extensive as some other restaurants of its kind, but that's a small sacrifice considering the other attractions. Set in an expanded corner storefront, Chun Soo Chang opens up into a bright and cheery setting. Unlike many other Korean restaurants I've visited, this one has four tables designed for cooking in place. Ask for one of these tables when you make your reservation, or go in on a slow night and perhaps you will find one free. In the center of these tables is a gas burner. Your waitress will light the burner and place what looks like an inverted cast-iron wok on top. This wok is really a grate, with a trough along its edge into which the meat juices drain. The meat itself is set over the grate, and you cook it to your own taste. In the case of bulkogi, marinated strips, not only the meat, but slivers of raw onion will seer in the intense heat of the gas flame. The result is some of the best grilled meat I've ever tasted.

In addition to the bulkogi, grill an order of marinated beef short ribs. The flavorful beef tears easily from the bones. There are several pork dishes on the menu, which also sets Chun Soo Chang apart from other local Korean restaurants. Seafood does not get a lot of attention from domestic Korean restaurants, but that flaw is remedied here as well. Choices range from clams or crabs in a spicy soup broth to various fish. The hot broths are a culinary focal point in traditional Korean dining. Chun Soo Chang even offers one that the menu says will "chase hangover."

Dinner should begin with an appetizer, perhaps steamed or fried dumplings with a thickened soy sauce accented with slivers of onion, peppers for heat, and garlic. And be sure to order one of the noodle dishes. Beebeem nang myon brings cold slender noodles mixed with slices of cucumber, which may be my digestive tract's natural enemy, but was so good I found it hard to say "enough." The waitress warned me that I might find the noodles too highly seasoned, but in fact, they were a refreshing counterpoint to the meat.

Korean tastes run to the highly seasoned, as kimchi, the pickled cabbage that is almost a national mania, demonstrates. Kimchi is in just one of the nearly dozen separate bowls that are ringed around the center of your table. Choices can include sliced daikon radish with mild peppers, cold cooked potatoes, sweet marinated whole anchovies, bean sprouts, and pastalike fish curd.

Chun Soo Chang serves delicious Korean food, and it's fun to eat here. Expect to spend only about $10 per person, plus tax and tip.

K/Rating 19/20: Decor 3.5/4, Service 5/5, Food 8.5/9, Value 2/2

DAE HO

Korean

2741 West Devon, Chicago
Telephone: (312) 274-8499

Hours: Wednesday–Monday 11–11. Cards: MC, V, house accounts. Street parking. Wine and beer. Handicap accessible. Private party room for up to 40 people. Troubleshooter: Suk H. Shin (owner). Inexpensive.

Though the decor has grown a bit threadbare over the years, this still remains one of my favorite Korean restaurants. The food is fresh and plentiful, and while the menu offers Chinese selections, I usually stay with the Korean choices. Lest the idea of something as foreign as Korean cuisine alarm you, rest assured it is an easy style of food to enjoy. Tasty finger foods, such as fried mandu, or dumplings, are a good way to start. They look like stuffed three-cornered hats, and each order is ample for two or three people.

The real heart of Korean dining lies in the preparation of barbecued beef dishes. Among my favorites is bulkogi, charbroiled sirloin steak marinated for a full day in a slightly sweet soy sauce. Senjuk is a Korean version of shish kebab, flavored by a marinade of soy sauce, sugar, ginger, garlic, and onion, then sizzled over open coals. A more unusual selection is bee-beem-bop, a beef and vegetable casserole with rice topped with a fried egg. It is a most interesting preparation and I urge you to include it among your choices. A variety of pork, chicken, and seafood specialties, as well as meat and noodle broths—substantial enough to be meals in themselves—are part of the menu.

K/Rating of 16/20: Decor 2/4, Service 3.5/5, Food 8.5/9, Value 2/2

LANNA THAI

Thai

5951-55 North Broadway, Chicago
Telephone: (312) 878-1155

Hours: Tuesday–Friday, 11–10, Saturday–Sunday noon–10. Cards: AE, MC, V. Reservations accepted. Casual dress. Street parking. Full bar service. Troubleshooters: Wilyveun Turatone and Eddie Yichaikul (owners). Inexpensive.

Lanna Thai is brightly lit and modestly decorated with art and artifacts from the owner's native Thailand. This is a good restaurant for newcomers to this food, because the seasoning tends to be on the less peppery end of the scale. The negative side is that if you really want it hot, it's difficult to get the owners to go along, apparently out of fear that you really do not know how hot, hot can be.

In any event, go to Lanna Thai with a party of four or more so you'll have an opportunity to taste a number of dishes. Satay is typical of Thai restaurants; here the seasoned pork or chicken is grilled on skewers and served in a spiced peanut sauce as an appetizer. Among other choices on the appetizer menu are egg rolls and spring rolls, noodles, squid tempura, and deep-fried tofu. The spring rolls are a mix of vegetables and mild Oriental sausage stuffed inside a dough wrapping, picked up and eaten like a taco. The best appetizer of the lot is mee krob, deep-fried noodles that must be seen and tasted to be believed. Rice noodles are quickly stir-fried with meat and seasonings; the temptation is to snack on these like potato chips; the satisfaction is far greater.

After appetizers, try one of the soups. My favorite, which has become a benchmark for me in measuring Thai restaurants, is the tom yum koong, shrimp in a moderately hot, spiced broth.

Thai curries are not always hot; they are made with a base of coconut milk, its sweetness playing on the tongue and palate in counterpoint to the other flavors.

To round out a dinner, order one of the beef dishes, such as the larb neur with its mix of meat, roasted rice, and vegetables. The real specialty is a whole deep-fried fish, which on your check is well worth the few extra dollars. Red snapper comes topped with either a spicy sauce (which, like the others, is not as spicy as you might fear) or a sweet-and-sour sauce.

Lanna Thai is a good bridge to the unique food of Thailand in a setting that could make the unadventurous eater comfortable with the exotic.

K/Rating of 17/20: Decor 3.5/4, Service 4.5/5, Food 7/9, Value 2/2

PASTEUR

Vietnamese

4759 North Sheridan Road, Chicago
Telephone: (312) 271-6673

Lunch: daily noon–2:30. Dinner: 5–10. Cards: AE, MC, V. Reservations suggested. No-smoking section. Street parking can be difficult. No alcoholic beverages. Handicap accessible. Troubleshooter: Tuan Nguyen (owner). Moderate.

At Pasteur there is a sense of nostalgia for what never can be again, namely, the Vietnam that existed what now seems a long time ago. There is a sadness in the faded photographs of Saigon street scenes, and in the music. But that is countered by the obvious enthusiasm and pleasure with which customers are greeted by owner Tuan Nguyen and his family.

The menu highlights several house specialties, but even when you go with the regular list, there are no mistakes to be made. The traditional Vietnamese spring roll is a delicate, almost translucent rice paper wrapped around a filling of rice noodles, bean sprouts, and small pieces of shrimp. The spring roll is taken in hand and dipped into a sweet plum sauce that is enhanced by the slight bite of peppers and topped with ground peanuts. Even better among the appetizers is an omelet called banh xeo. Folded almost like a crêpe, it is filled with shrimp, mushrooms, pork, bean sprouts, and other ingredients. The idea is to cut off a piece, wrap it in a large lettuce leaf, and dip into a somewhat thin but sweet sauce. The appetizer choices are many and varied, but another one I tasted was deep-fried shrimp with tapioca root. This is listed as a house specialty and for good reason. The flavors are absolutely marvelous; the shrimp and sticks of yam are held together by a light binding.

Other courses lie ahead. Some of the cooking is reminiscent of Thailand. While peppers are used, there is not the fiery heat characteristic of Thai cooking. For example, stir-fried chicken can be ordered with a seasoning of lemongrass and peppers. But the jalapeño-style peppers have been carefully seeded and washed, which removes most of the potential heat, and leaves in its wake a sautéed pepper with only a hint of its former self and a lovely sweet aftertaste. It balances perfectly with the mild chicken and other flavors.

K/Rating of 18.5/20: Decor 3/4, Service 5/5, Food 8.5/9, Value 2/2

Tokyo Marina

Japanese

5058 North Clark, Chicago
Telephone: (312) 878-2900

Hours: daily 11:30–11:30. Cards: MC, V. Reservations accepted. Casual dress. No-smoking section. Ample street parking. Full bar service; imported Japanese beers and sake. Semiprivate rooms for up to 35 people.
Troubleshooter: Noboru "Jim" Asato (owner).
Moderate.

Tokyo Marina offers just about anything you can find at any of Chicago's better Japanese restaurants, but at a near-budget cost. Diners can sit at the sushi bar or at wood-topped tables in either of two main dining rooms.

The menu lists only some of what is available. Before ordering, check the handwritten list of special fish and other seafood, as well as various kinds of maki, the seaweed-wrapped sushi that can contain anything from avocado to omelet. If you choose to order à la carte, sit at the sushi bar and tell the chef what you want. More economical, and with nearly as much variety at hand, are combination platters that include sushi with mackerel, yellowtail, octopus, tuna, and other toppings, depending upon what is fresh and available.

This restaurant is perfect for grazing, so try several appetizers. Chicken yakitori delivers two large skewers of grilled poultry and vegetables. The tempura I tasted was a bit too oily, but otherwise the vegetables and shrimp were cooked perfectly. One of the best choices is scallop butteryaki. Large sea scallops are stir-fried in butter with sliced button mushrooms. A dish like this would be perfectly at home in an elaborate French or Continental setting.

Tokyo Marina serves noodle dishes, soups, casseroles such as sukiyaki, and a quartet of "nabes," which are vegetable-and-meat one-pot meals, often cooked at tableside. Service can be oddly sluggish. But considering the value, Tokyo Marina should be on your list of regular haunts for Japanese food.

K/Rating of 16/20: Decor 3/4, Service 3.5/5, Food 7.5/9, Value 2/2

Suburbs: North

LINCOLNWOOD
SKOKIE
EVANSTON
WILMETTE
GLENVIEW
WINNETKA
GLENCOE
DEERFIELD
HIGHLAND PARK
HIGHWOOD

BONES

American

7110 North Lincoln, Lincolnwood
Telephone: (312) 677-3350

Hours: Monday–Thursday 11:30–11, Friday–Saturday 11:30–midnight, Sunday 3–10. Cards: AE, CB, DC, MC, V, LEYE. Reservations suggested. Parking lot and street parking. Full bar service. Private party rooms for parties of 25–100 people. Troubleshooter: Rich Melman (owner). Moderate.

You know all the diet warnings about cholesterol and fats, but no one can go to Bones and eat like a monk! If you are no stranger to this culinary cornucopia of calories, you know the temptations. But if you have never known the sensual delight of gnawing, gnashing, and "gnoshing" on hickory-smoked ribs or on barbecued chicken with meat that practically falls from the bones, or the pleasures of a barbecue sauce as thick and sweet as syrup, then I promise you a real treat.

Bones is almost always busy, which means you really should phone ahead for reservations. Otherwise, prepare for a stackup that makes Friday afternoons at O'Hare look like an ant hill. To its credit, the handsome sports bar is as good a place as any to wait.

Once seated amidst a mix of dark woods and cartoon drawings of celebrities handpainted on the walls, a waitress will be by to take your drink order and offer menus. The menus are fairly short, limited by and large to barbecued baby back ribs and beef ribs, and chicken either barbecued or broiled. Daily specials flesh out (no pun intended) the choices. Whole barbecued duck has been a regular feature recently, and it is often an instant sellout. Three-way chicken gives you a taste of barbecued chicken, broiled chicken, and chicken teriyaki. These are whole chickens, which means that unless you have the appetite of Andre the Giant, you'll bring home lots of leftovers. In fact, that's probably true for the rib slabs, too, which may be to ribs what the Hope diamond is to costume jewelry. In addition to how the ribs are cooked, the key to success, as must seem obvious, lies in the sauce. At Bones, there are two kinds. Spicy, which is really kind of sweet, and mild, which is, well, mild. As for the teriyaki sauce, stick to Japanese restaurants for this stuff.

Desserts are lavish and excessive, including something called skoog pie that is built of layers of ice cream, caramel, pecans, and chocolate. Or you could try something "simpler," like the strawberry ice cream pie with a purée of strawberries and a crunchy graham-cracker crust.

If all of this is not enough, someone with a pin identifying her as the Hospitality Schmoozer comes around with a large bowl of fried chicken for the asking. Oh, by the way, Bones also features at least one seafood selection. Broiled whitefish was offered the night I visited. I did not taste it. Why bother?

K/Rating of 16.5/20: Decor 3.5/4, Service 3/5, Food 8/9, Value 2/2

THE CHARCOAL OVEN

American

4400 Golf Road, Skokie
Telephone: (312) 675-8062

Lunch: Monday–Friday 11–3. Dinner: Monday–Friday 5–10, Saturday–Sunday 4–10:30. Cards: AE, CB, DC. Reservations accepted. No-smoking section. Full bar service. Handicap accessible. Entire restaurant available for private parties. Troubleshooter: Phil Georgousses (owner). Moderate.

I am going to reveal a secret. The Charcoal Oven no longer has a charcoal oven in its kitchen. Nonetheless, this restaurant remains one of the North Shore's most enduring dinner spots. Owner Phil Georgousses has been here for forty years, and I think his number one waitress and baker, Loretta Szumniak, has been here for almost as long. She is the one responsible for the grandmother rolls that come out steaming hot from the kitchen, just waiting to be laden with butter. She also gets the credit for most of the desserts, including berry pies with crusts like shortcake and cheesecakes awash with flavor.

An appetizer of spicy Greek sausage is brought in addition to whatever else you order. The menu lists twenty or more main-courses. Lake perch has been among the recent choices, sweet without being drowned in butter. Another favorite is calf's liver sautéed in butter and served with slivered onions.

Though some foods, such as the sausage or sautéed chicken livers, can be a bit oily, a whole roasted duck has skin that is crisp and crackling, concealing dark and moist meat. This dish is great as is, although the accompanying fruit sauce complements the poultry, without overpowering it. If your taste is for beef, a generous shish kebab brings tender grilled meat cubes that have been marinated in a complex mix of herbs and spices, oil, and just a little vinegar for sharpness. All dinners come with two fresh vegetables.

K/Rating 19/20: Decor 3.5/4, Service 5/5, Food 8.5/9, Value 2/2

THE TOWER GARDEN AND RESTAURANT

Continental

9925 Gross Point Road, Skokie
Telephone: (312) 673-4450

Hours: Monday–Friday 11:30–10, Saturday 4:30–11, Sunday 11:30–7:30. Sunday brunch served through midafternoon. Cards: AE, CB, DC, MC, V, house accounts. Reservations required. Jackets required for gentlemen. No-smoking section. Parking lot. Full bar service; cocktail lounge. Private party and banquet facilities for up to 200 people. Troubleshooter: Reinhard Barthel (owner). Expensive.

The Tower Garden and Restaurant has had its ups and downs in the past few years, but now seems to have found a focus. Gone are the barbecued ribs and other froufrou that caused some confusion as to what this restaurant was really all about. A new chef has worked to create a menu that is more wide ranging and sophisticated than previous ones. The menu pays tribute to current cooking trends, such as Cajun-inspired monkfish New Orleans, prepared in a spicy, peppery sauce. But there are also the classic French recipes, including duck breast Madagascar with a green peppercorn sauce flambéed with cognac. The ducks, by the way, come from a real showpiece, a large rotisserie at the front of the dining room. Pale white Provimi veal can be ordered à la Normande, with a flaming of Calvados in a sauce similar to that used for the duck. Or try the veal in a mushroom-laden chasseur sauce for something a bit bolder.

Trout comes from a holding tank to insure freshness. Walleyed pike Doria is a classic recipe with capers. The menu is filled out with perhaps a dozen other choices, ranging from cuts of steak to poultry and a hearty venison ragout called rehpfeffer Allemand, to underscore its German origins.

An order of oysters Rockefeller, Bienville, or Provençale is a fine way to begin your dining. Desserts can be as lavish as kirshwasser torte, available from time to time, or as simple as fresh berries in season. The wine list at The Tower remains one of the best in the area; in fact, this restaurant has been educating suburban diners about wines for more than twenty years.

K/Rating 17.5/20: Decor 4/4, Service 4/5, Food 7.5/9, Value 2/2

Davis Street Fish Market

American Seafood

501 Davis Street, Evanston
Telephone: (312) 869-3474

Hours: daily 11:30–11. Friday–Sunday country breakfast 8–2. Cards: AE, CB, DC, MC, V. Reservations only for parties of 5 or more. Street parking can be difficult. No-smoking section. Full bar service; limited wine list but many domestic beers. Handicap accessible. Troubleshooters: Steve Prescott and Harold Miller (managers). Moderate.

Sometimes I think that ordering fish in a restaurant is like buying insurance. I must have ten different insurance policies: whole life, half life, universal, home, auto. You name it and I've probably got it. And I can't tell you what any of them mean.

A competent insurance agent is important to me, to explain all of the cash values, surrender values, and anything else in small print. Along that same line, a good waitress in a fish restaurant is as important to me as what's on the menu. I like knowledgeable explanations to help sort through all the different kinds of fish. What do I know? It could be chopped liver!

The point is I like Davis Street Fish Market because I had a waitress who probably *forgot* more about fish than the old man and the sea ever knew. Selections are all listed on two large blackboards. When anything becomes sold out, bingo, out comes some guy with a large eraser at the end of a stick and wipes out the price. That way you know you won't be able to order any red haired-barracuda or whatever. But hold on for a minute! My waitress was better than the blackboard. She could talk about which fish were oily and which were drier, which fish were firm and which were flaky. She probably knows which ones can do the backstroke.

Oh, by the way, I ordered shrimp and crawfish étouffée. That's kind of a Cajun rice casserole. Served in a large soup tureen, the étouffée was rich and buttery, a dish you want to savor down to the last drop.

For dessert, I wasn't so impressed with the Lone Star cheesecake, even if it was made with the most famous beer out of Texas. But I did like the pecan pie, which is about as southern as you can get without an accent.

K/Rating of 18.5/20: Decor 4/4, Service 5/5, Food 7.5/9, Value 2/2

BLIND FAITH CAFE

Vegetarian

525 Dempster, Evanston
Telephone: (312) 328-6875

Hours: Monday 10–10, Tuesday–Sunday 7 am–10 pm. No cards. No reservations. No smoking in restaurant. No alcoholic beverages. Handicap accessible. Troubleshooter: David Lipschutz (owner). Inexpensive.

Do you remember when you were little how your mother urged you to "eat all your vegetables"? Mom doesn't exactly prowl the tables at Blind Faith Cafe, but certainly she's there in spirit at this most famous vegetarian restaurant in the Chicago area.

In the past, vegetarians had the reputation for being spindly folks who were likely to be involved in arcane politics and certainly were big readers of theosophy. Of course, there was never any truth to that profile then, nor is there now. Go into Blind Faith Cafe, or any other vegetarian restaurant for that matter, and chances are you will find the same cross section of people you see in any other eatery.

Indeed, you don't have to be a vegetarian to enjoy Blind Faith Cafe. Just go for the good food, lots of it, and most of it at extremely reasonable prices. Sure, the dinnertime salad bar at $6.95 is a bit high considering its somewhat meager choices, but if all you want is a salad bar, go to Wendy's.

Begin with one of the appetizers like tempeh fingers. These will remind you of fried mozzarella sticks, except that they are made with tempeh, a fermented soybean product. The taste is pleasant, the texture, cheeselike. The hummus and tabbouleh have the kind of authenticity you will find in better Middle Eastern restaurants and make great predinner snacking.

Soups include miso (a Japanese soy soup), vegetarian chili, or the soup of the day. Mushroom barley soup, a recent special, comes in a clear stock with lots of chewy slices of the fungus and delicious kernels of grain.

Food substances like tofu or tempeh, because they are so neutral, can show up in any number of ways. You might want to try sautéed tempeh, a delicately flavored dish in which the tempeh looks like stir-fried chicken and has a slightly oriental flavor, no doubt from a soy-sauce seasoning. The firm little tempeh nuggets are mixed with broccoli, onion, and mushrooms atop a bed of brown rice. There is also a vegetarian jambalaya, awash with everything you expect in a jambalaya except the meat. This one definitely proves vegetarianism does not mean "bland"!

One of the direct meat imitations at Blind Faith Cafe is pecan scallopini. This is not a bowl of nuts. A patty of texturized vegetable protein (TVP) is grilled, laden with a brown sauce and melted mozzarella, and served on a bed of linguine. When the recipe does not have to be imitative, things can be even better. Pasta with pesto is redolent with fresh basil and garlic. Instead of pine nuts, the recipe uses cashews, which may not be the way it's done in Genoa but is still quite good.

As you might expect, Blind Faith Cafe can accommodate special diets. It's really an interesting change from standard dining. And, who knows—you might just want to jog 10K or so after dinner!

K/Rating 17.5/20: Decor 3.5/4, Service 4.5/5, Food 7.5/9, Value 2/2

JILLY'S CAFE

American Contemporary

2614 Greenbay Road, Evanston
Telephone: (312) 869-7636

Dinner: Tuesday–Thursday 5–9, Friday–Saturday 5–10:30. Sunday brunch 10:30–2. Cards: MC, V. Reservations required. Casual dress, but no jeans. No-smoking section. Parking lot and street parking. Wine and beer; several wines by the glass. Restaurant available for private parties of up to 45 people Tuesday, Wednesday, Thursday. Troubleshooters: Jill Sigrist and Larry Quaglia (owners). Moderate.

Stucco walls and wood beams set the Continental country style. The food is contemporary, with a nod toward modern French. The rather concise regular menu is supplemented by daily specials. Recent choices included a delicious home-smoked platter of sliced duck, turkey, and chicken served with a fruity raspberry vinaigrette that was not so sharp as to mask the smoked poultry flavors. Pasta, made on the premises, is stylish and not overcooked. The fettuccine Alfredo, served as an appetizer, has a touch of gorgonzola at the heart of its cheese sauce. Somewhat less successful is escargots, black olives, and goat cheese on a bed of fettuccine. Here the problem is a conflict between the sharp salty flavor of the olives and the mildness of the snails, which are simply overpowered. The ambitious menu also offers baked brie en croute on the regular appetizer list, and such dishes as marinated shrimp and Cajun-style andouille sausage, and broiled lamb sausage in an eggplant-and-spiced-tomato sauce as specials.

An excellent hand is at work on the sauces. Perhaps one of the better dinner choices is slices of roasted duck breast ($14.95) in a cherry and cognac sauce. All entrées are served with your choice of soup or salad and come with an appropriate selection of fresh, lightly cooked vegetables.

Desserts are tempting. Recent choices were a moist carrot cake, apple tart, and chocolate prune cake.

K/Rating 17.5/20: Decor 3.5/4, Service 4.5/5, Food 7.5/9, Value 2/2

CAFE PROVENCAL

French

1625 Hinman, Evanston
Telephone: (312) 475-2233

Dinner: Monday–Thursday 6–9:30, Friday–Saturday 6–10. Cards. AE, CB, DC, MC, V. Reservations required. Jackets required for gentlemen. No-smoking section. Valet and street parking. Full bar service; excellent list of 250 wines. Private party facilities for 14–30 people Monday–Thursday. Troubleshooters: Leslie Reis (chef/owner) and Henry Adaniya (maître d'). Expensive.

When Cafe Provencal opened a decade or so ago, it was a pioneer among North Shore restaurants, bringing the kind of elegance in dining usually limited to the city. In that intervening time, French and Continental restaurants have become almost commonplace, though the really good ones are still the exception rather than the rule.

As it has from the beginning, Cafe Provencal remains an exception. Owner Leslie Reis has assembled a first-class staff, front and back. And, if good food is the goal, Cafe Provencal is remarkably successful. Consider an appetizer of torte aux legumes Provencal ($6.95). At the center of a large platter sits a small wedge of artichoke mousse topped with a coulis of vegetables, all napped in a lusciously herbaceous tomato sauce redolent with basil and a lingering touch of mint. For something a bit more substantial, try ravioli de homard aux thyme ($8.95). Here the large, freshly made raviolis are plumped with fresh lobster pieces. The raviolis come in a saffron-and-thyme wine sauce that looks like it is related to a lobster bisque and tastes almost as good.

Other appetizer selections include smoked salmon ($8.95) served with cornmeal pancakes, kind of an American version of blinis. Carrying out the theme, the salmon is topped with crème fraîche and American caviar. For the truly rich in dining there is canard roulé ($8.95), duck breast and foie gras garnished with onion confit flavored with wild cherries.

Fresh seafood is at the heart of the daily specials. Recently, Norwegian salmon ($24.95) was presented Niçoise style, with peppers, tomatoes, onions, and olives. Striped bass ($24.95) might come grilled with a similar saucing, which works handsomely with this neutral-flavored fish.

One evening, diners were served magret grillé ($24.95). Slices of medium-rare duck breast were fanned in a semicircle on a platter with thick slices of duck sausage and sweet red cabbage. The sauce was a reduction of tomato, with the distinct flavor of honey and the slight bite of vinegar. The honey flavor was a bit out of balance, though not cloying.

Grilled fillet of beef is done in a mustard, shallot, and tarragon sauce. Roasted pheasant, saddle of lamb, and veal chop in a Château Neuf-du-Pape sauce have been other recent entrées.

Desserts include a Cafe Provencal signature selection, chocolate génoise layered with raspberry purée. Something a bit lighter, though no less elegant, are the dual small pots of delicious crème brûlée and satiny chocolate mousse.

K/Rating 19/20: Decor 3.5/4, Service 5/5, Food 9/9, Value 1.5/2

SIAM SQUARE

Thai

622 Davis, Evanston
Telephone: (312) 475-0860

Hours: Monday–Thursday 11–10, Friday–Saturday 11–10:30, Sunday 4–9. Cards: AE, DC, MC, V. Reservations accepted. No-smoking section. Free parking at First Rotary Center (between Grove and Sherman), usually ample street parking. Wine and beer. Handicap accessible. Private party facilities. Troubleshooter: Sunanta (Susy) Laddaglom (owner). Moderate.

As with other Asian cuisines, Thai foods are best enjoyed with a large party so the diversity of the menu can be experienced. Starting with appetizers, be sure to order spring rolls. I prefer the fresh to the fried; a thin rice-paper wrap encases crisp bean sprouts and other vegetables and a ribbon of mild sausage and is topped with a sweet plum glaze.

Traditional to Thai dining are satays, skewered grilled meats served with a slightly peppery peanut sauce. Chicken satay brings several thin strips of turmeric-spiced chicken. To round out the appetizer selection, order fried tofus with chicken or pork in a moderately spicy brown sauce.

For an unforgettable soup, try one of the tom yams. These are fiery hot in seasoning, with an aftertaste of fresh lemongrass. Order the shrimp or chicken version for something so good you might be tempted to ask for seconds.

There are several other dishes you may want to get to know at Siam Square, including the curries. Let your own taste be your guide, and specify whether you want something seasoned mild or hot. The kitchen will happily comply. Thai noodle dishes offer a near endless fascination. My favorite is pad Thai, translucent rice noodles with lettuce for crispiness, bean sprouts for texture, and bits of egg to bind everything together. Variations may include different meat choices.

K/Rating of 18/20: Decor 3.5/4, Service 4/5, Food 8.5/9, Value 2/2

DARUMA

Japanese

2901 Central, Evanston
Telephone: (312) 864-6633 or 834-6636
Other location is listed below.

Lunch: Tuesday–Saturday 11:30–2:30. Dinner: Tuesday–Thursday 4:30–10, Friday–Saturday 4:30–11, Sunday 4:30–9. Reservations only for parties of 6 or more. Street parking. Wine and beer, including Japanese sake, beers, plum wines. Handicap accessible. Troubleshooter: Shozo Sakata (owner). Moderate.

The restaurant is not all that large, which means that some tables are fairly close to each other. That's a problem only if you are a nonsmoker seated close to a table full of smokers. The menu is rather extensive and carries good descriptions of the various sushi and sashimi combinations. The sushi is delivered on a traditional hardwood serving block, with attention to appearance as important as attention to taste and texture. Each order comes with a dab of wasabi (horseradish) and thin slices of vinegared gingerroot.

Dinner choices include such Japanese standards as tempura, teriyaki chicken, beef, or fish, and the steaming meat and vegetable casserole called sukiyaki. The sukiyaki at Daruma is as good as they come, an artful presentation as well as a gustatorially satisfying one. Breaded pork cutlet, a virtual classic in Japanese cookery, receives excellent treatment. A light breading covers the pale, mild meat, and a syrupy blend of soy and ginger is the dipping sauce. Fish is important to Japanese cuisine, as one might expect from an island nation. Fish entrées vary according to season and availability, but buttery baked salmon is regularly offered, along with a range of grilled fish dishes. Service can be inept, in sharp contrast to the elegant simplicity of the foods.

Daruma has a second location at 1851 West Golf Road (312-310-8877), Schaumburg.

K/Rating of 16.5/20: Decor 3.5/4, Service 3/5, Food 8/9, Value 2/2

NEW JAPAN

Japanese

1322 Chicago Avenue, Evanston
Telephone: (312) 475-5980

Lunch: Tuesday–Saturday 11:30–2:15. Dinner: Tuesday–Thursday, Sunday 5–9:15, Friday–Saturday 5–10:15. Cards: AE, CB, DC, MC, V. Reservations suggested. Street parking. Full bar service. Handicap accessible. Semiprivate party room available for up to 50 people. Troubleshooter: Hisao Fukui (owner). Moderate.

This was one of the first restaurants in the Chicago area to blend the culinary traditions of East and West. New Japan's food is traditional

Japanese in many respects, but with some decidedly French accents. The crab croquettes ($11.50) are a perfect example. The chef finishes a béchamel sauce with onions, mushrooms, and cream to create a buttery richness. The result is a sharp contrast in textures: the ruggedness of the breaded crabmeat cakes balanced against the silkiness of the sauce that hangs languorously to each bite. Contrast is an extremely important aspect of Japanese food preparation. A platter of sushi is a picture of visual contrasts. There are rice balls topped with slices of different colored fish and platters of maki, rice formed into cylinders around a filling and wrapped in sheets of dark green seaweed. Sukiyaki, the classic stew of beef, noodles, and vegetables, comes in a lacquered bowl with the ingredients arranged in circular patterns, perhaps to symbolize the completeness of such dining. Cabbage, for example, is wrapped around a center of dark green spinach, each cabbage leaf unfolding in succession as you grasp it with chopsticks.

The dining room makes appropriate use of bleached blond wood for trim and accent. Rice-paper screens decorate some of the walls. The floor is a cinnamon block tile, somewhat austere considering the nearly ephemeral mood created by the rest of the decor.

K/Rating of 16/20: Decor 4/4, Service 3/5, Food 7.5/9, Value 1.5/2

WALKER BROS. ORIGINAL PANCAKE HOUSE

Pancakes

153 Greenbay Road, Wilmette
Telephone: (312) 251–6000
Other locations are listed below.

Hours: Sunday–Thursday 7–10:30, Friday–Saturday 7–midnight. No cards. Reservations weekdays only for larger parties. No-smoking section. Handicap accessible. Private party room for up to 30 people only for early breakfast meetings. No alcoholic beverages. Troubleshooter: Ray Walker (owner). Inexpensive.

The short and sweet of it is that there are no better pancakes made and served anywhere than at Walker Bros. Stained-glass fanciers will love the atmosphere, but the real reason to be here should be self-evident. Best of the best is the apple pancake, an oven-baked affair oozing butter and glistening with melted sugar and a dusting of cinnamon. But the fact is that no matter what your choice, you cannot order anything but good food.

Walker Bros. can also be found at 1615 Waukegan Road, Glenview (312-723-0220) and at 825 Dundee Road, Arlington Heights (312-392-6600).

K/Rating of 20/20: Decor 4/4, Service 5/5, Food 9/9, Value 2/2

CONVITO ITALIANO

Italian

1515 Sheridan Road
(Plaza del Lago), Wilmette
Telephone: (312) 251-3654
Other location is listed below.

Lunch: Monday–Friday 11:30–2:15, Sunday 11:30–3. Dinner: Monday–Thursday 5–9, Friday–Saturday 5–10, Sunday 4–8. Cards: AE, MC, V. Reservations accepted. Casual, but neat dress. No-smoking section. Free parking lot. Wine and beer; good Italian wine selection. Handicap accessible. Troubleshooter: Nancy Bardocci (owner). Moderate.

Though first impressions seem to indicate that restaurant service is not much more than an afterthought at Convito Italiano, the reality of sitting down to lunch or dinner reveals something else. True, the place gives the impression of being more devoted to its Italian take-out lines than it does to in-house service. The restaurant section is somewhat out of the way, more or less isolated from the food-store area.

For a reason I have not determined, service people do not take your orders. Instead, when you check in for a table, you are given a menu and asked to make your choices before you are seated. I think this more than a little odd, if not downright inhospitable.

That aside, choosing is not too difficult because the menu is rather short, supplemented only by a couple of daily specials listed on a chalkboard. An appetizer of sliced eggplant with a topping of melted cheese and tomato sauce is simple in concept, but quite satisfying in texture and flavors.

The entrée choices are mostly pastas, though diners can choose some meats from the chalkboard. Recently, chicken with gorgonzola cheese sauce was a delicious selection. In contrast, pasta with vegetables in a tomato cream sauce had all the charm of a canned soup. On the more positive side, spaghetti pomodoro e basilico hit a culinary bull's-eye. Fresh noodles were bathed in a luxuriant tomato sauce. The flecks of basil were more than visual enhancement; the sweet pungency of the herb gave an added measure of freshness to the pasta.

A colorful, though small house salad in a simple vinaigrette accompanies the dinner. Desserts include a moist and flavorful Italian chocolate torte. On balance, for a restaurant that doesn't seem to be able to make up its mind about being a real restaurant, Convito Italiano offers some genuinely good Italian fare on the North Shore in what may be the closest thing you can find here to a trattoria.

Convito Italiano has a second location at 11 East Chestnut Street (312-943-2984), Chicago.

K/Rating of 16/20: Decor 3/4, Service 4/5, Food 7.5/9, Value 1.5/2

THE GRILL ROOM

American

222 Greenwood, Glenview
Telephone: (312) 967-1222

Hours: Tuesday–Sunday 11–10. Cards: AE, CB, DC, MC, V, house accounts. Reservations required. Casual, but neat dress. Free valet parking. Full bar service; cocktail lounge; excellent wine list. Private party room available for 10–140 people. Troubleshooter: Ben Witte (chef). Moderate.

The Grill Room is actually one-half of Palm Beach (see below). Since both restaurants are serviced out of the same kitchen, a similar standard of excellence applies. Consider something as prosaic as fried onion rings. They are wide-cut onion rings, maybe just half a dozen from each onion, that have been dipped into an egg-and-cream batter and then deep fried. The result is a thick and tasty coat around a hot and sweet onion; nothing namby-pamby or effete . . . just onions about as good as they get.

Other appetizers include a half slab of barbecued ribs, and escargots sautéed in butter and imaginatively served inside a hollowed-out loaf of warm sourdough bread. The idea is to enjoy the snails, and then tear off pieces of the loaf to soak up the buttery sauce.

The heart of The Grill Room is, as one would expect, given over to steaks, ribs, and chops. The largest steak is an eighteen-ounce center-cut strip ($19.95). A delicious bordelaise sauce studded with truffles goes beyond the capabilities of ordinary steak restaurants. In addition you can get a 20-ounce lobster (about $10), a large cut of prime rib, and a thick, meaty swordfish steak with béarnaise ($14.95).

Desserts on the pastry cart include a wonderful Baileys Irish Cream chocolate torte. The Grill Room is a restaurant to put on your dining list.

K/Rating of 18.5/20: Decor 4/4, Service 4/5, Food 8.5/9, Value 2/2

PALM BEACH

French

222 Greenwood, Glenview
Telephone: (312) 967-1222

Hours: Tuesday–Sunday 11–10. Cards: AE, CB, DC, MC, V, house accounts. Reservations required. Jackets requested for gentlemen. Free valet parking. Full bar service; cocktail lounge; excellent wine list. Private party room available for 10–140 people. Troubleshooter: Ben Witte (chef). Expensive.

The name Palm Beach might suggest trendy American, but chef Ben Witte is true to the roots of classical French, tempered only by a certain lightness that is more a refinement than an attempt at the avant-garde. Thus fresh Dover sole is presented either amandine or meunière, while a breast of capon can be ordered broiled with Dijon mustard glaze or poached with a cream sauce studded with morel mushrooms.

Continental tradition can also be found among the appetizers, which include oysters on the half shell, a house pâté, snails in garlic butter, and oysters Florentine. Soups include a cooling vichyssoise, classic crock-baked French onion, and velvety lobster bisque. One of the better tests of a restaurant kitchen's capabilities is the house pâté, which should be fresh and firm. The version here has a smooth texture, despite the "country-style" menu description. The flavors are balanced and the seasonings are perfect, however.

Among entrées, several specials not on the printed menu are offered each evening. Recently, noisettes of lamb were served in a clear rosemary sauce. The meat had a bright, appetizing flavor; the rosemary was obviously fresh. Like all the entrées, the lamb came with a lovely bouquet of fresh vegetables on handsome china. The carrots still had their crunch and the thin slices of zucchini were garden fresh. Medallions of veal in a chasseur, or hunter's, sauce is given an interesting twist. In most recipes, the chasseur is thickened with a roux. At Palm Beach, Chef Witte wisely prepares a tomato concasse, which he uses to lightly bind sautéed slices of mushrooms and shallots. There was no flaw with the chasseur, but I think it a bit too powerful for the delicate veal.

Desserts include some marvelous tarts and fresh berries. A chocolate torte, however, was a shade dry. My request for warm sabayon, even though not on the menu, was met with graciousness. As much as I appreciated the effort, I would be less than honest not to point out that it was too heavily sweetened to be a perfect success.

See listing opposite for sister restaurant, The Grill Room.

K/Rating of 18.5/20: Decor 4/4, Service 5/5, Food 7.5/9, Value 2/2

GUSTO ITALIANO

1470 Waukegan Road at Carillon Square, Glenview
Telephone: (312) 729-5444
Other location is listed on next page.

Hours: Monday–Thursday 11–10, Friday–Saturday 11–11, Sunday 4–9. Cards: AE, DC, MC, V. Reservations only for parties of ten or more. No-smoking section. Parking lot. Full bar service. Handicap accessible. Troubleshooters: Ciro Esposito and Debbie Dubin (owners). Moderate.

Italian

Readers of earlier editions of this book may remember Seven Hills. Although it went out of business a few years ago, its influence is still being felt at Gusto Italiano, where family members are continuing some of its culinary traditions. The influence of Seven Hills is apparent as soon as you are seated and a basket of dinner rolls is brought to the table. These are the same crusty hard rolls with a soft doughy center, all buttery and studded with bits of fresh roasted garlic. There's not a better dinner roll anywhere.

But fight off the temptation they pose and think about a selection of appetizers. If the choice is too tough, order a house platter. You'll get delicious baked clams, hot spinach bread, deep-fried mozzarella cheese with a crumb coating, and a buttery artichoke with a light breading. If that's not enough for the trenchermen at your table, try an order of fried calamari or scungilli (conch) salad. They'll even take a dinner-size portion of eggplant rollatini and cut it down to appetizer size. That rollatini is scrumptious, the pancake-thin layers of pounded eggplant rolled around a filling of ricotta cheese and spinach, topped with mozzarella and a tangy tomato sauce.

The Gusto Italiano dinner menu is otherwise rather conventional on first reading. But the cooking is anything but prosaic. Consider the crisp-skinned chicken Vesuvio, a quarter of a fryer covered with bits of garlic and served with roasted potatoes. There is nothing greasy about this chicken Vesuvio. The pastas are exceptional, with the linguine with clam sauce a classic of its kind. There is no unwanted pool of sauce, but rather just bits of clam meat clinging to the fresh-cooked pasta.

Be sure to save room for dessert. A house special not on the menu is a double chocolate Italian torte. Other choices include four kinds of cheesecake, some ice creams, torte inglese, and a luscious Grand Marnier torte.

Gusto Italiano has a second location at 345 West Northwest Highway (312-705-0130), Palatine.

K/Rating 19/20: Decor 3/4, Service 5/5, Food 9/9, Value 2/2

DRAGON INN NORTH

Chinese (Mandarin)

1650 Waukegan Road, Glenview
Telephone: (312) 729-8383

Hours: Monday–Thursday 11:30–9:30, Friday 11:30–11:30, Saturday 5–11:30, Sunday noon–9:30. Cards: AE, MC, V. Reservations suggested. Free parking in lot. Casual, but neat dress. No-smoking section. Full bar service; small cocktail lounge. Handicap accessible. Semiprivate party room for 20–45 people. Troubleshooter: Jeanette Sih (owner). Moderate.

Dragon Inn North was a pioneer among Mandarin and Szechwan restaurants. First opened in the 1960s by a partnership of women (that in itself was unusual at the time) in a far southern suburb, this northern enclave followed in the early seventies and continues to prosper. The secret to the restaurant's success is not entirely dependent upon its food. Rather, it is the management's close attention to detail, a practice that has been passed on from original owner Susan Sih to her daughter, Jeanette. The restaurant has always been very well kept, and there has never been any complacency about the foods or the way things are served. Though this restaurant has scores (if not hundreds) of regulars, newcomers can always count on a gracious welcome. Experienced diners will be satisfied with the rich array of choices; first-timers to the cuisine will find attentive service and the gracious Ms. Sih anxious to explain anything that may appear too exotic.

The menu offers more than fifty entrées, plus appetizers and soups. Among my favorites are the Peking duck, which requires a twenty-four-hour advance notice, and the smoked tea duck, with its dusky flavor and darkened meat. Sizzling rice soup and shrimp toast are two good selections with which to open your meal.

K/Rating of 18.5/20: Decor 4/4, Service 5/5, Food 7.5/9, Value 2/2

La Boheme

French

566 Chestnut (The Laundry Mall), Winnetka
Telephone: (312) 446-4600

Lunch: Tuesday–Saturday 11:30–2. Dinner: Tuesday–Saturday 6–10. Cards: AE, CB, DC, MC, V. Reservations suggested. Jackets and ties requested for gentlemen. Lot parking and street parking difficult. Full bar service; extensive choice of wine by the glass. Handicap accessible. Private party rooms on Sunday for 50–100 people, smaller groups of 20–50 people Tuesday–Saturday. Troubleshooters: Peter Karas and Chris Skafidas (owners). Expensive.

Ever since it opened in 1979, La Boheme has been one of the handsomest restaurants on the North Shore. Food and service, however, were hit and miss. Consequently, I had never considered the restaurant among the top rank. Not, that is, until now. Under new ownership, and with chef Didier Durand in charge of the kitchen, La Boheme is serving dinners deserving of recognition.

The cooking style is elaborate without being heavy. Sauces are reductions of stock and meat juices, seasoned with reliance on fresh herbs. Venison is a good example of what is served here. The medallions are napped in a dark currant demi-glace studded with dried fruits and rippled leaves of what I suspect are cèpes. Fruit sauce is not uncommon with venison. Consider a sauce Cumberland, for example. But chef Durand goes a step beyond, forcing a deeper flavor from his currant base. The result is something lighter than a syrup, but still full enough to cling to each piece of venison. As with most of the entrées, the venison comes with a buttery rich souffléed potato, baby carrots, and delicious julienned zucchini that has the look and even the texture of al dente pasta.

This sort of artistry is also seen in roasted lamb loin in a Provencale sauce. The sauce is actually more of an essence, a reduced mixture of onions, tomatoes, and garlic . . . especially garlic. Slices of the still pink, but not undercooked meat are fanned around the center of the serving platter.

Marinated salmon is an excellent appetizer choice. The paper-thin salmon is as fragile as fine lace, resting in a light oil flavored with the strength of fresh ginger and splashed with lime juice to assuage intensity. An assortment of pâtés brings forcemeats of chicken, duck, rabbit, and veal in a generous portion. Textures range from country rough to the near creaminess of mousse.

K/Rating of 19/20: Decor 3.5/4, Service 5/5, Food 8.5/9, Value 2/2

WINNETKA GRILL

64 Green Bay Road, Winnetka
Telephone: (312) 441-6444

Dinner: Monday–Friday 5:30–9, Saturday 5–9. Cards: AE, CB, DC, DISC, MC, V. Reservations suggested. Parking lot. Full bar service. Will host private luncheons for a minimum of 45 people. Troubleshooters: John Stoltzman and Henry Markwood (owners). Expensive.

American

The decor is modish neoclassic. Tables tend to be closer than you might prefer for a very intimate evening, but this is not a quiet French restaurant, after all. No, Winnetka Grill is part and parcel of the American cuisine. I'm not talking about Yankee pot roast here. I mean grilling over mesquite charcoal and an emphasis on domestic ingredients. The cooking is stylish, often understated in its elegance. Favorites have been a pasta appetizer with Wisconsin gorgonzola and toasted walnuts in cream. The Grill's version of ceviche might be Cape Hatteras bay scallops marinated in lime juice. Other choices can include veal chop in Marsala wine sauce and veal medallions in lemon sauce.

K/Rating 15/20: Decor 3/4, Service 3.5/5, Food 7/9, Value 1.5/2

KING LONG

910 Green Bay Road, Winnetka
Telephone: (312) 441-5171

Lunch: Monday–Friday 11:30–2. Dinner: Monday–Thursday 5–10, Friday–Saturday 5–11, Sunday 4–10. Cards: AE, MC, V. Reservations accepted. No-smoking section. Ample street parking. Full bar service. Handicap accessible. Private parties for up to 15 people. Troubleshooter: Ronie Maa (owner). Moderate.

Chinese

By almost any definition, the menu at King Long is conventional at best. Even though little here appears trendsetting, what is being prepared is cooked with care and sometimes excellence.

Diners can opt for an à la carte choice of appetizers, or take a combination platter that puts together egg rolls, fried won tons, shrimp toast, skewered strips of beef, and meaty butterflied prawns. Though nothing among this selection would win a culinary award, the shrimp toast is noticeably plump and juicy, the prawns buttery, and the egg roll good and crisp.

There is at least one menu selection that goes beyond the commonplace. Tucked away on a back page of the menu under the heading "House Special" is a northern-style hors d'oeuvre platter. This appetizer assortment delivers an artistic design of vegetables arranged in concentric circles with regard to color, shape, and texture. Worked into the visual design are scallops, shrimp, and abalone, all lightly steamed so as not to intrude on the delicacy of the whole. The dish is as much a feast for eye as it is for palate.

Entrée choices return to the conventional, albeit well prepared. Garlic chicken easily lives up to its name. The good-sized portion of meat and vegetables is given an ample douse of fresh garlic, but done in balance. For something spicy, try King Long beef, a house namesake in which the meat is stir-fried and served with a spicy, peppery, but again well-balanced brown sauce. For vegetable lovers, a platter of black mushrooms with bamboo shoots could prove irresistible. King Long is generous in its use of the chewy oriental mushrooms that are central to this dish. And mu-shu, which is found on just about every Chinese menu, gets respectful treatment in the King Long kitchen.

K/Rating 17.5/20: Decor 3.5/4, Service 4.5/5, Food 7.5/9, Value 2/2

AMERICAN JOE'S

American

378 Park Avenue, Glencoe
Telephone: (312) 835-4720

Dinner: Tuesday–Thursday 5:30–8:30, Friday 5:30–9, Saturday 5:30–9:30. Cards: MC, V, house accounts. Reservations recommended. Casual, but neat dress. No-smoking section. Street parking. Full bar service; moderate listing of American wines. Private party room for 35–40 people. Troubleshooter: Lee Keating (owner). Moderate.

American Joe's is a standout in virtually all respects. The dining areas invite casualness, which, if nothing else, has become an American way of life. Service is generally well informed and cordial. The cooking is superior.

The menu changes often. Recently, entrées ranged from Southern-style catfish to roast duck in a port wine sauce. Dinners include hot breads and side vegetables. But some à la carte appetizers are not to be missed. Pasta shells with a filling of duck sausage and goat cheese is an occasional evening special you should snap up when offered. The handmade shells are warm and chewy, the filling a marvelous blend of subtle seasonings. Other appetizers could include grilled shrimp and shiitake mushrooms, stone-crab claws, and fresh crab cakes.

Seafood gets prominent exposure on the American Joe's menu. Sautéed rainbow trout may come with pecan butter; catfish can be ordered blackened or with a cornmeal dusting. Scallops have been served with an orange-and-pecan sauce, which indeed shows that contrivance has not eluded American Joe's. More natural is salmon with basil butter.

One of the tastiest choices is a spicy chicken jambalaya made with an authentic andouille sausage. This mild Cajun sausage picks up some of the flavors of the jambalaya. The roast duck with port wine sauce is a somewhat straightforward presentation, with a good balance of flavors in the sauce. Simpler is boned breast of chicken grilled over coals and served with a mild salsa and herbs that reflect the influence of the Southwest. Other dinners might include strip steak with ale and onion sauce or lamb chops with fresh rosemary.

Desserts include flourless chocolate cake, a margarita mousse, or bread pudding with cranberry sauce, among rotating selections.

K/Rating 18.5/20: Decor 3.5/4, Service 5/5, Food 8/9, Value 2/2

SHAW'S BLUE CRAB

American Seafood

660 Lake Cook Road, Deerfield
Telephone: (312) 948-1020

Hours: Monday–Thursday 11–10, Friday 11:30–11, Saturday 5–11, Sunday 4:30–9. Cards: AE, CB, DC, MC, V, LEYE. Reservations suggested. No-smoking section. Free parking lot. Full bar service; good wine list. Handicap accessible. Troubleshooter: Rich Melman (owner). Moderate.

If you go into the building and turn right, you're headed into Ed Debevic's (see page 34). And you know what that means! But if you turn left instead, you walk into Shaw's Blue Crab, one of the really hot spots on the North Shore.

Though not quite as lavish in decor as its big brother downtown (see Shaw's Crab House on page 17), Shaw's Blue Crab still has plenty to offer in the way of atmosphere and mood. The central bar is a great place for pairing off or for joining a group in conversation. The large dining areas, like the bar, have an East Coast traditional oyster-house look about them.

Seafood, of course, is what Shaw's Blue Crab is all about. Everything is absolutely fresh. Walk over to the raw bar on an early evening and check out what is available in clams and oysters. Except for some expensive seasonal specials, such as Florida stone crabs, most everything on the menu is modestly priced. Dinners include choice of soup or salad, although à la carte appetizers do add to the fixin's. In fact, I think the Maryland crab cake is just about the best to be found this side of The Chesapeake.

As for those dinners, the house namesake is Shaw's Blue Crab stew ($13.95). The potent fish broth is seasoned liberally with the kind of peppers and spices that sneak up on you. The broth is chock full of coarsely cut vegetables, the kind that suggest a family around the kitchen table chopping ingredients as they wile away an afternoon in conversation. The heart of the stew, of course, is the fish. In this case, it's a large cut-up king crab in the shell, a smaller lobster tail, oodles of clams, mussels, fish, and just enough whole shrimp in the shell to make things respectable. Eat all of this at one sitting and they'll have to roll you home!

Other entrées run the gamut from fried or sautéed frog legs, sea scallops, and the like, to a seafood and pasta platter. For those who eschew seafood in any form, a sirloin steak and two whole baked chicken recipes are on the menu. Try the garlic chicken and you'll wonder why they don't put the word "chicken" somewhere in the name of the restaurant. As for desserts, the Key lime pie tastes as sweet-tart as it would in good old Islamorada.

K/Rating of 18.5/20: Decor 4/4, Service 4/5, Food 9/9, Value 1.5/2

ADA'S

Delicatessen

405 Lake Cook Road, Deerfield
Telephone: (312) 564-4446

Hours: daily 6 am–10 pm. Cards: MC, V. No reservations (wait can be long at peak periods). Parking lot. Troubleshooter: Marvin Kornich and Joel Spatz (owners). Inexpensive.

I recently realized that you can learn some interesting secrets about your close friends when you eat with them at a delicatessen. For instance, I learned that a very good friend eats corned beef on *white* bread. I came across this astounding bit of information at Ada's, which probably dosen't look like any deli you've ever seen. It has an art deco motif with broad strokes of plum and gray, terraced seating areas, brass rails, and circular mirrors spaced evenly along one wall. The place resembles a nightclub where a hostess might come out selling cigars and cigarettes. Instead, waiters offer corned beef, pastrami, and seltzer. The usual deli sandwiches are made unusual at Ada's because they cure their own meats. The chopped liver could use a bit more chicken fat if it is to really be like Mama used to make, but I suppose there are certain sacrifices to be made in a cholesterol-conscious world. The soups have that real kitchen-made quality; mushroom barley may be the best west of the Hudson! Potato pancakes, however, fall flat, with a puréed rather than grated texture. Incidentally, they'll pack most everything to go.

K/Rating 18/20: Decor 4/4, Service 4/5, Food 8.5/9, Value 1.5/2

Hunan Garden

Chinese

130 South Waukegan Road, Deerfield
Telephone: (312) 480-0577

Hours: Tuesday–Friday 11–10, Saturday 11:30–11, Sunday 11:30–9. Cards: AE, DC, MC, V. Reservations suggested. Free parking in shopping mall lot. Full bar service. Handicap accessible. Private party facilities for up to 75 people. Troubleshooter: Jerry Liu (owner). Moderate.

Except for an occasional lapse in service, it's hard to find a flaw in what justifiably is one of the best Chinese restaurants in any of the Chicago suburbs. During the few years the restaurant has been in this ordinary-looking shopping mall, the menu has developed and grown into as sophisticated a listing of regional Chinese cuisine as most diners could want. Among appetizers, the onion cake is really special, especially when seasoned with just a bit of soy sauce. The whole fish is always as fresh as can be. There are a half-dozen ways that it can be prepared, ranging from mild steaming to a spicy-hot version with a vegetable garnish. Speaking of vegetables, there are enough here to keep even the dedicated vegetarian diner coming back for more. My favorite is the garlic eggplant, called yu-hsiang on the menu. A similar dish, with a bit of pork and bean curd added, is almost a meal in itself. For real splurging, try the Peking duck by advance order. Right from the menu, try Hunan lamb or kung-pao lamb, the latter sautéed with onion, bamboo shoots, and peanuts.

K/Rating of 18.5/20: Decor 3.5/4, Service 4/5, Food 9/9, Value 2/2

Timbers Charhouse

American

295 Skokie Highway, Highland Park
Telephone: (312) 831-1400

Hours: Monday–Thursday 11:30–10, Friday 10–11, Saturday noon–11:30, Sunday 4:30–8:30. Cards: AE, MC, V. Reservations accepted. No-smoking section. Free parking lot. Full bar service; good selection of wines and beers. Handicap accessible. Private party room for up to 65 people. Troubleshooter: Jim Errant (owner). Moderate.

Timbers is a very Western-style American eatery, with the emphasis on meat and fish. There's no fancy saucing, except what goes on the ribs. There's no pretense of preparing a "cuisine." They do food here! Well, yes, I should point out there is some mesquite grilling. But it isn't affectation as much as a natural choice to enhance those heartier fish and meats that can stand up to this wood's singular type of flavoring. Timbers simply offers basic good eating, without too much in the way of frills.

The soups are the hearty kind, not some insipid little broth with a French kitchen pedigree. Even the salads are substantial. The house salad is a good mix of greens and tomatoes with your choice of excellent dressings. The romaine salad is a large lengthwise cut of the lettuce, so that the leaves form a boat for the dressing. It's an imaginative way to serve a salad, which shows more than a little thought went into concepts. Desserts can be lavish; the great American favorite, hot fudge sundae, comes with a sauce that is both hot and fudgy. Other choices are similarly mainstream American.

One more note: There used to be a health club on the spot now occupied by Timbers. It was torn down to make way for construction of the restaurant. Since the only stretching I'm usually interested in is for a second helping, I consider the demolition a real moral victory!

K/Rating 17.5/20: Decor 4/4, Service 4.5/5, Food 7/9, Value 2/2

FIRST STREET PIER

American Seafood

1876 First Street, Highland Park
Telephone: (312) 432-1200

Hours: Tuesday–Sunday 5–10. Cards: AE, DC, MC, V, house accounts. Reservations suggested. Casual dress, but no shorts, tank tops, etc. No-smoking section. Ample lot and street parking. Full bar service; extensive wine list. Handicap accessible. Private party room for up to 175 people, or whole restaurant available. Troubleshooters: Arnie Morton (owner) and John Vrtiak (manager). Moderate.

At First Street Pier, food is handsomely presented and generally well prepared. Though fish is the primary draw, the menu calls upon the adjoining Morton's steak house (see page 37) for such choices as Sicilian grilled veal chop with a side of fettuccine. Other options include a grilled chicken half with or without a barbecue sauce, barbecued ribs in whole or half slab, and a combo of ribs and chicken.

Chalkboard specials have included grilled grouper and blackened redfish, which was not nearly as spicy as some versions. (I have come to think that "blackened" cooking is more a gimmick than a culinary discovery, but that's another matter.) Other possibilities range from linguine with shrimp and scallops the house-named shrimp Arnie's, in which shrimp in a wine and garlic sauce are served on a bed of pasta under a blanket of melted mozzarella.

First Street Pier desserts continue the kind of excellence that has been associated with this restaurant from the beginning, including the appropriately named chocolate velvet cake. All dinners come with your choice of salad, and potatoes or rice pilaf. Weeknight earlybirds (5:00–6:30) can take advantage of a special $9.95 dinner selection. With the trend toward lighter dining, First Street Pier meets a local need.

K/Rating of 16.5/20: Decor 4/4, Service 4/5, Food 6.5/9, Value 2/2

AEGEAN ISLES

Greek

561 Roger Williams Avenue, Highland Park
Telephone: (312) 433-5620

Hours: Tuesday–Sunday 4:30–11. Cards: MC, V. Reservations accepted. No-smoking section. Street parking. Full bar service; good selection of Greek wines. Handicap accessible. Available for private parties on weeknights. Troubleshooter: Angelo Papasteriadis (owner). Inexpensive.

This storefront restaurant has all the zip of a taverna, thanks to the handsome wall hangings and other Hellenic decor. As with most other Greek restaurants, diners will find a creditable combination platter. Of course, there are also such appetizers as saganaki (flaming cheese) served with the resounding cry of "opaa." Roast leg of lamb, while sometimes a bit stringy, is flavorful. But the real delight here is the Grecian-style seafood. Fresh sea bass or red snapper is especially rewarding. The fish is prepared simply, with just a hint of lemon and oregano to enhance its delicate taste. It's not on the menu as such, but if ordered in advance for a festive party, be sure to ask that the fish be served with a bouquet of fresh, coarse-cut vegetables.

For dessert, do not miss the bougatsa flambé, a delicious mix of pastry and custard flamed with Greek brandy. You'll have so much fun, you might just want to break all the plates!

K/Rating of 18/20: Decor 3.5/4, Service 5/5, Food 7.5/9, Value 2/2

CARLOS

French

429 Temple Avenue, Highland Park
Telephone: (312) 432-0770

Hours: Monday, Wednesday–Thursday, Sunday, two seatings 5:30–8 and 6:30–8:30; Friday–Saturday 5:30–9 and 6:30–9:30. Cards: AE, DC, MC, DISC, V, house accounts. Reservations required. Jackets required for gentlemen. No-smoking section. Valet parking. Full bar service, extensive wine list. Private party rooms for 5–22 people. Troubleshooter: Carlos Nieto (owner). Expensive.

This formerly drab storefront now houses an intimate French restaurant, warm with the color of plums and touches of brass, soft with velvet, sparkling with decorative glass. The food is in the style of nouvelle cuisine with its extra-light sauces, decorative flourishes in presentation, and emphasis on flavor contrasts. In one appetizer, a delicate feuilleté pastry shell holds pieces of crabmeat matched with a lightly flavored pineapple sauce—your palate must work over the flavors to understand what has been presented. A similar effort is required if you choose the mousse St. Jacques with two sauces. The scallop essence is ever so light, hardly discernible in its nap of beurre blanc and beurre rouge, underscoring the chef's technique in creating a mousse so airy it virtually dissolves in your mouth.

Entrées reflect unexpected blends of tastes and textures. Whitefish may be grilled and served in a pink peppercorn sauce whose bite contrasts with the neutral fish. Veal and mushrooms go together as well as any two ingredients, so the success of veal Madeira should come as no surprise. What is surprising is the intense flavor of the greatly reduced Madeira sauce accompaniment; underneath the veal rests a wisp of potato pancake, like an edible doily, absorbing juices and flavors. Desserts are from the cart.

K/Rating of 20/20: Decor 4/4, Service 5/5, Food 9/9, Value 2/2

LITTLE SZECHWAN

Chinese

1900 First Street, Highland Park
Telephone: (312) 433-7007

Dinner: Monday–Thursday 5–9:30, Friday–Saturday 5–10:30, Sunday 5–9. Cards: AE, MC, V. Reservations suggested. No-smoking section. Parking lot and street parking. Full bar service. Handicap accessible. Troubleshooters: Simon Lin and Phil Chiu (owners). Moderate.

White tablecloths set the tone here. Decorative accents include a large aquarium. The menu concentrates on doing a few things well, rather than trying to recreate 5,000 years of Chinese culinary history.

For starters, the hacked chicken, served cold, is a real favorite; slices of breast meat come on a bed of shredded lettuce with a peppery peanut sauce on top. This dish is a real appetite stimulant. Taiwanese chicken rolls are finger foods; deep-fried bean-curd skins encase layers of shredded chicken. The flavor is rather mild but the texture quite interesting.

It is difficult to go wrong with any of the main-course selections and chef recommendations. Three treasures brings together beef, shrimp, scallops, and stir-fried vegetables in a light black bean sauce. Beef with orange peel has been one of my regular dishes in recent years. The version at Little Szechwan successfully combines the sharp flavor of the cooked orange skin with sautéed pieces of tenderloin and a cache of seasonings to make for exciting dining. In addition to the printed menu, the restaurant features a few nightly specials; they will also prepare dishes at a customer's request, depending upon availability of ingredients.

K/Rating of 18.5/20: Decor 4/4, Service 5/5, Food 7.5/9, Value 2/2

Yu Lin's Chinese Dumpling House

Chinese (Mandarin)

1636 Old Deerfield Road, Highland Park
Telephone: (312) 831-3155

Hours: Sunday–Friday 4:30–9:30, Saturday 4:30–10:30. No cards; personal checks accepted with proper identification. Reservations suggested. No-smoking section. Parking lot. Full bar service. Handicap accessible. Troubleshooters: Yu Lin and C. P. Hsueh (owners). Moderate.

Yu Lin's Chinese Dumpling House gets better and better in more ways than one. In terms of decor, the old cowboy look (left over from a previous rib-house ownership) is gone, replaced by subtle accents from the orient. Food continues to be some of the best Chinese fare available on the North Shore, with a menu that seems constantly to expand horizons. Indeed, regular diners here have come to expect more than the ordinary.

Many of the dinners are "firepot," with meats and vegetables cooked, almost fondue style, at the table. Some of these require at least a day's advance notice because of the elaborate preparation of ingredients. One thing that tends to set this place apart from most other Chinese restaurants is the special use of sauces; they are not just some liquid to absorb rice, but a serious contribution to the balance of flavors that the kitchen staff is trying to achieve.

One more note: Yu Lin's Chinese Dumpling House is perfect for special, but not necessarily expensive or dressy occasions. Children always seem to enjoy Yu Lin herself and her not-always-as-visible husband, C. P. And if you should be at a loss for what to order, let Yu Lin be your personal guide across this enchanting land of culinary delights.

K/Rating 19/20: Decor 3.5/4, Service 5/5, Food 9/9, Value 1.5/2

Froggy's

French

306 Greenbay Road, Highwood
Telephone: (312) 433-7080

Lunch: Monday–Friday 11:30–2. Dinner Monday–Thursday 5–10, Friday–Saturday 5–11. Cards: CB, DC, DISC, MC, V. Reservations only for parties of 6 or more. Casual dress, but no shorts or T-shirts. Street parking can be difficult. Full bar service; wine list includes 50 California chardonnays. Private party facilities for up to 50 people. Troubleshooter: Gregg Mason (owner). Moderate.

Why hasn't someone opened a French restaurant where diners need not take out a second mortgage to pay for dinner? Well, someone has.

Froggy's is a bargain-basement-priced French restaurant that manages to hang on to quality. You can have dinner for two here for $25 to $30, and that includes appetizer, house salad with your entrée, coffee, and even some of the house wine. One of the neat little dessert pastries could add a couple of dollars more to the tab.

The menu leans toward nouvelle cuisine and changes each month. Seafood is often featured in challenging and delicious ways. For instance, grilled trout in white wine sauce and a French seafood chowder à la bouillabaisse might be served one month. At another time you might find medallions of sole stuffed with a sole mousse and seasoned with green peppercorns, or sea bass braised in white wine with scallions and pearl onions. Duck appears roasted with grapes and raisins, or with a fresh mint and vodka sauce. In other words, imagination is the key at Froggy's, and while some dishes ask that the diner be a bit adventurous, this restaurant is never boring.

K/Rating 18.5/20: Decor 3.5/4, Service 5/5, Food 8/9, Value 2/2

ALOUETTE

French

440 North Green Bay Road, Highwood
Telephone: (312) 433-5600

Dinner 5–10. Cards: AE, CB, DC, DISC, MC, V. Reservations accepted. Jackets required for gentlemen. Parking lot. Full bar service; cocktail lounge; extensive selection of wines. Private party room for up to 45 people, or entire restaurant for up to 100 people.
Troubleshooter: Christian Zeiger (owner).
Expensive.

When he is not traveling through France researching new recipes, chef Michel Coutrieux is in the kitchen, where a new menu is created each day. The restaurant, which opened in 1977, is as handsome as ever with its country-inn motif. What is different about Alouette today is the style of cooking. Chef Coutrieux is a master at understatement. He does not allow his sauces to overwhelm his meats, fish, or poultry. That, of course, is how it should be in any context, but at Alouette an even more minimalist approach is taken. Sweetbreads, perhaps the most difficult of all meats to prepare and serve properly, come out golden in a light egg batter. The delicate crayfish sauce barely clings to the small nuggets of crayfish that garnish the sweetbreads. Dover sole, which seems made for sauce meunière, is a study in classic seafood perfection.

Where understatement characterizes appetizer and dinner courses at Alouette, the desserts tend to go the other way. A sugar glaze on a raspberry tart with custard is superfluous, even out of balance. Similarly, crème brûlée, its satiny texture a welcome finish, is overly sweetened by a glazed topping.

K/Rating of 18.5/20: Decor 4/4, Service 5/5, Food 7.5/9, Value 2/2

LITTLE ITALY

Italian/Sicilian

47 Highwood Avenue, Highwood
Telephone: (312) 432-0070

Dinner: Tuesday–Thursday 4–10, Friday–Sunday 4–11:00. Cards: MC, V. Reservations only for parties of 6 or more. No-smoking section. Parking at city lot and street parking. Full bar service. Handicap accessible. Restaurant available for private parties of up to 55 people on Monday. Troubleshooter: Sam Visconti (owner). Inexpensive.

Typical of Highwood's Italian restaurants, Little Italy has what you would expect: red tablecloths, art prints, even a waitress with a sense of humor. Naturally, a restaurant like this will have its regulars, but even first-time visitors are made to feel right at home. The cooking is strictly home-style Sicilian. Thus, sauces tend to be spicy, sweet, and garlicky. Take your waitress's recommendation for dinner, particularly if she suggests veal Marsala; the deglazed sauce is rich with fresh mushrooms and the full flavor of Marsala wine. Veal parmigiana is traditionally prepared with a blanket of smooth-flavored tomato sauce and cheese. Veal piccante is less successful because the sauce lacks the proper balance between butter and tart lemon.

Among appetizers, toasted ravioli is a snack novelty akin to fried won tons. Spinach is terrific cooked in oil with lots of assertive fresh garlic. Other appetizers range from mussels in red or white sauce to assorted antipasti platters. Desserts, such as as ricotta-filled cannoli, have that homemade touch. The wine list holds some excellent choices.

K/Rating of 16/20: Decor 3/4, Service 4/5, Food 7/9, Value 2/2

MEANDERIN' MANDARIN

Chinese

258 Green Bay Road, Highwood
Telephone: (312) 433-7210

Hours: Tuesday–Sunday 5–10:30. Cards: MC, V, house accounts. Reservations suggested. No-smoking section. Street parking can be difficult. Full bar service; good wine list. Limited private party facilities. Troubleshooter: Kurt Youngman (owner). Moderate.

This is not your usual Chinese restaurant by any description. For one thing, the owner is not Chinese; however, the cooking staff is. Second, the restaurant is right in the heart of a community that for years has been known as a mecca for Italian restaurants. And third, although the food is nominally Chinese in most instances, there remains a personal stamp on preparations that goes beyond the ordinary.

Yes, the menu has egg rolls and fried rice and other clichés of the cuisine. But try an order of shao mai, steamed dumplings filled with a light forcemeat of shrimp and pork. Even if you always like your dumplings plain, splash on a little of the light soy-and-ginger sauce with bits of scallion. And while you are still on the appetizer course, try orange glazed ribs, more sweet than orangy, in a thick sauce that tastes like it has been cooked all day to form its syrupy state.

Owner Kurt Youngman, he being the Meanderin' Mandarin of the restaurant's sobriquet, will quite likely stop by your table to describe any of several specials not on the printed menu. The asparagus and shrimp goes far beyond its prosaic name. The shrimp is quickly cooked in a mildly seasoned chicken broth lightly thickened with cornstarch. Diagonal slices of the asparagus are finished in the final turning of the dish, then everything is quickly served to preserve texture.

Speaking of texture, try an order of mu shu, either pork, beef, chicken, or vegetable. There is no oversteaming of filling here. The julienned veggies retain their sharp crunch and freshness. The hoisin sauce is painted, not poured onto the thin pancake. It's a refreshing approach to an old standard.

The Meanderin' Mandarin version of Mongolian beef reminds me of how good simple dishes can be. The sauce is a bit sweeter than I prefer, but otherwise nicely balanced in seasonings and spices. The beef is impeccably tender. Another example of the kind of understatement to be found here is orange chicken. This is not to be confused with a chicken version of orange beef. There is no thick, dark, spicy sauce to be seen. Instead, the sauce is clear, hardly visible, but nevertheless clinging to each piece of stir-fried chicken. The flavor is rich with garlic; the orange essence apparently comes from zest and perhaps a little juice. The orange's presence requires some culinary detective work to ascertain. In short, it is there to underscore, not to disguise.

Understatement seems to be the key to virtually all the cooking at Meanderin' Mandarin. The menu is a little pricy by some Asian-restaurant standards, but the overall experience is worth it.

K/Rating 18.5/20: Decor 3.5/4, Service 4.5/5, Food 9/9, Value 1.5/2

Chicago:
West & Northwest

WEST

Mrs. Levy's Delicatessen

Delicatessen

233 South Wacker (Concourse Level, Sears Tower), Chicago
Telephone: (312) 993-0530

Hours: Monday–Friday 6:30 am–7:30 pm, Saturday 10–6, Sunday 10–5. No cards. No reservations. No-smoking section. Parking in nearby garages or lots. No alcoholic beverages. Handicap accessible. Troubleshooter: Steve Katz (manager). Inexpensive.

There really is a Mrs. Levy, though I've never actually seen her working behind the counter. In any event, this is a large and pristine sort of environment for a deli. But considering the fact that Mrs. Levy's carries the entire weight of The World's Tallest Building (Sears Tower) overhead, it is lucky that it is able to maintain some traditional touches. Specialties include meat blintzes, matzoh ball soup, corned beef on rye, and more. Service is exemplary. This is a fine way station for breakfast, lunch, or an early dinner before or after going up to the observation deck some 1,400 feet above the city.

K/Rating of 17.5/20: Decor 3/4, Service 5/5, Food 7.5/9, Value 2/2

Tap and Growler

American

901 West Jackson, Chicago
Telephone: (312) 829-4141

Hours: Monday–Thursday 11–11, Friday 11–midnight, Saturday 3:30–midnight. Cards: AE, MC, V. Reservations accepted. Casual, but neat dress. No-smoking section. Valet parking at lunch, ample street parking at dinner. Restaurant is a showcase microbrewery and full service bar that includes restaurant brewed and bottled beers, plus wines, mixed drinks. Banquet facilities for up to 80 people. Troubleshooter: Ralph Vaivada (owner). Moderate.

One of the best things to happen to beer lovers since the invention of foam has been the growth of so-called microbreweries. These are fairly small operations; in some instances the word "tiny" might be overstating the case. Microbreweries are often combined with restaurants, where brewing is limited to only the small amount needed to serve customers. One such operation here is Tap and Growler. The decor is trendy open duct work and there is plenty of scattered seating, most of which has a view of the four or five large brewing kettles where the Tap and Growler beers and ales are produced.

The food leans toward casual fare. Most noteworthy are the large dinner pies, generally priced from about $9 to $11, depending upon what's in them. The beef pot pie is loaded with large chunks of savory beef, tender meat that even remains a little bit rare deep inside. A smattering of vegetables adds some depth to the smooth gravy that bathes the meat. Other selections include chicken, a seafood chowder pie with scallops, shrimp, and fish, and Growler pie, flaky pastry encasing salmon, mushrooms, cabbage, and onions.

Additional entrées include roasted pan oysters with mushrooms and bacon in a thyme cream sauce, delicious grilled flank steak, meat loaf, and an array of daily choices. Appetizers are fine for grazing, though a portion of fried cheese balls struck me as skimpy. Fried oysters at $5.25 are also overpriced, but otherwise make fine nibbling with a glass or growler of beer. Save some room for desserts, which include an incredible caramel cheesecake.

None of the beers will wean me from my two Wisconsin favorites, though some of the food within this microbrewery/restaurant concept is fine.

K/Rating of 15.5/20: Decor 3.5/4, Service 4/5, Food 7/9, Value 1/2

LOU MITCHELL'S

American

565 West Jackson, Chicago
Telephone: (312) 939-3111

Hours: Monday–Friday 4:30 am–4 pm, Saturday 4:30 am–7:30 pm. No cards. Street and parking lot. Casual dress to suit and tie. Troubleshooters: Lou Mitchell and Nick Noble (owners). Inexpensive.

If Lou Mitchell had decided to become a violin maker, Stradivari would probably have been his model. Had he become a jeweler, he no doubt would deal exclusively in unflawed stones.

But Lou Mitchell is in the breakfast business and serves just about the best there is to find in Chicago. Lou has been making breakfasts for hundreds of thousands of Chicagoans and visitors to the city for about sixty years. Most any day you'll find Lou up front greeting customers and passing out small boxes of Milk Duds to people on their way out. He employs two full-time bakers who do nothing but make fresh buns, breads, sweet rolls, and other pastries from scratch. Even his jams and jellies are house made. His French vanilla ice cream is 18 percent butterfat, which may not put it on the surgeon general's healthy foods list, but then you do have to splurge once in a while!

The restaurant is known for the enormous breakfasts it serves to Chicago's early risers. Lou's fluffy three-egg omelets are made from double-yolk eggs. If the zoning laws would allow it, he probably would raise his own chickens behind the restaurant. Nonetheless, his omelets are spectacular creations, served in the individual pans in which they have been cooked.

Pancakes and waffles are among the other favorites. Try rolled pancakes with apples, sour cream, and pure maple syrup, or a fluffy-light Belgian waffle made with real malted milk. The breakfast specials are served all day, but if something more conventional is your lunch preference, you might want the roast chicken swabbed with a barbecue-style sauce. Other choices include roast loin of pork with fresh sage dressing, baby broiled beef liver, and fried fillet of sole.

But it is really the eggs, waffles, and pancakes that make Lou Mitchell's famous; if you don't try one of them, you will have missed what all Chicago talks about.

K/Rating of 18.5/20: Decor 3.5/4, Service 4/5, Food 9/9, Value 2/2

ZINCS

French

555 West, Madison (Presidential Towers), Chicago
Telephone: (312) 902-2900

Hours: Monday–Friday 11:30–2:30, 5–10, Saturday 5–11. Sunday brunch: 11–2:30. Cards: AE, CB, DC, MC, V, house accounts. Reservations for dining room only. Casual, but neat dress. No-smoking section. Free valet and garage parking. Full bar service; good wines by the glass. Handicap accessible. Private party room for up to 50 people, atrium room up to 300 people. Troubleshooter: Richard L. Valente (owner). Moderate.

Zincs's menu lists the traditional brasserie range of foods, including such basics as steak and pommes frites, beef carbonnade, choucroute, and duck confit. The last of these is done in a classic roasted manner, the dark meat resting on a bed of cooked lentils in a seasoning of the bird's own natural juice and fat. The carbonnade is the kind of eating one enjoys best on a cold, blustery day, with its dark stewlike sauce and sizzled slivers of onion on top of a cut of beef that benefits from long, slow cooking.

Among other entrée choices are several evening specials. Recently, couscous came at the center of a platter that included delicious tastes of roast chicken, a navarin of lamb, a bouquet of vegetables, and spiced sausage. Going in an entirely different direction, the kitchen wrapped salmon and amberjack together in puff pastry and served the package in a watercress beurre blanc.

Delicious appetizers include duck raviolis, lightly napped in a tomato cream. A platter of wild mushrooms comes with bits of prosciutto, garlic, and shallots in a brandy sauce. Though the preparation seems elaborate, the woodsy flavor of the mushrooms is never lost. Veal sausage, which comes from Paulina Market, is served with warm homemade potato salad in a mustard-mayonnaise base; it is about as good as potato salad can ever be. The mushroom barley soup is made with a clear chicken stock redolent with a host of flavors.

Desserts include an excellent flourless chocolate cake with a dense, fudgy texture. For something less sweet, savor the lemon tart, with its tangy, sunny feeling.

K/Rating of 19.5/20: Decor 4/4, Service 4.5/5, Food 9/9, Value 2/2

DIANNA'S OPAA

Greek

212 South Halsted, Chicago
Telephone: (312) 332-1225

Hours: daily 11 am–2 am. Cards: AE, CB, DC. Reservations suggested, mandatory on weekends. Free parking in supervised lot across street. Full bar service. Semiprivate party facilities for up to 200 people weekdays, up to 50 people on weekends. Troubleshooter: Petros Kogeonos (owner). Moderate.

Petros Kogeonos is probably the most flamboyant character in Chicago's Halsted Street South Greektown neighborhood. Everyone is "cousin" to Petros. But aside from the character of its proprietor, Dianna's Opaa creates one of the cheeriest settings in Chicago for good Greek food. The restaurant looks like a Greek town square brought indoors. Waiters bustle back and forth between tables and kitchen calling out "Opaa!" ("Olé!") with each flaming of the popular appetizer saganaki (kasseri cheese flamed with brandy). The best deal in the house is the combination platter. Or if there are several in your group, order family style and get avgolemono soup, Greek salad with tomatoes, lettuce, and feta cheese, saganaki, gyros, pastitsio, moussaka, dolmades, rice, and vegetables, plus braised lamb or beef.

K/Rating 17.5/20: Decor 3.5/4, Service 4.5/5, Food 7.5/9, Value 2/2

RODITYS

Greek

222 South Halsted, Chicago
Telephone: (312) 454-0800

Hours: Sunday–Thursday 11–1 am, Friday–Saturday 11–2 am. Cards: AE. Reservations suggested. Valet parking or nearby lot. Full bar service. Private party room for up to 25 people. Troubleshooters: Perry Senopoulos and Pete Isouklas (owners). Moderate.

I think it would be difficult for almost anyone to blind-taste food from a number of Greek restaurants and identify where it came from. With very few exceptions, the food at Chicago's Greek restaurants is similarly prepared and served. True, one restaurant may prepare fish better than another, or a salad may be more attractive, a soup more pungent. But on balance, there is more similarity than difference among the Greek restaurants I know and enjoy. The differences that do exist are created primarily by the personalities of the owners. They are all in their own way ebullient, gregarious, loquacious hosts who oversee their domains perhaps much as ancient Greek kings ruled their city-states.

At Roditys, the character of the restaurant also comes from the clientele. On a typical evening it may range from orthodox priests and businessmen to families with dark-eyed grandmothers and small babies swaddled against an intruding chill. Yet the non-Greek who craves good food can find a home-away-from-home at Roditys. Service is flawless. Foods may take time to reach your table, but here that is a sign of fresh preparation, not a lax kitchen staff.

I have been impressed here by the fresh deliciousness of red snapper hot from the broiler. Lamb, a meat given soul by the Greeks, is braised, broiled, roasted, barbecued. It comes mixed with beef in gyros, on the bone as a chop, or roasted and sliced from the loin, leg, or shoulder. Order typical Greek casseroles like pastitsio or moussaka, stuffed grape leaves called dolmades, or spinach pie with the tongue-twisting name spanakopita. Another tongue twister to say, but a balm to the tongue, is taramasalata. This is a creamy fish roe salad, light pink in color and with the sweet saltiness of the sea mixed in with tart seasonings. Old favorites on the menu range from saganaki for an appetizer to baklava and custard for dessert. Then sit back and enjoy a hot draft of strong Greek coffee.

K/Rating of 17.5/20: Decor 2.5/4, Service 5/5, Food 8/9, Value 2/2

COURTYARDS OF PLAKA

Greek

340 South Halsted, Chicago
Telephone: (312) 263-0767

Hours: Sunday–Thursday 11–midnight, Friday–Saturday 11–1 am. Cards: AE, CB, DC, MC, V, house accounts. Reservations suggested. Free valet parking. Full bar service. Troubleshooters: Chris Liakouras and Dimitri Dokolas (owners). Moderate.

Unlike any other Greek restaurant in Chicago, Courtyards of Plaka is a genuinely sophisticated approach to the better aspects of Hellenic cuisine. True, you will still find such basics as moussaka and pastitsio, even gyros and saganaki. But when the waiter ignites the brandy to flame the saganaki, no one dares call out "Opaa!"—anymore than one would shout "Voilà!" in a fine French restaurant.

Diners can choose a combination dinner, but the real pleasure is in ordering à la carte so that you may try some special dishes. For instance, kreatopita is delicious lamb and beef baked inside a flaky phyllo pastry and napped in a light cream sauce. Additional lamb treatments are also recommended: Double-cut lamb chops are a joy, served simply with rice pilaf or panfried potatoes, plus a vegetable. Sliced roast leg of lamb is baked with spaghetti and tomato sauce, then simmered in a crock. Shish kebab may not be indigenously Greek, but that doesn't hamper its popularity, whether as skewered chunks of lamb, pieces of chicken, or even shrimp flamed at tableside. Other seafood, such as fresh snapper or sea bass, is broiled in the simple, naturally flavored Greek fashion.

Appetizers are so good, you may be tempted to make a meal of them. If so, choose taramasalata (fish roe spread) and melitzanosalata (crushed eggplant and garlic) for starters. Be sure to try the fried sweetbreads: delicious morsels locked inside a breaded crust, but still silky within. Desserts include some of the often-found Greek delicacies like baklava laced with honey, cinnamon, and nuts; thick chocolate custard; and delicate cream caramel. There's even a Greek version of cream Napoleon, not on the printed menu but offered by the waiter when available. A full bar and limited wine list complement dinner selections.

K/Rating 18/20: Decor 4/4, Service 5/5, Food 7/9, Value 2/2

GREEK ISLANDS

Greek

766 West Jackson, Chicago
Telephone: (312) 782-9855
Other location is listed below.

Hours: Sunday–Thursday 11–midnight, Friday–Saturday 11–1 am. Cards: AE, CB, DC, MC, V. Reservations only for large parties. Attendant parking fees. Full bar service. Private party room for up to 30 people. Troubleshooters: Mike Scafidi and Gus Couchell (owners). Moderate.

There is no abatement of the partisan rivalry that exists among Chicago's Greek restaurants; it may be even more intense than the rivalry between the Cubs and the Sox. The restaurants proudly advertise their support, plastering windows with letters, photographs, and endorsements. There is probably no Greek restaurant in Chicago with as vocal a following as the Greek Islands. The restaurant foreswears most of the gimmicks such as bazoukis and belly dancers, but they do have baklava. As with its competitors in the Halsted Street South Greektown area, the food here is abundant and reasonably priced.

My lack of enthusiasm in the first edition of this book for the fish at Greek Islands has been washed away by subsequent experiences with broiled sea bass, served with lots of oregano and lemon and beautifully boned at tableside by a waiter with the dexterity of a cardiac surgeon. In addition to the seafood, you will find the ubiquitous array of Greek foods—braised lamb, loin and leg of lamb, souvlaki, pastitsio, moussaka, and all the rest. Combination platters are the best buys; they give you several different foods and lots of it.

Greek Islands has a second location at 300 East 22nd Street (312-932-4545), Lombard.

K/Rating 17/20: Decor 3/4, Service 4/5, Food 8/9, Value 2/2

PARTHENON

Greek

314 South Halsted, Chicago
Telephone: (312) 726-2407

Hours: daily 11–1:30 am. Cards: AE, CB, DC, MC, V, house accounts. Reservations only for parties of 6 or more. Parking lot and street parking. Full bar service. Semiprivate party facilities available for up to 150 people (except Friday–Saturday). Troubleshooters: Chris Liakouras and Gregory Karabia (owner). Inexpensive.

Venerable is a word usually not applied to Chicago's Greek restaurants, but by the standards of Greektown I suppose it is fair to so describe the Parthenon. Open since 1968 and just now in its adolescence, the Parthenon has long been one of the most popular Hellenic dining spots in the city. The place fits right in with its companions in South Halsted's Greek neighborhood in terms of food quality and value. Appetizer portions are large enough to split between two people! Try dolmades (the traditional rice-stuffed grape leaves that come eight or nine to the order) or the creamy little baked cheese pies deep fried to a light golden color. The owners here claim to have invented saganaki, the popular fried cheese flamed with Greek brandy. I cannot verify the claim, but their saganaki is in a portion large enough for two, with a mild flavor free of the harsh saltiness sometimes found in this dish.

For fish lovers, the Parthenon serves a lovely red snapper priced at market rate. Lamb is, of course, another specialty; one option comes with artichoke in a mildly tart egg-lemon sauce. Braised lamb is served with a bouquet of mixed vegetables. The imported Greek wines make up in price what they may lack in finish.

K/Rating of 17/20: Decor 3/4, Service 4/5, Food 8/9, Value 2/2

NORTHWEST

DON JUAN

Mexican

6730 North Northwest Highway, Chicago
Telephone: (312) 775-6438

Hours: Monday–Thursday 11–10, Friday–Saturday 11–11:30, Sunday 11–9. Sunday brunch: 11–3. Cards: AE, CB, DC, MC, V. Reservations accepted. No-smoking section. Parking lot across the street. Full bar service; specialties include fresh fruit margaritas, piña coladas, sangria, Mexican beer. Handicap accessible. Private parties accepted. Troubleshooter: Maria Josefa Concannon (owner). Inexpensive.

For all their popularity, most Mexican restaurants are about the same. When one comes along that is a cut above the rest, that's time for a celebration of sorts. Well, bring on the hats and horns for Don Juan. The menu here differs from most of the Mexican restaurants you already know. If you insist on burritos and enchiladas, you'll find them. But enjoy some chicken mole or a chile relleno for a change of pace. The chicken mole has a dark, mysterious, almost bitter, flavor. The sauce is a blend of unsugared chocolate and spices, beautifully thickened so that it bathes the tender roasted chicken. I have never had tastier beef in any Mexican restaurant than the carne asada at Don Juan. It tastes as if it has been marinated in complex seasonings. The chile relleno is delicious, a large green bell pepper stuffed with ground seasoned beef. Combination platters will bring tacos, enchiladas, or tostadas in varying styles. Diners can also order these items à la carte.

For dessert, do not miss the flan, the Spanish custard in slightly burnt caramel sauce. Don Juan's version is as refreshing as they come.

K/Rating 18/20: Decor 3/4, Service 5/5, Food 8/9, Value 2/2

RISTORANTE ITALIA

Italian

2631 North Harlem, Chicago
Telephone: (312) 889-5008

Hours: Tuesday–Sunday 4–11. No cards; house accounts. Reservations suggested. Street parking. Full service bar with Italian wines. Private party room for up to 60 people. Troubleshooter: Joe Lollino (owner). Moderate.

A nice touch of homemade seems to mark Ristorante Italia. From the more than one dozen appetizers, the best of the lot may be mussels marinara, a large bowl of tender steamed mussels in a delicious crimson sauce. For a good texture contrast, try an order of panzerotti; it is something like a double folded pizza, but with a crust puffed full and flaky. Ristorante Italia's version of arancini, the deep-fried Sicilian rice balls, comes with less ground sausage and seasonings than others I've tasted. The menu boasts that Pina, the cook, will prepare whatever you may have a taste for, even if it is not listed. After taking a look at her bustle about the kitchen, I believe it. But within that printed list are some top choices. Just look at the many pasta selections ranging from puttanesca (be sure to ask why this is called the "prostitute's pasta") to chewy gnocchi. You will also find one of the most lavish (and expensive) zuppa di mare served in any Chicago restaurant.

Calamari with pasta in white sauce is excellent; the sauce, which clings to every strand, is rich with butter, oil, and garlic. Hickory smoked shrimp (gamberi alla griglia) is coated with a seasoned bread crust, but not so thick as to limit the enjoyment of the shrimp. Chicken Vesuvio is the kind you want to pick up by the piece and dig into right down to the bone; order it with the oil drained away for the best texture and flavor. If veal or eggplant parmigiana is to your taste, Ristorante Italia is an excellent place to order them. Nice accents with dinner include a basket of hot tomato bread.

K/Rating 17.5/20: Decor 3/4, Service 5/5, Food 7.5/9, Value 2/2

ARCADIA

Polish

2943 North Milwaukee, Chicago
Telephone: (312) 342-1464

Hours: daily 10–10. No cards. Reservations accepted. Street parking can be difficult. Full bar service; imported and domestic beers, wines, cognacs, and vodkas. Private party room available. Troubleshooter: Walter Kowynia (owner). Inexpensive.

Arcadia is one of those rare restaurants that can almost transport its customers into another world. The world is that of Poland; it is not unusual in this still heavily Polish neighborhood north of Logan Square to hear Polish spoken among diners and waiters.

This place is a good refuge for budget diners looking for a complete dinner from soup to dessert for as little as $6. For a dollar less you can order à la carte, but the extra expense is easily worth the soup, vegetables, coffee or tea, and dessert. Beginning with the soup, you can have your choice of a clear broth chicken noodle or a traditional Polish mushroom. The chicken soup is laden with slender noodles amidst a smattering of vegetables. The mushroom is the stuff of which reputations are made. It speaks of Middle Europe, dark, thick forests with soft earth beneath your shoes and the woodsy smell that nurtures these fungi. A sprinkling of fresh dill atop the broth adds its own complexity to the aroma and flavor of this not-to-be-missed soup.

Dinner entrées can be as classic as kielbasa and sauerkraut, stuffed cabbage, or pierogis. What would Polish dining be without duck? The menu tells you the Arcadia bird is stuffed with apples. In fact, it is a prune and apple stuffing, with a tartness that works as counterpoint to the fattiness of the duck. Dessert choices seem limited to gelatin or ice cream. If you keep asking as I did, the waiter may be able to come up with something else from the kitchen, such as a cherry torte, which unlike the previous courses, did not have that homemade quality.

K/Rating 16.5/20: Decor 3/4, Service 4.5/5, Food 7/9, Value 2/2

Suburbs: West & Northwest

OAK PARK
ELMWOOD PARK
HINSDALE
GENEVA
ELGIN
NORRIDGE
ROSEMONT
NILES
DES PLAINES
ARLINGTON HEIGHTS
WHEELING
PALATINE
LONG GROVE
LAKE ZURICH
LAKEMOOR

WEST

PHILANDER'S

Seafood

1120 Pleasant Street, Oak Park
Telephone: (312) 848-4250

Dinner: daily from 5:30. Cards: AE, CB, DC, MC, V, house accounts. Reservations suggested. Jackets requested for gentlemen. No-smoking section. Valet parking and street parking. Full bar service; good wine list. Private party facilities for 25–200 people. Troubleshooter: Dennis Murphy (owner). Expensive.

Philander's features one of the western suburbs' best selections of seafood, presented in an elegant, high-ceilinged, turn-of-the-century bar and restaurant. Entrées offer a moderately broad choice of fish and shellfish, plus a number of steaks, chops, and poultry dishes. The restaurant avoids the standard "surf and turf" clichés, but manages to bridge the combo gap with carpetbagger steak as an alternative. Tracing its ancestry to New Orleans, this dish combines the succulence of a juicy grilled- or broiled-oyster stuffing with an ample cut of steak. Philander's serves a popular bouillabaisse, which should not be confused with the Marseilles variety. The stock here is a sweet tomato and fish broth, overflowing with mussels, oysters, clams, and crabs.

As with all seafood houses worth their bric-a-brac, Philander's serves a variety of daily specials. Finnan haddie, when available from the north Atlantic waters off Scotland, is recommended for its dark smoky flavor enhanced by a cream butter sauce. Although dinners include a house salad, potato, and vegetable, the repertoire of appetizers and desserts is tempting enough to run up a higher check than might seem likely at first glance.

K/Rating 17/20: Decor 4/4, Service 4/5, Food 7.5/9, Value 1.5/2

PORTOFINO

Italian

2434 North Harlem, Elmwood Park
Telephone: (312) 453-1060

Hours: Monday–Saturday 4–11. Cards: AE, DC, MC, V. Reservations accepted. No-smoking section. Street parking or in free lot behind restaurant. Full bar service; good Italian wine list. Troubleshooter: Tony Demarinis (owner). Moderate.

You literally have to search out Portofino. Barely visible from the street, except for a moderate identifying sign, Portofino is tucked away in Catherina Mall, a small shopping area that seems about as unbusy as the restaurant.

This is one restaurant that deserves more exposure. The fairly large dining room has a few nautical accents to underscore its namesake, the town of Portofino on the Ligurian coast, south of Genoa. Actually, among the region's greatest claims to culinary fame is the creation of pesto, the sauce that depends upon basil for its singular flavor. And so basil shows up in the cooking at Portofino. For example, an entrée called veal broccoli offers more than just those two ingredients. The meat is topped with mozzarella, large pieces of fresh broccoli, slices of red tomato, and a windfall of aromatic fresh basil leaves, then baked in the oven. The result is a satisfying bouquet of tantalizing flavors.

The liberal use of fresh herbs (and not only basil, to be sure) shows up in other dishes at Portofino. Consider one evening's special of sautéed chicken seasoned with rosemary and garlic and a spectrum of other ingredients, including a mild homemade Italian sausage.

Seafood offerings rotate regularly on the menu. Zuppa di pesce includes crab legs, squid, mussels, and shrimp. A recent evening's special, admittedly more expensive than most of the menu, substituted a large lobster tail for the crab legs. The tomato sauce that makes up the broth for this fish stew was smooth, mild, unmistakably Italian.

By the way, among appetizers, don't miss the delicious fried calamari, with a light batter that makes them as easy to nibble on as any finger snack. All dinners come with soup or salad; the escarole with garbanzo beans is a treasure. Dinners also include a side of mostaccioli.

K/Rating 18/20: Decor 4/4, Service 5/5, Food 7/9, Value 2/2

THE CYPRESS

500 East Ogden Avenue (Route #34 exit on Tri State Tollway), Hinsdale
Telephone: (312) 323-2727

Hours: Monday–Sunday 11:30–10:30. Cards: AE, CB, DC, MC, V. Reservations suggested. No-smoking section. Ample free parking in adjacent lots. Full bar service; three bars plus piano cocktail lounge; extensive wine list. Handicap accessible. Private party facilities for up to 175 people. Troubleshooter: E. J. Applegate (owner). Moderate.

American

The Cypress is a big, rambling sort of place that can seat as many as 450 people. Despite the size, it is one of the most convivial places I've visited in a long while. The food, which is the heart of the matter, is largely basic American with a few embellishments here and there. The large menu lists several cuts of beef, a good amount of seafood, ribs, liver, and the like. Dinners come with a house salad and potatoes. Like many other restaurants, The Cypress serves daily specials. But unlike others, you can call their specialty hotline (986-8050) for a rundown on what's cooking!

K/Rating 17.5/20: Decor 3.5/4, Service 5/5, Food 7.5/9, Value 1.5/2

302 WEST

American

302 West State, Geneva
Telephone: (312) 232-9302

Lunch: Tuesday–Saturday 11:30–2. Dinner: Tuesday–Friday 6–9, Saturday 6–10. Cards: AE, MC, V. Reservations mandatory. Casual dress. Street parking. Full bar service; intimate cocktail lounge located in loft above dining room; extensive list of wines, cognacs, armagnacs. Entire restaurant available for private parties Sunday and Monday with custom-tailored menus for any occasion. Note: Menu changes every 4 to 6 weeks. Troubleshooters: Catherine and Joel Findlay (owners). Expensive.

Housed in a former bank building, 302 West takes good advantage of the high ceilings and open spaces to create a pleasant, comfortable dining atmosphere.

Food leans toward the contemporary American style with imaginative use of ingredients. The kitchen does a marvelous job with an appetizer of roasted garlic. A full head is roasted until each clove is softened. You can eat it right from the skin, or dab some with a knife onto the warm bread that is delivered with the garlic. A log of herbed cheese is a good match with the garlic, as are some briny Niçoise olives for a little added bite. Among other appetizer selections is a mild seafood sausage in a beurre blanc sauce. The seafood is slightly coarse, making for an appealing texture. Carpaccio, bellon oysters on the half shell, and tuna tartare are also offered.

The fine house salad is a mix of butter lettuce, a crush of gorgonzola cheese, and pine nuts in a light tarragon vinaigrette. An à la carte soup course may also be ordered.

The excellence continues in the preparation of the entrées. A grilled veal chop comes with wild mushrooms in a Madeira sauce. Slices of roasted duck arrive at the table still pink, accompanied with a fruity peach chutney and, as with all entrées, a bouquet of lightly cooked, crisp vegetables. The restaurant seems to excel at seafood. Grilled fillet of sole brings a large piece of yellow sole with a crown of ground almonds; the richness of the brown butter sauce is broken by a splash or two of lime juice. If you have a taste for grilled tuna, the 302 West version is flawless. The tuna steak is grilled with tomatoes, onions, and peppers, a combination as natural as blue skies at morning. Other fish choices include mahimahi, grouper, and others, depending upon the availability.

Desserts serve as fitting climax to preceding courses. Selections are made fresh daily and can include cheesecake, mousse, and various tortes. Chocolate lovers will revel in the selections.

Service at 302 West is not as sophisticated as the food preparation, though it is friendly and accommodating.

K/Rating 17.5/20: Decor 4/4, Service 4/5, Food 8/9, Value 1.5/2

DIETERLE'S

German

550 South McLean Boulevard, Elgin
Telephone: (312) 697-7311

Lunch: Tuesday–Friday 11:30–4. Dinner: Tuesday–Thursday 5–10, Friday–Saturday 5–11, Sunday noon–8. Cards: AE, CB, DC, MC, V, house accounts. Reservations suggested. Casual dress, but no shorts or tank tops. Free parking lot. Full bar with excellent selection of German beer and wine. Handicap accessible. Private party room for 50–200 or more people. Troubleshooters: Ulrich and Edna Dieterle (owners). Moderate.

Dieterle's is done up in Black Forest–inspired half timbers and beams, but not laid on so thickly that it's like a visit to The Seven Dwarfs. You could start with an appetizer as prosaic as shrimp cocktail, or as traditionally German as pickled tongue. But the house relish tray that comes with all dinners includes some of the tastiest liver pâté you are ever likely to enjoy, making an à la carte choice superfluous.

Entrées include several American-style beef and seafood choices, but it was the German portion of Dieterle's menu that attracted me. One of the best selections is duck à la Deutsch. Half a duckling is roasted to a golden crispness and served with a lavish portion of Bavarian red cabbage and a bread dumpling nearly the size of a tennis ball. The duck is marvelously flavored, not too fatty. The red cabbage is cooked gently with apples and just a hint of such aromatics as cinnamon and cloves. Naturally, Dieterle's features schnitzels and other staples of the German larder—kassler rippchen, Thuringer sausage or bratwurst platters, and liver with German fried potatoes. The liver is tender and sweet, and, like all else, in ample portion. Desserts include apple strudel, though it is a commercial rather than a house-made product.

K/Rating of 17.5/20: Decor 3/4, Service 4.5/5, Food 8/9, Value 2/2

NORTHWEST

GIANNOTTI

Italian

8422 West Lawrence, Norridge
Telephone: (312) 453-1616

Hours: daily 11:30–11:30 (bar open until 2 am). Cards: AE, DC, DISC, MC, V, house accounts. Reservations required. Casual, but neat dress. Valet parking. Full bar service; show lounge; extensive wine list. Private party facilities for up to 40 people. Troubleshooter: Victor Giannotti (chef). Moderate.

The Chicago area's best Italian chef is back in business. Vic Giannotti, whose restaurant wanderings over the last ten years have sent his fans scurrying, is cooking again at the restaurant that bears his family name. The dining room is done in tasteful art deco with color accents of plum and mauve. Tables tend to be crowded fairly close, but that just gives you a chance to see all the wonderful foods being brought out from the kitchen. In addition to the dining room, there is an adjacent lounge with dancing.

Over the years, the Giannotti benchmark for me has been veal piccante, the premium meat sautéed to a golden crust in butter and lemon juice, then served with a sprinkling of roasted pine nuts. It's still being served the same way, and though other restaurateurs have tried to duplicate this dish, they have never done it as well as you will find it done at Giannotti.

That's just one out of many outstanding tempters. Start with an appetizer of rolled eggplant stuffed with ricotta cheese and just about the best tomato sauce anywhere for a surprisingly low $1.50. Actually, the menu is studded with such bargains. A huge bowl of steamed mussels is under $7.00, and half a loaf of delicious pizza bread is just $3.00.

Full dinners include salad or soup and a side vegetable or pasta. Among pastas, do not miss homemade cavatelli, a cousin of gnocchi. The cavatelli come simply mixed with broccoli in a light bath of olive oil and garlic. The texture and flavors are perfect, although because of the heat of the pasta, the broccoli can lose some of its crispness.

Any given evening will showcase perhaps a dozen choices not on the printed menu. Chef Giannotti likes to combine new ingredients with traditional methods. For example, he prepares swordfish Vesuvio, a variation on the popular chicken Vesuvio. At the same time his menu will offer giambotta, a "paisan" feast of broiled Italian sausage with roasted peppers in a sauce heady with wine, onions, and mushrooms, plus dark roasted potatoes.

K/Rating 19.5/20: Decor 4/4, Service 5/5, Food 8.5/9, Value 2/2

CAFE DE PARIS

French

5550 North River Road in the Hotel Sofitel O'Hare, Rosemont
Telephone: (312) 678-4488

Lunch: Monday–Friday 11:30–2. Dinner: Monday–Thursday 6–10:30, Friday–Saturday 6–11. Cards: AE, CB, DC, MC, V. Reservations required. No-smoking section. Ample parking. Full bar service; excellent list of French wines. Handicap accessible. Private party facilities. Troubleshooter: Jean Pierre Legand (maître d'). Expensive.

As the name suggests, this is a French restaurant, but more than that, Cafe de Paris and the hotel in which it is housed are owned by a French company that is bringing true authenticity to French dining opportunities in the O'Hare area.

Cafe de Paris is handsomely decorated with wall tapestries and chandeliers. When the dining room is busy, there is an unfortunate din that is out of step with the finesse that characterizes the food. The cookery is excellent, almost without flaw, although decidedly expensive. Among the less extravagantly priced appetizers is a pheasant-and-sweetbread terrine served with an odd combination that works: a sauce, perhaps of honeydew or a similar melon, garnished with curls of cantaloupe for color. Or consider escargots, but not in the common garlic butter sauce. Instead, these little nuggets come in a distinctive red wine sauce with a small serving of eggplant mousse. The Cafe de Paris kitchen staff has a fine eye for color and placement. Each serving, no matter what the preparation, looks as if it is ready to be photographed.

The fairly short menu lists a dozen entrée selections, divided evenly between seafood and meats. Fillet of sole comes with a filling of salmon mousse in a red wine sauce less forceful than that which bathes the snails. More interesting, I think, is shark with a mild ginger sauce and shards of fresh fruit. Medallions of veal and sweetbread with a honey sauce studded with pink peppercorns is a superb preparation. The sauce is actually a veal demi-glace enhanced with honey, a flavoring that works especially well with the sweetbreads.

Desserts reflect the same talent displayed in other courses. Fig mousse and mango coulis is one of the most exotic desserts I have ever sampled.

One more note: When I visited Cafe de Paris, two companions were on strict, no-cholesterol diets that eliminated all sauces made with butter, cream, or eggs. When the goal is classic French cuisine, that is limiting, indeed. But to the great credit of the kitchen staff, a veal-stock mustard sauce, created within minutes, proved to be tasty accompaniment to two fish entrées.

K/Rating 16.5/20: Decor 3/4, Service 3.5/5, Food 8.5/9, Value 1.5/2

Zofia's Polish Restaurant

Polish

6873 North Milwaukee, Niles
Telephone: (312) 647-7949

Hours: Sunday–Thursday 11–10, Friday–Saturday 11–11. Cards: AE, CB, DC, MC, V. Reservations suggested. Casual, but neat dress. Free parking lot. Full bar service; good selection of Polish beers. Handicap accessible. Troubleshooter: Zofia Niewiarowski (owner). Moderate.

When it comes to hearty foods at good value, it's hard to top a Polish restaurant. One of the best is Zofia's. There's a faded, dark look to the main dining room, what with its old-fashioned embossed ceiling and deep-toned vinyl furniture. Yet it is comfortable and welcoming nonetheless. The food is served in large portions and is quite good within its limitations. Things tend to get starchy with Polish and other East–European style cooking, so this is no place for calorie counters.

Start your dinner with a cup of homemade soup. If mushroom is being served, be sure to order this genuine treat. The broth is thick and loaded with fresh mushroom slices. You will find traditional Polish roast duckling served Wednesday through Sunday. Or try an order of beef in horseradish gravy. Two large slices of thick, well-cooked meat are covered with a thick, creamy horseradish sauce. There's nothing delicate about the way it is prepared; this is good, basic eating. As with all dinners, the beef comes with vegetables on the side. Pierogis, filled with meat, cheese, or potato, are delicious and can be ordered as a side dish or as a full dinner. Desserts are homemade. The kolaczki, akin to a fruit tart, is my favorite of offerings that include cheesecake and a layered apple cake.

K/Rating of 17.5/20: Decor 3/4, Service 5/5, Food 7.5/9, Value 2/2

Mykonos

Greek

8660 West Golf Road, Des Plaines
Telephone: (312) 296-6677

Hours: Sunday–Thursday 11–11, Friday–Saturday 11–midnight. Cards: AE, CB, DC, MC, V, house accounts. Reservations only for parties of 4 or more. Valet parking. Full bar service; good selection of Greek wines. Handicap accessible. Troubleshooter: Demetrios (Jim) Meragas (chef-owner). Inexpensive.

The restaurant has more of a taverna feel, coupled with an outdoor cafe and garden in warm weather, that gives it an unusual sophistication for a suburban restaurant. Yet, thanks to reasonable pricing, Mykonos remains a favorite for families. The combination dinner is the best bargain, but if you order à la carte you can taste some good things not on the combo. Although the menu seems to mimic virtually every Greek restaurant, there remains that perceptible difference in seasonings that makes Mykonos a restaurant I enjoy returning to as often as possible.

Among outstanding menu items is the Athenian chicken, roasted to a turn, with a side order of artichokes in a rich lemon cream sauce as an added bonus. Among appetizers, the traditional flaming cheese, saganaki, is rather salty. A full-flavored garlic spread is great when smeared on thick slices of crusty bread. Spinach puffs are particularly tasty, with the delicious filling piping hot inside a phyllo pastry crust.

K/Rating 18.5/20: Decor 4/4, Service 5/5, Food 7.5/9, Value 2/2

EDOYA

Japanese

1285 South Elmhurst Road, Des Plaines
Telephone: (312) 593-2470

Lunch: Monday–Saturday 11:30–2. Dinner: Monday–Saturday 5–10:30. Cards: AE, CB, DC, MC, V. Reservations suggested. Parking lot. Full service bar. Handicap accessible. Private party facilities include small tea rooms for 4–30 people. Troubleshooters: Sadao and Barbara Kojima (owners). Moderate.

Edoya is one of a number of Japanese restaurants in the northwestern suburbs catering to a growing ethnic population with a taste for the foods they left behind. Limited menu descriptions in English supplement the Japanese names that most non-Japanese customers do not understand. But, depending upon your waitress's fluency in English, you may still not have a clear idea of what you are ordering until it arrives.

There is little problem with à la carte sushi or sashimi selections, however, since diners are given a card that pictures and names several different types. Or choose a mixed platter and you will be served a good assortment. Dinners begin with a traditional light broth with scallions and bean curd. The sukiyaki is a typical rendition, with a stock that reflects the Japanese penchant for sweetness. Beef teriyaki brings handsomely grilled meat to the table in a pleasant sauce; the chicken teriyaki is even better.

Among the more esoteric choices at Edoya is one of the noodle dishes, really a noodle soup called nabeyaki udon. This is a basic stock, very mild in flavor, but rich with meat, vegetables, and the broad udon noodles central to the dish.

K/Rating 16.5/20: Decor 4/4, Service 3.5/5, Food 7.5/9, Value 1.5/2

DELANEY & MURPHY

American/Steaks

3400 West Euclid in the Woodfield Hilton and Towers, Arlington Heights
Telephone: (312) 394-2000 or 394-3090

Lunch: Monday–Friday 11:30–1:30. Dinner: Monday–Saturday 5:30–10. Cards: AE, CB, DC, DISC, MC, V. Reservations suggested. Casual dress, but no jeans, shorts, T-shirts. No-smoking section. Valet parking or hotel lot. Full bar service; extensive wine list. Two private party rooms for 8–40 people. Troubleshooter: Robert Falor or Heather Walsh (managers). Expensive.

It's not much of a secret that beef is back. The time is here again when you can satisfy your craving for a big, thick, juicy steak and not have people think you are some kind of culinary Neanderthal.

Among the newer restaurants out to satisfy this pent-up desire for real meat is Delaney & Murphy. The room is large, with high ceilings and an understated refinement. Seating is in deep comfortable chairs at large, well-spaced tables, so that even when the restaurant is busy, the noise is not distracting.

The menu is weighted toward the beef option, to be sure, but those who shy away from such fare will be satisfied with a good choice of seafood, including fresh red snapper and swordfish treated to the charcoal grill, scrod, Cajun-style shrimp, scallops, and lobster tails.

But at the bottom line, this is a beef restaurant. The house specialty—advertised as the chef's special at the top of the menu and also recommended by my waitress—is a steak called grilled pepperloin with mustard sauce. Never mind that there is no such cut as "pepperloin." What they are trying to suggest is that the meat is the tenderloin with a pepper-flavored mustard sauce.

The pepperloin is okay, but I really think Delaney & Murphy ought to be making more of a big deal about their prime filet mignon or excellent veal chop. To take first things first, diners who order the house special will get three ample slices of meat cooked to order. The beef comes out in a hot broiler pan, which means that when sauce is poured on the side it literally sizzles and splatters. This does nothing for the sauce or the meat, and I think the sauce should be offered in a separate bowl. Otherwise, it seems like little more than a good-quality commercial steak sauce. If the imagery is pepper and mustard, it needs more of a kick in both directions. And without the sauce, even though the menu says the beef has been "Marinated for 48 Hours, Rolled in Rock Salt and Special Seasonings . . . ," it tastes just like any other good cut of beef to me. This is not to suggest that grilled pepperloin with mustard sauce is somehow not enjoyable. Just don't go in expecting the be-all and end-all of pepper steak.

As for the filet mignon, it is a superb piece of meat with excellent natural flavor, certain to please any steak lover. And the veal chop, which is treated to a good dose of seasonings and a charcoaled crust, is similarly satisfying. Among appetizers, fresh crab cakes come two to the order and may look massive, but are really light and delicate in flavor and texture. The Caesar salad needs some work, mostly more garlic and anchovies to give it bite. Desserts include cheesecakes, ice creams, and chocolate fudge tortes.

K/Rating 17/20: Decor 4/4, Service 5/5, Food 6.5/9, Value 1.5/2

LE TITI DE PARIS

French

1015 West Dundee Road, Arlington Heights
Telephone: (312) 506-0222

Lunch: Tuesday–Friday 11:30–2. Dinner: Tuesday–Thursday 5:30–9:30, Friday 5:30–10:30, Saturday 5:30–11. Cards: AE, CB, DC, MC, V. Reservations required. Jackets requested for gentlemen. Parking lot. Full bar service; wine list with 300 bottlings, some by the split or glass. Handicap accessible. Semiprivate party room for up to 35 people. Troubleshooter: Pierre Pollin (chef-owner), Judith Pollin (co-owner), Erich Rauch (maître d'). Expensive.

A new location for this longtime favorite northwestern suburb restaurant has added the space and sophistication its previous bistro lacked. The decor is now in keeping with the food. Chef Pierre Pollin supplements his printed menu with an extensive listing that changes regularly. From a selection of hors d'oeuvres, a cold vegetable terrine blends mousse of carrot, spinach, turnip, and mushroom in a near-ephemeral loaf. The platter comes with a summer-fresh tomato coulis and a delicious avocado mayonnaise. Or for something hot, try a terrine of sweetbreads and wild mushrooms, bound in a forcemeat of veal and mushrooms. This is a particularly successful way to begin dining. Other choices may be a duck fois gras either sautéed or cold, a seafood cassoulet, or the house pâté.

Soup and salad are à la carte, though entrées do come with a handsome vegetable accompaniment. One of the better salads brings together sharp-flavored watercress and other greens with a round of toasted goat cheese and bits of crisp bacon, all in a warmed vinaigrette.

Meat eaters will find sliced beef tenderloin in a shallot-wine sauce, lovely rack of lamb perfumed with thyme and mustard-vinegar sauce, and a handful of other options. But Le Titi de Paris is best-known for the variety of its fine seafood preparations. Dover sole comes from the grill with a nap of spinach sauce that serves as the perfect complement. North Sea turbot is bathed in a light lobster demi-glace. All entrées come with a vegetable mousse, a tricolored layering of carrot, broccoli, and turnip. On the other side of the handsome oversized platter, diners might find a thin slice of roasted eggplant rolled up much like a blini. Other recent choices have included grilled fresh tuna with an orange-rosemary sauce and roasted baby pheasant on cabbage with a sauce of green peppercorns.

Desserts include a satisfying dense apple tart, a selection of chocolate indulgences, creams, and berries. The wine list is marvelous.

K/Rating 18/20: Decor 4/4, Service 4.5/5, Food 8/9, Value 1.5/2

DON ROTH'S IN WHEELING

American

61 North Milwaukee, Wheeling
Telephone: (312) 537-5800

Lunch: Monday–Friday 11:30–2:30. Dinner: Monday–Thursday 5:30–9:30, Friday 5:30–10:30, Saturday 5–11, Sunday 4:30–8:30. Cards: AE, CB, DC, MC, V. Reservations suggested. Casual dress, but no shorts, jeans, etc. Free parking lot. Full bar service; modest wine list. Handicap accessible. Private party facilities for up to 40 people. Troubleshooter: Don Roth (owner). Moderate.

If there is a dean of Chicago restaurateurs, that person most certainly would be Don Roth. Roth's family goes back to the early twenties and the renowned, though now departed Blackhawk. The restaurant was made famous by coast-to-coast broadcasts of band remotes in the early days of radio. And it was home to the famous spinning salad bowl.

Though that is now history, Don Roth remains active at his restaurant in suburban Wheeling. The spinning salad bowl has been replaced by the salad bar, a salad bar that remains one of the best in the area, at a time when this feature has become largely passé in other contexts. The menu is rather short, with the emphasis on American simplicity. In addition to the regular dinner menu, Don Roth's in Wheeling offers several fresh fish and seafood specials. Diners also will find an excellent raw bar.

K/Rating of 17.5/20: Decor 3.5/4, Service 4/5, Food 8/9, Value 2/2

BILLY AND COMPANY

American

124 South Milwaukee, Wheeling
Telephone: (312) 541-6160

Lunch: Monday–Friday 11–4. Dinner: Monday–Friday 5–11, Saturday 5–midnight, Sunday 4–10. Cards: AE, CB, DC, MC, V. Reservations preferred, mandatory on weekends. Valet parking and parking lot. Full bar service; disco lounge until 2 am daily. Handicap accessible. Limited private party accommodations; call for details. Troubleshooter: William Moss (owner). Moderate.

The eclectic menu is basic American, if that description can include Jewish chopped liver, Grecian pork chops, and Italian veal scallopini. As diverse as the menu is, this is a fine family-style restaurant. My absolute favorite on the menu is John's peppercorn steak, a remnant from an old Chicago restaurant now long gone. Scores of whole peppercorns are pounded into the raw meat, then the meat is grilled so that juices and pepper blend into tangy goodness. This is the very best pepper steak in the entire Chicago area! All dinners come with salad and a side of potato or pasta. Seafood, chops, and poultry make up the bulk of the menu. Desserts are spectacular, if not garish.

K/Rating 17.5/20: Decor 2.5/4, Service 5/5, Food 8/9, Value 2/2

BOB CHINN'S CRAB HOUSE

American Seafood

393 South Milwaukee, Wheeling
Telephone: (312) 520-3633

Lunch: Monday–Friday 11:30–2:30. Dinner: Monday–Thursday 4:30–10:30, Friday–Saturday 4:30–11:30, Sunday 3–10. Cards: AE, CB, DC, MC, V. Reservations accepted. No-smoking section. Free parking lot. Full bar service; antique long bar and whirling tropical fans; excellent selection of wines and beers. Semiprivate party facilities. Troubleshooter: Bob Chinn (owner). Moderate.

This restaurant's biggest fault used to be the long wait for tables. Now, since a major renovation and expansion, diners are moved in and out almost like so many widgets on a conveyer belt. Once in the hands of a waitress, however, things become much more cordial.

The food preparation remains about as good as ever, though in some instances things are a little expensive. For example, the deep-fried seafood sampler appetizer for $5.95 should, at that price, be chock full of all sorts of shrimp, scallops, and clams. It isn't. Instead there are overly breaded nuggets of various soft fish. Better appetizers come from the raw bar, where a fabulous choice of crustaceans awaits.

Soups are delicious. The seafood gumbo is the kind of dish that sneaks up on you. Your first spoonful fills the mouth with comets of flavor. Then, when you think things are about to subside, a rush of pepper seasoning takes hold. This one is a real winner.

Entrées change regularly, as do prices, which depend upon market conditions. Recently whole steamed or broiled lobster has been a feature. Bob Chinn's Crab House really knows how to serve traditional lobster. After outfitting you with a bib to catch all the juices, your waitress will bring out a large wooden platter with the lobster butterflied and most of the shell cracked. The rest is up to you. Savor each delicious bit, saving the best for last. Crack into the claws and remove the meat from the shell for the kind of dining that makes lobster the supreme treat it can be.

For fish lovers, Pacific ahi tuna is a good choice. The large cut of tuna steak comes fresh from the fire, complete with grill marks. The fish is topped with a seasoned cracker-crumb mix that leaves just a bit of saltiness and, perhaps, the flavor of Worstershire on the tongue.

Desserts include several chocolate goodies, cheesecake, ice cream, and Key lime pie, which is too sweet.

K/Rating of 17.5/20: Decor 3.5/4, Service 4.5/5, Food 8/9, Value 1.5/2

Le Francais

French

269 South Milwaukee, Wheeling
Telephone: (312) 541-7470

Hours: Tuesday–Sunday 5:30–9:30. Cards: AE, CB, DC, MC, V. Reservations required. Valet parking. Full bar service; small cocktail lounge; excellent wine list. Troubleshooter: Doris Banchet (owner). Expensive.

Chef Jean Banchet never seems satisfied with his achievements: He constantly strives for improvements, even though Le Francais is already recognized as one of America's few genuinely great restaurants. Diners are treated to an array of more than two dozen evening specials paraded out on magnificent platters by the always well-informed waiters.

Sauces are Banchet's forte, whether a simple red wine, an esoteric sea-urchin butter, or anything in between. (In the past, Banchet's intense reductions of sauces sometimes resulted in too much saltiness, but that problem has largely been eliminated.) Le Francais's patrons have come to expect ingredients unavailable elsewhere in Chicago. Thus fresh fish and vegetables are flown in daily from sources around the country, and other ingredients are imported when required. Often main-course platters will hold two or even three entrées, perhaps two cuts of veal, or a small squab resting in a pastry boat flanked by breast of mallard on one side and pheasant on the other. Even side dishes, such as carrot mousse or mushroom mousse sauced with hollandaise, are sublime demonstrations of Banchet's quest for excellence.

Desserts stand up to the same rigorous demands. Pastry crusts flake almost with a snap, yet are light as air. Fresh seasonal fruits and cream fillings are wedded together. Half a dozen chocolate gâteaux, tortes, and similar delights are always available, as is Le Francais's exquisitely delicious strawberry Napoleon, the best in the Midwest.

K/Rating 20/20: Decor 4/4, Service 5/5, Food 9/9, Value 2/2

Amourette

French

2275 Rand Road, Palatine
Telephone: (312) 359-6220

Lunch: Monday–Friday 11:30–2:30. Dinner: daily from 5. Cards: AE, CB, DC, MC, V. Reservations suggested. Parking lot. Full bar service; good wine list. Troubleshooter: Christian Zeiger (owner). Moderate.

Amourette just goes to show that there is always room for another good French restaurant. And one so reasonably priced means you can go back again and again without worrying about next month's car payment. It is a cozy sort of place, convivial, casual, but with style. Cooking follows the best direction of modern French cuisine. One intriguing appetizer is small rock shrimp sautéed with oyster mushrooms. These are the kind of shrimp that seem surf fresh, cooked in a butter sauce flecked with small mushrooms. Other choices include scallop ceviche, crab cakes sautéed with pecans and scallions, and a fine pâté platter combining a chicken blend with pistachios and a more flavorful duck terrine with wedges of chèvre and brie cheeses alongside. But my favorite first course is a leek, tomato, and salmon tart. The tart, a little smaller than a compact disc, sits in a pool of warm champagne butter sauce laced with julienned carrots and other colorful vegetables. Two wedges of salmon rest on top. This dish is a visual delight and a culinary triumph.

Dinner choices range from roast rack of lamb to quail with a confit of duck leg in a sauce that includes raisins and pears. Veal scallops are served in a thyme and honey sauce, and salmon has been featured recently with a topping of lingonberries and orange slices. It is amazing how well the strong fruits work with this flavorful cold-water fish. As with every other course, each dinner plate is a stunning composition.

Desserts are as exciting as previous courses. Crème brûlée is silken. Chocolate is given proper due.

K/Rating 18.5/20: Decor 3/4, Service 5/5, Food 8.5/9, Value 2/2

VILLAGE TAVERN

American

Old McHenry Road, Routes 53 and 83, Long Grove
Telephone: (312) 634-3117

Hours: Monday 11:30–5, Tuesday–Thursday, Sunday 11:30–midnight, Friday–Saturday 11:30 am–2 am. Cards: AE, DISC, MC, V. No reservations. Street parking. Full bar service. Handicap accessible. Private party room for up to 125 people. Troubleshooters: Bill and Norma Sayles (owners). Inexpensive.

Depending upon the night you visit the Village Tavern, you could run into an auction of antiques, a Dixieland jazz band, a sing-along, or just a casual party. It's that kind of place. When was the last time a waitress stopped taking your order so she could join in singing "Happy Birthday" to a group of revelers nearby? And chances are, rather than becoming annoyed, you would pitch in and sing, too. The atmosphere is casual and boisterous. You cannot go home hungry. Try the eighteen-ounce T-bone ($11.95) or a half-pound chopped beefsteak with sautéed onions ($6.25). Chicken is skillet fried, country style ($6.25). Or order some of the barbecued beef ribs ($5.95) for some "get right down to it and dig in" eating. A good lineup of salads and sandwiches rounds out the menu, and although some foods could use zippier seasonings, the Village Tavern still has enough zesty happenings to keep it the fun place it has been for years.

K/Rating 16.5/20: Decor 3.5/4, Service 5/5, Food 6/9, Value 2/2

D & J Bistro

French

First Street Bank Plaza, 466 South Rand Road, Lake Zurich
Telephone: (312) 438-8001

Lunch: Tuesday–Friday 11:30–2. Dinner: Monday–Friday from 5:30, Saturday from 5. Cards: AE, MC, V. Reservations accepted Friday, Saturday; weeknights only for parties of 4 or more. Casual dress. Parking lot. Full bar service. Semiprivate party facilities for up to 25 people. Troubleshooters: Dominique and Jacqueline Legeai (owners). Moderate.

Tucked away in an ordinary strip shopping mall is a delightful new French restaurant where the food is excellent and prices moderate. The decor is pleasantly country French, though the vinyl trim on chair backs and seats fails to carry through on the theme.

The Japanese chef, Masato Suzuki, certainly knows his way around French cuisine. His cooking has flair and reveals a sure talent.

Diners may order à la carte, or choose from the entire menu to build a five-course prix-fixe dinner of appetizer, soup, salad, entrée, and dessert for a very reasonable $19.50. It's quite the bargain, although even when ordering à la carte everything is reasonably priced, especially considering the quality of ingredients and preparation.

A seafood terrine ($4.25) is the best of the several appetizer choices I have tasted. Two large nuggets of fish, one salmon and the other lobster, are centered in a mild vegetable mousse, napped in a smooth saffron sauce. The textures are in perfect balance with the flavors. A bit heartier is an order of raviolis stuffed with a duck forcemeat and served in what tastes like a tomato-based reduction of the duck's juices. Other choices include an imaginative broiled fillet of sole topping a salad of mixed greens and dressed with a vinaigrette. A selection of house pâtés, snails in garlic butter, steak tartare, and blue point oysters round out the rather extensive appetizer selection.

When it comes to preparing main courses, D & J Bistro really shines. Grilled swordfish, the gashes firmly drawn, was done peppercorn style, as if it were steak rather than fish. The notion works well, proving once again how adaptable swordfish is. Broiled quail comes with a mild house sausage in a reduced wine sauce that works perfectly with the other ingredients.

Desserts can be as formal as an assortment of cheeses or as simple as caramel custard. The wine list is long on imagination and value. I do not want to make a bigger issue of this than need be, but service can be inattentive.

K/Rating 15.5/20: Decor 3.5/4, Service 2/5, Food 8/9, Value 2/2

LE VICHYSSOIS

French

220 West Route 120, Lakemoor
Telephone: (815) 385-8221

Hours: Wednesday–Thursday 5:30 until last seating at 9, Friday–Saturday until last seating at 10, Sunday 4:30 until last seating at 9. Cards: AE, CB, DC, MC, V. Reservations mandatory. Parking lot. Full bar service; extensive list of French, German, and American wines. Handicap accessible. Troubleshooters: Bernard and Priscilla Cretier (owners). Expensive.

Just as the French know that some of their nation's best restaurants lie outside of Paris, so, too, do Chicagoans know that traveling a few miles out into the country can often yield some marvelous dining. A trip to Le Vichyssois is just such an outing. Lakemoor is nothing more than a wide spot in the road, but to one side is a small, whitewashed country inn where chef Bernard Cretier is doing some award-winning cooking. His style is firmly in the nouvelle manner, but without doctrinaire convention. The house namesake, vichyssois (*sic*) is a lovely way to begin your meal. Follow it with a country-fresh pâté of coarsely ground duck meat. Sauces show up especially well in seafood choices such as trois poissons nantais. For something very special, try the veal steak with a sauce of morels. Service can sometimes be a bit slow, but this is the country after all, sans big city sophistication . . . except in the food, that is!

K/Rating of 19/20: Decor 4/4, Service 4/5, Food 9/9, Value 2/2

CHICAGO: SOUTH

NEAR SOUTH
SOUTH

PRAIRIE

American

500 South Dearborn, Chicago
Telephone: (312) 663-1143

Hours: Sunday–Thursday 6:30 am–11 pm, Friday–Saturday 6–midnight. Cards: AE, MC, V. Reservations suggested. Casual dress, but no shorts, jeans, sneakers. No-smoking section. Valet parking. Full bar service; good list of Midwestern beers and American wines. Handicap accessible. Private party facilities available. Troubleshooter: Paul Stepan (owner). Expensive.

Despite its name, Prairie evokes the city, not the country, with sophisticated decor and the suggestion of Frank Lloyd Wright architectural influence. Window views are of traffic on Congress Parkway rather than the Great Plains.

The cooking at Prairie is right on the mark. The menu changes with the seasons, but the emphasis is always on simplicity, with only as much embellishment as the chef perceives is necessary. But the foods are far from spartan. Appetizers can be as prosaic as Sheboygan sausage with a warm potato salad to something as ambitious as a terrine of smoked trout or one of chicken and vegetables. The latter is served with a red bell pepper mayonnaise that underscores the light flavor of the terrine. The smoked trout, on the other hand, comes with a dill mayonnaise, stronger, more assertive, but in step with the smoky flavor of the fish.

Salads are à la carte and range from a simple mix of greens to sliced grilled breast of duck, pork loin with apple-caraway dressing, and roasted rack of lamb with blue cheese, fresh asparagus tips, and greens.

If you prefer your rack of lamb in the more traditional entrée form, the Prairie kitchen version is first class. Four ribs in a light herbal seasoning of rosemary come napped in a reduction of the lamb's natural juices. Though there is a smattering of red meats and poultry, freshwater fish from the Midwest is also showcased. Baked walleyed pike is outstanding. The fish is stuffed with a medley of vegetables and wild rice, all complemented with a very mild parsley sauce. Fans of Door County fish boils will find an elegant rendition of that singular culinary event. White fish is broiled and served with an accompaniment of root vegetables. Another success is baby coho salmon, as mild as this fish has ever tasted, served with bacon, leeks, and walnuts as platter companions.

Desserts can be as elaborate as a walnut caramel schaum torte or as American as homemade deep-dish apple pie.

K/Rating of 18.5/20: Decor 3.5/4, Service 5/5, Food 8/9, Value 2/2

Printer's Row

American/Eclectic

550 South Dearborn, Chicago
Telephone: (312) 461-0780

Lunch: Monday–Friday 11:30–2:15. Dinner: Monday–Saturday 5:30–10. Cards: AE, CB, DC, MC, V. Reservations recommended. No-smoking section. Street parking. Full bar service; lounge and wine bar. Troubleshooter: Mike Foley (owner). Expensive.

This is the best thing to happen to the south Loop area since paved streets and street lamps. The menu is so tantalizing that deciding what to choose is a labor of love. Among appetizers might be a vegetable ravioli, fat stuffed pillows of pasta loaded with a mixture of crisp julienned vegetables, napped in a delicate tomato-butter sauce. Another example of creativity is steamed asparagus, not with an ordinary hollandaise, but with a butter sauce enhanced by just enough fresh orange juice for a subtle aftertaste.

Seafood might include grilled salmon in pink peppercorn sauce with leeks. (Salmon has a rich enough flavor to accept the strong flavors of the peppercorn sauce without being overwhelmed.) A similar imaginative use of ingredients is demonstrated in the preparation of scallops in a saffron broth, and in a terrine of duck garnished with sweet raisins. Among entrées, sweetbread ragout is a standout, a new use of an innard that great chefs have always considered challenging. The ragout is served with a deglazed red wine sauce finished with cream and sorrel. Duckling with corn crêpes and pork tenderloin with onion, mint, and citrus fruits are other examples of the lengths to which creativity has been extended at this welcome new restaurant.

K/Rating 20/20: Decor 4/4, Service 5/5, Food 9/9, Value 2/2

Gennaro's

Italian

1352 West Taylor, Chicago
Telephone: (312) 243-1035 or 733-8790

Hours: Thursday 5–9, Friday–Saturday 5–10, Sunday 4–9. No cards. Reservations recommended. Casual dress. Street parking. Full bar service. Troubleshooter: John Gennaro, Jr. (owner). Inexpensive.

Gennaro's remains a tribute to the old Taylor Street Italian district. Like so many neighborhood restaurants, there is a certain clubbiness that permeates the place, although as an outsider, I have always found the greetings and service congenial. Still, the locked front door and buzzer entry creates an almost siegelike atmosphere in an area undergoing social change.

The menu here does not appear extraordinary at first glance. But everything served is fresh, hot, and homemade. Seasonings are mellowed, well married in the sauces. Something as commonplace as veal parmigiana is exceptionally delicious; the cheese topping is perfectly enhanced by a deep red tomato sauce that tastes as if it had been cooked for hours at slow simmer. The veal itself is tender, well textured, and ample. To really experience the excellence of Gennaro's, you must order an à la carte specialty. Homemade gnocchi are not to be missed. These little potato dumplings are rich and chewy and, I am sure, sinfully fattening, but as pleasurable a way to put on weight as I can think of. The gnocchi are bathed in that wonderful, full-bodied tomato sauce, the backbone of Gennaro's kitchen creations. Other homemade pastas are raviolis, stuffed manicotti, and broad noodles. Spumone and tortoni are offered for desserts, but the cannoli, made in house, is the standout.

K/Rating 19/20: Decor 3/4, Service 5/5, Food 9/9, Value 2/2

It's Greek to Me

Greek

306 South Halsted, Chicago
Telephone: (312) 977-0022

Hours: Monday–Thursday, Saturday 11–1 am, Sunday 11–midnight. Cards: AE, CB, DC, MC, V, house accounts. Reservations suggested. Casual dress. Free valet parking. Beer and large selection of Greek wines. Facilities for semiprivate parties. Troubleshooter: Dennis Salafatinos (owner). Inexpensive.

The saying "It's Greek to me" is used to designate confusion or unawareness of something. But there is no confusion at all about the good cooking and festive air at this restaurant of the same name. It's Greek to Me is as handsome as any restaurant on the Greektown strip, and more so than many. The terraced dining area with its bright, airy spaciousness, gives one the feel of outdoors; all that is missing is the warmth of the Mediterranean sun.

Many of the Greek restaurants are doing a generally good job, even though some cater more directly to tourists. It's Greek to Me is one of the few that seems determined to win and keep its ethnic Greek-American business. The menu is somewhat more expansive than the norm, presenting specialty dishes beyond the usual pastitsio, moussaka, gyros, and the like.

If you want to try a bit of this and that as you sit down for dinner, order a combination of appetizers for $4.75 per person. Within minutes, a platter laden with tidbits will arrive from the kitchen. There will be some fish roe spread called taramasalata, and its garlic laden cousin, skordalia. Both are fantastic when spread like cream cheese on hard-crusted bread. Savor the spinach pie with the jaw-breaking name of spanakopita, the filling encased in a buttery phyllo crust. The dolmades, grape leaves stuffed with ground meat and rice, are great when eased down with a bit of wine. For more gusto, taste the melitzanosalata, a zesty eggplant salad. There are also simple little delights such as lima beans and wedges of feta cheese with tomatoes.

You can order a combination dinner platter, too, for a taste of the staples. If you are more adventurous, try the lamb exohiko, which is lamb prepared with a stuffing of artichoke hearts, pine nuts, feta cheese, tomatoes, and peas. Or order lamb gemisto for $7.95, stuffed with a forcemeat of ground beef laden with pine nuts and raisins. Shrimp Mediterranean is a delicious blend of shellfish and seasonings in a cream-based wine sauce, the whole shrimp absorbing all the flavors. Desserts range from baklava to custards.

Service is courteous and on the mark, although sometimes it can be just a little rushed.

K/Rating of 18.5/20: Decor 4/4, Service 4/5, Food 9/9, Value 1.5/2

SEVEN TREASURES

Chinese

2312 South Wentworth, Chicago
Telephone: (312) 225-2668

Hours: daily 11–2 am. No cards. Reservations accepted. Street parking. No alcoholic beverages. Troubleshooter: Chung L. Au (owner). Inexpensive.

Think of Chinese food, and chances are you think of rice as the accompaniment. But in fact there is also a whole world of Chinese noodles, pasta if you will. Take a look at the two menus at Seven Treasures, one with the same large list found at most conventional Chinese restaurants, and a smaller one with a selection of soups, dumplings, and noodles. Begin with the dumplings in oyster sauce, a large platter of some of the best dumplings I have ever had. These are made with a nearly transparent dough, as thin as a sheet of paper. They are filled with chopped mushrooms and meat or whole tiny shrimp. The light oyster sauce clings to each delicious dumpling as you enjoy its sensual taste and texture. Try an order of braised noodles with a light topping of fresh ginger and snips of scallions. Chinese braised noodles have a texture not unlike "al dente" Italian pasta, yet the flavors and seasonings make them unmistakably oriental. For contrast, accompany noodles with a small side order of duck with crisp skin and meat that practically falls from the bones.

Choosing main courses at Seven Treasures can be difficult, because all the selections are so tempting. If you want to eat like the local customers, try one of the soups. They range from a clear broth to rice soup, to soup and noodles, with a wide choice of toppings from which to choose. Though largely Cantonese, the menu does list some of the spicier Szechwan dishes that offer more pronounced seasoning. Yet Cantonese dining still has its charms: a large portion of stir-fried beef in a thick brown gravy with a topping of Chinese broccoli, leafy spinach, and other green vegetables.

A large part of the Seven Treasures kitchen is open to view through the front window of the restaurant, so you can actually see the preparation of many of the foods. The restaurant is brightly lit, not unlike a cafeteria or coffee shop of the 1950s. But what really makes Seven Treasures distinctive is that this is where the locals go.

K/Rating 17.5/20: Decor 2.5/4, Service 4/5, Food 9/9, Value 2/2

SOUTH

ARMY AND LOU'S

422 East 75th Street, Chicago
Telephone: (312) 483-6550

Soul Food

Hours: Wednesday–Saturday 11–10, Sunday 9–10. Cards: AE, CB, DC, MC, V. Reservations accepted. No-smoking section. Parking lot. Full bar service. Handicap accessible. Semiprivate facilities for 15–100 people. Troubleshooters: Mr. and Mrs. Charles Cole (owners) and Ron Ballinger (manager). Moderate.

Soul food comes from the heart as well as from the kitchen, and when folks talk soul food in Chicago, Army and Lou's is one of the first restaurants mentioned. The greens, boiled beans, and buffalo fish get traditional attention here. Fried chicken comes in large portions, steaming hot and crisp. Smothered chicken is real fixin's in soul kitchens, and Army and Lou's serves it right, not only with giblet gravy, but with a cornbread dressing, too. Right on the money are the barbecued ribs topped with a spicy sauce, the meat practically falling from the bones. And long before anybody up here in Chicago ever heard of Paul Prudhomme, Army and Lou's was teaching lots of folks about Cajun and Creole cookin'! One of the best selections, not often thought of as soul food, is Creole gumbo. This savory stew of crabmeat, chicken, rice, vegetables, and spicy seasonings is as perfect a gumbo as I have ever had. An extra cup of gravy can be requested for even more flavor and goodness.

Army and Lou's uses separate deep-frying vats for chicken, fish, and potatoes. That way flavors are protected from each other. All beef is Prime. Dinners include soup, salad, two vegetables, fresh hot rolls, and muffins. À la carte desserts such as peach cobbler and ice cream are worth the extra cost.

K/Rating of 17/20: Decor 3/4, Service 5/5, Food 7/9, Value 2/2

NUEVO LEON

1515 West 18th Street, Chicago
Telephone: (312) 421-1517

Mexican

Hours: daily 8–3 am. No cards. Street parking. No alcoholic beverages. Troubleshooters: Danny and Raul Gutierrez (owners). Inexpensive.

Don't look for trendy atmosphere at Nuevo Leon. Located in the heart of the old Pilsen neighborhood, this is the kind of Mexican restaurant that serves families with children in arms, young couples, street people as well as turistas looking for something better than that served at more glitzy emporiums. The menu is typical of most Mexican restaurants, emphasizing tacos, enchiladas, and so on. In fact, a neon sign out front notes that this is a "taqueria," a place for snacks as well as meals. You should do well with whatever you choose.

The menu features a number of Mexican soups and stews, the kind with a deep homemade flavor. The real standout, however, is chicken mole. The sauce has the underpinnings of unsweetened chocolate, without which mole would not be mole. And, yes, there is the essence of peppers, but not so hot as to upset the balance. Nuevo Leon is quite the Mexican experience!

K/Rating 16/20: Decor 2/4, Service 4/5, Food 8/9, Value 2/2

TOSCANO

Italian

2439 South Oakley, Chicago
Telephone: (312) 376-4841

Hours: Tuesday–Thursday 11–11, Friday 11–midnight, Saturday noon–10, Sunday 2–10. Cards: AE, DC. Reservations ?????. Street parking (sometimes difficult). Full bar service. Private second-floor dining room available for up to 70 people; entire restaurant seating up to 175, may also be taken on advance notice. Troubleshooter: Thomas A. Scapillato (owner). Moderate.

The small Italian Christmas lights are gone. So too are the plastic greenery and the mural of Venice and its Grand Canal. What is left is what was there sixty-five years ago. Toscano has been restored back to its art deco roots. The booths have been replaced with tables and bentwood chairs; the tin ceiling has been restored to its original glory; the walls have been recovered. But the food is still that deftly prepared Italian fare with an emphasis on the north but without the trendiness of newer northern Italian restaurants.

New to the menu is a house creation, veal carciofi, plus appetizers such as spinach ravioli with shrimp and plum tomatoes in a basil sauce. The Tuscan sauces characteristic of northern Italy are thick and meaty, with less tomato acidity than sauces south of Rome. The menu lists the usual pastas—spaghetti, lasagne, and ravioli among others. The lasagne is typically meaty; garlic is used sparingly. Among other recommended selections on the menu is the chicken toscano mildly seasoned in a wine sauce; veal toscano is similarly prepared.

Like many truly good restaurants, Toscano has one or two specialties not listed on the menu. If you like the spice of hot peppers and garlic and the richness of olive oil, ask for their special sauce. Freshly chopped parsley and anchovy add some complexity, but order this sauce on a side pasta only, unless you really like your food hot.

K/Rating of 17.5/20: Decor 4/4, Service 4/5, Food 7.5/9, Value 2/2

BRUNA'S

2424 South Oakley, Chicago
Telephone: (312) 254-5550

Hours: Monday–Thursday 11–10, Friday–Saturday 11–11, Sunday 1:30–10. Cards: AE, MC, V, house accounts. Reservations suggested. Parking lot and street parking. Full bar service; extensive list of Italian wines. Troubleshooter: Luciano Silvestri (owner). Moderate.

Italian

The menu at Bruna's offers the typical mix of Italian dining—veal, chicken, pastas, a touch of seafood. Though specific combinations are listed, the fact is that most everything is interchangeable, since pastas and sauces are fresh. Try the pesto sauce with its heart of basil and oil; though it may seem too fragile to put up against a pasta as substantial as gnocchi, the contrast actually works extraordinarily well. The meat sauce here is the classic ragu, almost like a gravy in its intense richness, with the telltale aftertaste of nutmeg. The marinara sauce is a delicious tomato blend that lends itself to simple pastas or seafood. Try it with mussels, the ebony shells bathed in a pool of the full-flavored marinara broth. From a choice of appetizers, try the calamari salad with a fresh lemon vinaigrette. Baked clams come sizzling hot in their shells. The wine list is extensive and well annotated.

K/Rating 17.5/20: Decor 3.5/4, Service 4/5, Food 8/9, Value 2/2

MATEGRANO'S

1321 West Taylor, Chicago
Telephone: (312) 243-8441

Lunch: Tuesday–Friday 11–3. Dinner: Tuesday–Thursday 3–9, Friday–Saturday 3–10, Sunday 1–8. Cards: CB, DC, MC, V. Reservations suggested. Casual dress. Valet parking on Thursday and Saturday nights for evening buffet. Full bar service. Private party facilities for up to 50 people or 100 people in either of two separate rooms. Troubleshooter: Annette S. Mategrano (owner). Inexpensive.

Italian

Anybody who knows anything about budget Italian dining knows Mategrano's Thursday and Saturday night buffets. These all-you-can-eat extravaganzas are as much a party as anything else, with tables heaped high with dozens of house specialties, some familiar, some not always so. Annette Mategrano and her sister Millie Miccucio keep things moving along, and even on nights when the buffet is not offered, it is hard to spend much more than $8 to $10 a person; often you will spend much less.

Mategrano's is one of the old-timers in the long-established Taylor Street Italian community. The food is typical Neapolitan home cooking. Seafood specialties such as calamari, polpi, and, when it is available, baccala are among favorites here. Pastas are homemade. Braciole is one of the house specialties I could eat till Judgement Day.

K/Rating 17/20: Decor 3/4, Service 5/5, Food 7/9, Value 2/2

BACCHANALIA

Italian

2413 South Oakley, Chicago
Telephone: (312) 254-6555

Hours: Monday, Wednesday–Friday 11–11, Saturday 4–11, Sunday 4–9. No cards. Reservations suggested. Casual dress. Street parking can be difficult. Full bar service. Handicap accessible. Private party facilities only early Sunday and on Tuesday. Troubleshooter: Paula Pieri (owner). Moderate.

While there may be a few glitches in service from time to time, there is no mistaking the quality of the flavorful home-cooked foods at Bacchanalia. The basic tomato-meat sauce is marked by a liberal use of pepper, oil, and tomatoes and is particularly good served with gnocchi, little potato dumplings.

Among the other top-notch pastas, try tortellini verde, green spinach noodles twisted into little caps stuffed with creamy ricotta cheese. Virtually a meal in itself is manicotti, tubes of pasta stuffed with seasoned ground meat; the house meat sauce is used again to good effect. Other courses may not fare as well as the pastas. Veal limone is rather mild, and chicken Vesuvio is not garlicky enough for me. Among appetizers, the pizza bread is tasty, but the clams are too heavily breaded. You might try the arancini, breaded rice balls stuffed with sausage; they are not listed on the menu, so you will have to ask for them.

K/Rating of 16/20: Decor 2.5/4, Service 4.5/5, Food 7/9, Value 2/2

VERNON PARK TAP

Italian

1073 West Vernon Park, Chicago
Telephone: (312) 226-9878

Dinner: Tuesday–Thursday 5–10, Friday–Saturday 5–11, Sunday 4–9. No cards. No reservations. Ample street parking. Full bar service. Troubleshooter: Joseph Di Buono (owner). Inexpensive.

You have to look closely to find this place, hidden as it is in a row of modest older buildings across the street from the sprawling University of

Illinois Chicago Circle Campus. The inside is as plain as the exterior: A barroom up front looks like something out of the 1940s, and the back dining room is furnished with a catchall of wobbly tables and chairs. The Tufano family founded the restaurant over half a century ago and they still run the place; it is as casual as an Italian family dinner.

Blackboards list the various selections of the day. At first glance it seems basic Italian: spaghetti, veal, maybe a chicken dish, ravioli, lasagne, sausage. Entrée prices are very low, and if you go with a group and order family style you will pay even less. Begin with a small antipasto: a large crockery bowl gorged with greens, peppers, mozzarella cheese, black olives, thinly sliced salami, and tomatoes awash in oil. Next have some pasta, perhaps mostaccioli in an excellent marinara, or spaghetti in garlic and oil. For meat choices try veal parmigiana and chicken Vesuvio. The tomato sauce here is the slow-cooked kind, with a mellow tomato bite, an underscoring of garlic. If you have difficulty finding Vernon Park Tap, ask someone in the neighborhood to point the way—although some regulars might like to keep this place a secret.

K/Rating 15.5/20: Decor 2/4, Service 4/5, Food 7.5/9, Value 2/2

VILLA MARCONI

Italian

2354 South Oakley, Chicago
Telephone: (312) 847-3168

Hours: Monday–Friday 11–10, Saturday 5–11. Cards: CB, DC, MC, V, house accounts. Reservations accepted. Street parking can be difficult. Full bar service; domestic and imported wines. Private party room accommodates up to 50 people. Troubleshooter: Lillian Marconi (owner). Inexpensive.

If I were to describe the perfect casual restaurant, I would want it to be a family-owned-and-operated neighborhood place, with pleasant decor, friendly service, and really good food at excellent value. And if it happened to be Italian, that wouldn't be so bad.

This in a nutshell is Villa Marconi and what should really please the budget diner here, in addition to the good food, are the great prices. Low prices, of course, are meaningless if the food is not good. Fortunately, it happens to be generally top-notch at Villa Marconi. Fried appetizers such as calamari or zucchini sticks are virtually greaseless. Baked clams are steaming hot, succulent, and flavorful beneath a seasoned bread crumb blanket. The minestrone soup of fresh vegetables and homemade stock tastes like it has been slowly simmering all day.

From among a selection of pastas, the waitress was kind enough to suggest linguine with mussels, which was neither on the menu nor on the chalkboard. A large oval platter, the kind used for family-style dining, came out with more than two dozen mussels circling the edge. In the center was a mound of pasta, lightly oiled and garlicked, but not so much as to interfere with the fresh taste of the steamed mussels.

Among the entrées is chicken Vesuvio, a classic in its simplicity. Veal parmigiana is a large cutlet, like a golden pillow all puffed up in a light-flour-and-egg crust. Beef braciole is a bit different than the usual, wrapped with mortadella instead of milder prosciutto. But that's all right, since it showcases the talent of a creative kitchen.

Desserts include cheesecakes and Italian ice creams.

K/Rating 18/20: Decor 3/4, Service 5/5, Food 8/9, Value 2/2

MAPLE TREE INN

10730 South Western, Chicago
Telephone: (312) 239-3688

Hours: Tuesday–Saturday from 5. Cards: MC, V. Reservations suggested. No-smoking section. Street parking. Full bar service; wine by the glass or bottle; jazz and blues lounge on second floor. Limited private party facilities. Troubleshooter: Charlie Orr (owner). Moderate.

New Orleans/Creole/Southern

There is a style of New Orleans cookery that brings out its French roots, and there is a side that leans more toward the Cajun contributions. The latter seems to hold sway at the Maple Tree Inn.

To get things off to a good start, a dozen combined oysters is just right for a party of four, offering good tastes of delightful oysters Rockefeller with their blend of spinach, other greens, and a touch of Pernod. You'll also get the delicious oysters Bienville, named for the founder of New Orleans; the tasty oyster in the shell is blanketed by the rich butter-and-cream sauce that is the trademark of this dish. Among other delightful appetizers is a delicious crabmeat Remick, shreds of the meat in a remoulade-based pepper sauce. You would probably have to go all the way down to the Delta to find grilled shrimp and andouille sausage as good as it is here. Or if it is the peppery flavor you like, don't miss a platter of New Orleans boiled shrimp, perfect to tease the appetite for what's to come.

There are over a dozen entrées, ranging from something as simple as a strip steak to delicious shrimp or crawfish étouffée. For simpler fare you might find pompano sautéed in black butter being offered one night. It's a good presentation, the fish boned and butter fried, the black butter adding more in the way of color than flavor to the fish. In any event, it's a real pleaser. Ask owner Charlie Orr about the real house specialty and he'll immediately propose the Cajun jambalaya. Laden with rice, chicken, and lots of ham, it's a classic of its kind. Be sure to get dessert; the Mississippi mud cake and the bread pudding with whiskey sauce are my favorites.

K/Rating 18/20: Decor 3.5/4, Service 4.5/5, Food 8/9, Value 2/2

SUBURBS: SOUTH

OAK LAWN
CALUMET PARK
CALUMET CITY
LANSING
LOCKPORT

PALERMO'S

Italian

4849 West 95th Street, Oak Lawn
Telephone: (312) 425-6262

Dinner: Monday, Wednesday–Thursday 4–11:30, Friday–Saturday 4–1:30 am. Cards: AE, CB, DC, MC, V. Reservations required on weekends. No-smoking section. Free parking. Full bar service. Troubleshooters: Ben and Tony Palermo (owners). Moderate.

You probably have your favorite little family-run restaurant where the owners cater to your every need. Usually in such friendly restaurants, diners converse with complete strangers and even share tastes of food. This happens at Palermo's. On a typical evening, soon after I sat down, Ben Palermo asked if I wanted anything special. I asked him to make recommendations and ended up with more than ten courses, each better than the last.

Even though the menu states that "Fiesta Dinners" are only served to parties of four or more, our twosome got similar treatment. An excellent start was cold calamari salad, in which marinated baby squid was cut into small pieces. Next came stuffed escarole, steaming hot with a filling of mild sausage and melted mozzarella. Fried zucchini in a light batter followed, as did baked artichokes filled with a cheese sauce. We skipped the soup, and out came our first pasta course, seashell macaroni in a zesty marinara sauce. About this time we entered into conversation and taste sharing with the people at the next table. Then the fettuccine Alfredo was served, followed by sautéed shrimp in butter sauce, spaghetti marinara, and sautéed chicken. By the end of this trencherman's dream, all we could do was wave away dessert and motion for the check. What we didn't consume was packed to take home.

K/Rating 18.5/20: Decor 3.5/4, Service 5/5, Food 8/9, Value 2/2

GULFPORT DINER

Soul Food

12401 South Ashland Avenue, Calumet Park
Telephone: (312) 385-3100

Hours: Tuesday–Thursday 11–9:30, Friday 11–1:30, Saturday 4–10:30. Sunday: 5–9:30. Sunday brunch: noon–3:30. No cards. Reservations accepted, except for Sunday brunch. Full bar service. Handicap accessible. Troubleshooter: Charlie Taylor (chef-owner). Inexpensive.

There really are some diners still around! You remember those long and narrow restaurants. They had a row of counter stools and usually some booths opposite. Gulfport Diner is the real thing and then some. You won't find reduced sauces and exotic meats here. Instead, typical specialties are red beans and rice flavored with ham hocks, deep-fried catfish, and usually some shrimp jambalaya. With dishes such as the jambalaya, you'll find hints of the spicy foods of New Orleans. But chef Charley Taylor's cooking is not so much influenced by the Cajun bayou or the urban Creole as it is by Deep Dixie. So, his jambalaya is mild, yet still complex and delicious.

Taylor's style really shines with an original creation, lamb Biloxi, a frequent addition to the regular printed menu. Cubes of meat are simmered with green pepper, tomato, celery, and onion. He finishes the dish with a brown sauce worked from the freshly cooked juices of the lamb, thickens it lightly with a roux, and there is a new American classic. Or try the smothered chicken with rice, about the most Southern thing I can think of. A specialty is jack salmon à la Taylor. The fish is deep fried and served with a medley of tomatoes, green peppers, and onions cooked into a sauce and served on rice. Chef Taylor is not one to shy away from more delicate ways of cooking a fish, however. Baked red snapper comes with a mild Creole sauce, its acidic tomato base eased with sweetenings. Save room for dessert. I like the bread pudding best.

K/Rating of 18.5/20: Decor 4/4, Service 5/5, Food 7.5/9, Value 2/2

THE COTTAGE

Continental

525 Torrence Avenue, Calumet City
Telephone: (312) 891-8900

Lunch: Tuesday–Friday 11:30–2. Dinner: Thursday–Friday 6–10, Saturday 5–11. Cards: MC, V. Reservations required. Jackets requested for gentlemen. Free parking lot. Full bar service. Handicap accessible. Entire restaurant available for private parties on Sunday and Monday; private party room for up to 20 people. Troubleshooter: Jerry Buster (co-owner). Expensive.

Chef Carolyn Buster's cooking has never been better than it is now at this charming suburban retreat. Definitely worth a visit, The Cottage has evolved from a table d'hôte format into a semi à la carte menu. Many of the old favorites such as Cottage schnitzel, duckling with orange sauce and chutney dressing, and steak Madagascar are still featured, but now the menu has a greater depth and diversity, while still staying within its framework of from eight to ten entrées nightly.

What makes the restaurant even better are some of the fine appetizer and salad specials. Seafood raviolis feature a forcemeat inside a pillow of spinach pasta with an anchovy cream butter sauce Lamb sausages are grilled over coals, sauced with the juices of crushed sweet peppers, and served with minted lentils. Steamed sea scallops might come with a tarragon beurre blanc. Desserts vary from day to day but usually include exquisitely fine white and dark chocolate mousse, raspberry gâteau, and apple strudel with a delicate flaked crust. The wine list, overseen by maître d' Jerry Buster, has been deepened. In addition to the regular menu, a five-course dinner may be ordered with appropriately selected wines for a prix fixe, recently starting at $32.50.

K/Rating 20/20: Decor 4/4, Service 5/5, Food 9/9, Value 2/2

CAFE BORGIA

Italian

17923 Torrence, Lansing
Telephone: (312) 474-5515

Hours: Sunday–Thursday 11–11, Friday–Saturday 11–midnight. Cards: MC, V. Reservations accepted. Parking lot and street parking. No alcoholic beverages, but customers may bring in wine. Restaurant available for private parties of up to 50 people. Troubleshooters: Mike and Karen Jesso (owners). Inexpensive.

Cafe Borgia gives far south suburban diners an opportunity to enjoy some exceptional Italian cooking that may not be a renaissance, but still manages to satisfy.

In addition to the printed menu, each evening a handwritten poster lists specials for each course. The cooking is mostly that of Italy's north central region, though the menu is not limited to that area. For starters, Cafe Borgia's version of vittello tonnato is the only real disappointment. The tuna sauce has a distinctly canned taste. A bit more interesting is a wedge of polenta, its golden yellow centered on a deep-hued tomato-and-meat sauce. The Cafe Borgia version of pizza with four cheeses brings a thin, crisp crust blanketed with its quartet of melted toppings hot from the baking oven. This is the kind of pizza usually found only at so-called trendy gourmet Italian restaurants.

Salad is a refreshing mix of greens, tossed in a rich olive oil dressing. I had to ask the waiter for a pepper grinder and grated cheese, which should have been automatically offered with this course. Diners can also opt for soup, or for appetizers, which can be smaller portions of some of the full pasta courses. Penne, the tubular pasta, comes in a rich multiflavored cheese sauce. The fettuccine carbonara is made not only with pancetta, cheese, and egg yolk, but with slivers of grilled onion as well.

Cafe Borgia serves an interesting version of chicken Vesuvio, again demonstrating a bit of latitude with the conventional approach. In this version, a good helping of fresh rosemary is heaped onto the cut-up chicken, garlic, and potatoes before baking. Rosemary is hardy enough to stand up to the pungency of the garlic seasoning that characterizes a good chicken Vesuvio.

Chicken cacciatore holds closer to tradition, though mushrooms were missing one evening in the otherwise busy sauce. I suspect, however, that the kitchen may simply have been out of mushrooms, since I noticed they had been stricken from another entrée, too.

K/Rating of 16.5/20: Decor 3.5/4, Service 3.5/5, Food 7.5/9, Value 2/2

TALLGRASS

American Nouvelle

1006 South State Street, Lockport
Telephone: (815) 838-5566

Dinner: Thursday–Sunday 6–10. Cards: MC, V, house accounts, personal checks. Reservations mandatory. Jackets required for gentlemen. Ample street parking. Full bar service; wine list includes 185 American and French bottlings. Restaurant available for private parties for up to 40 people Monday–Wednesday. Troubleshooters: R. D. Burcenski and J. T. Alves (owners). Expensive.

Enter through a carpeted basement, then climb a flight of stairs. That's how you get inside Tallgrass. The floor is an old mosaic of small checked black-and-white tile. Dark, distinctively grained-wood paneling climbs more than halfway up the wall, meeting a clean line of mirrors that travels the rest of the way up to the antique tin ceiling. Dark green cloths grace each table in the small dining room, where hardly more than thirty-five or forty people can be served at any one time.

The food leans toward the nouvelle style, with some excellent choices. One night might bring an exquisite consommé of shrimp and lobster with a lingering taste of saffron and delicate angel hair pasta in the broth. Among entrées, try the rack of lamb, broiled to the palest of pinks and flavored with a bouquet of herbs. Other recent choices from a menu that changes often include poached lobster with orange and grapefruit segments in a citrus beurre blanc, medallions of prime veal dusted with crushed hazelnuts in hazelnut beurre blanc, or grilled medallions of Norwegian salmon with sea scallops and celery-sorrel butter sauce. For dessert consider a mousse of fresh berries wrapped in chocolate bark and drizzled with berry juice, warmed savory of fresh pear and nuts in a puff pastry with stilton cheese cream sauce, and white and dark chocolate torte with raspberry sauce.

K/Rating 17.5/20: Decor 4/4, Service 4/5, Food 8/9, Value 1.5/2

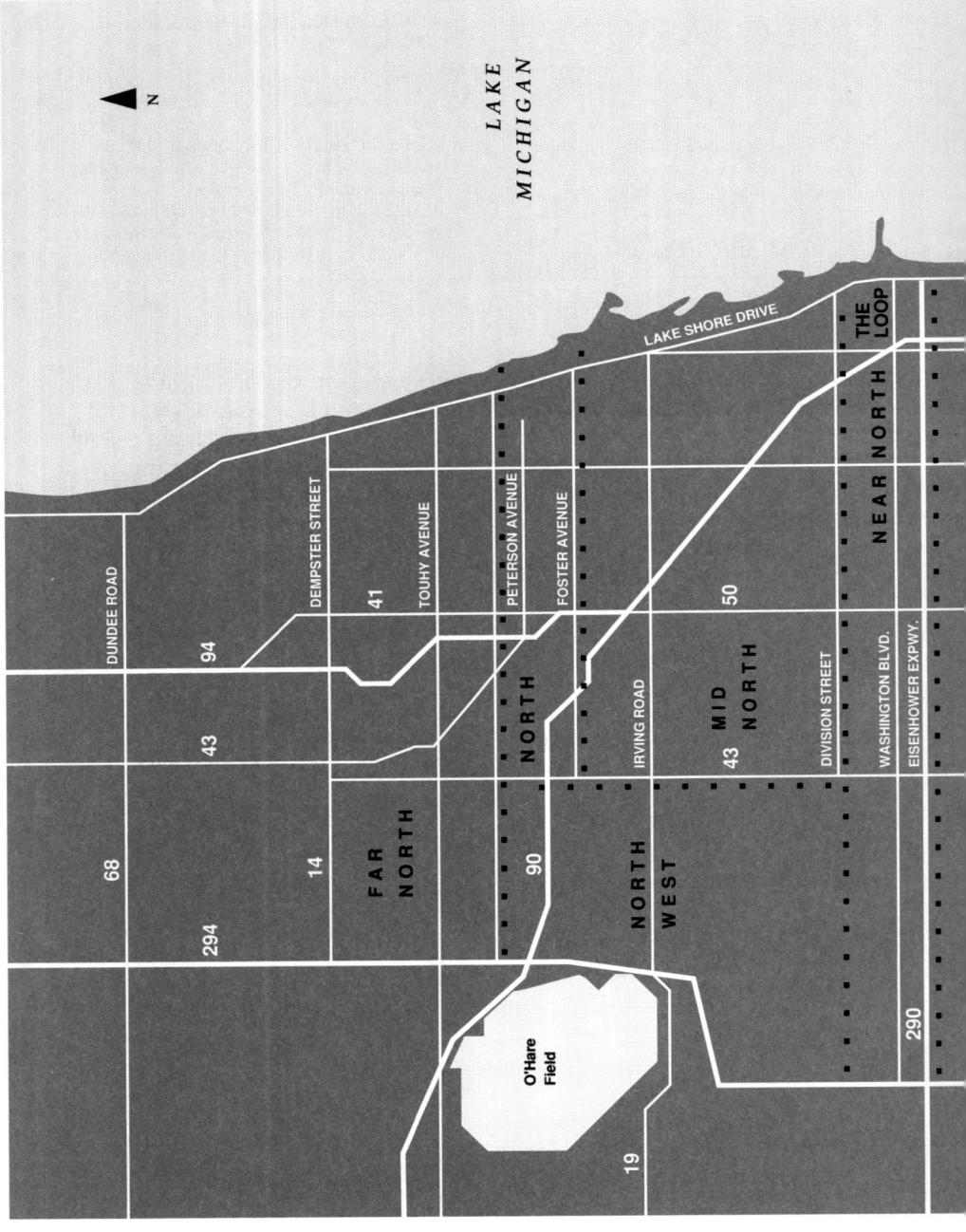

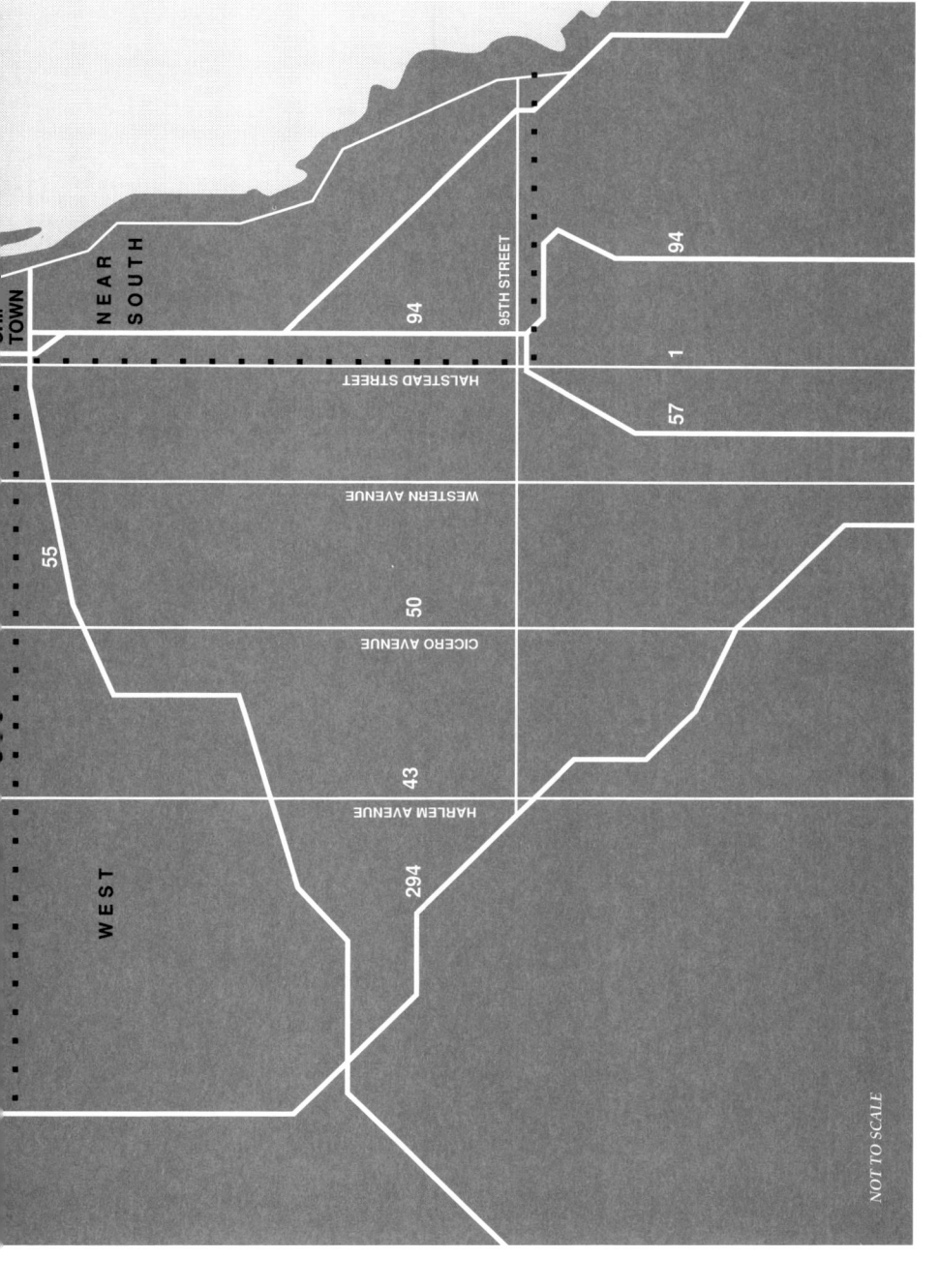

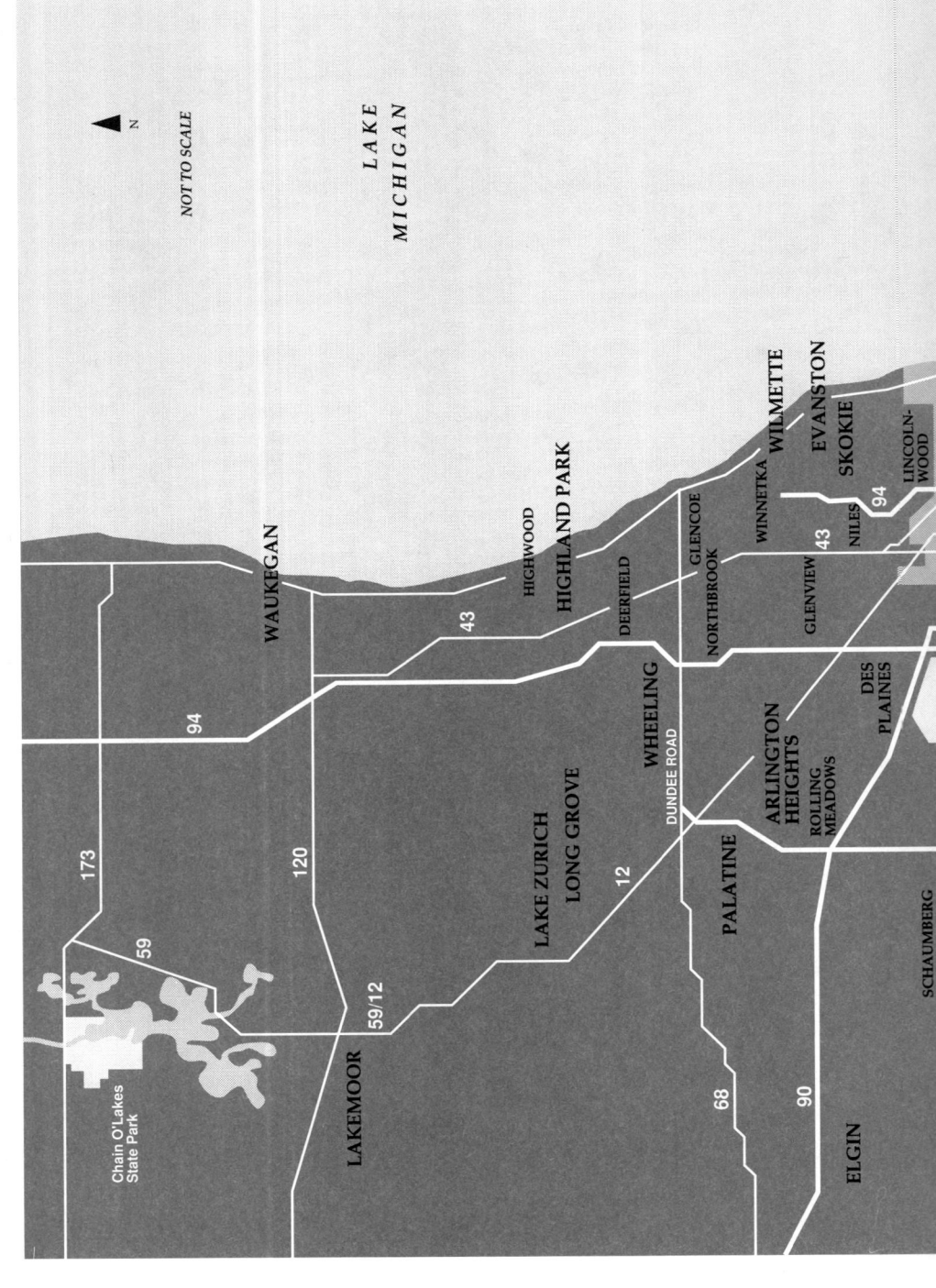

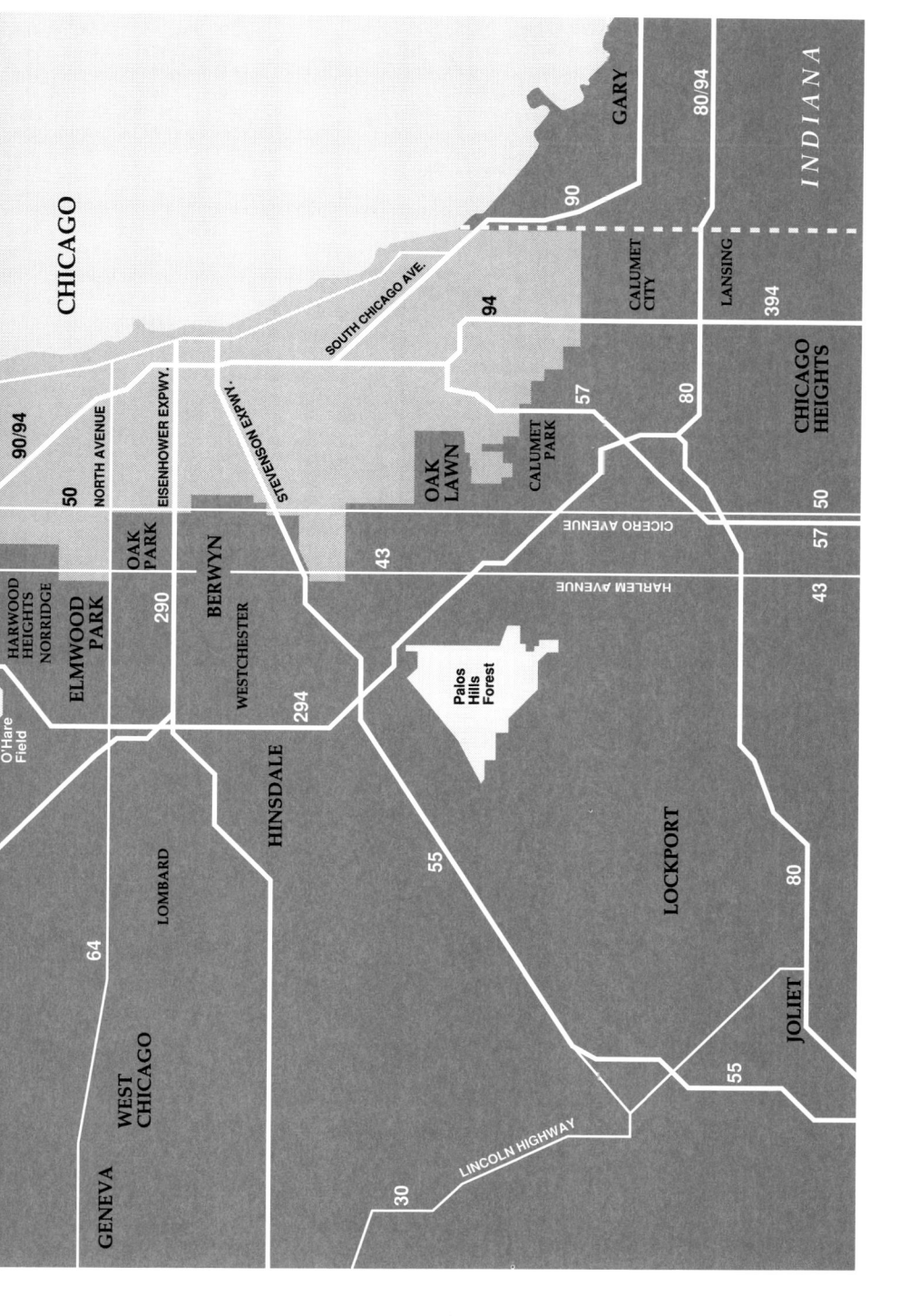

INDEX

RESTAURANTS IN ALPHABETICAL ORDER

302 West, 162
Ada's, 137
Aegean Isles, 140
Alouette, 143
Ambria, 85
American Joe's, 135
Amourette, 172
Ananda, 70
Ann Sather's, 82
Aqui mi Tierra, 77
Arbela, 111
Arcadia, 156
Army & Lou's, 182
Arnie's, 43
Avanzare, 58
Bacchanalia, 185
Beirut, 110
Biggs, 54
Billy and Company, 170
Binyon's, 10
Bistro 110, 56
Blind Faith Cafe, 123
Blue Mesa, 76
Bob Chinn's Crab House, 171
Bombay Palace, 65
Bones, 120
Bruna's, 184
Cafe Ba-Ba-Reeba, 87
Cafe Borgia, 192
Cafe de Paris, 165
Cafe Provencal, 125
Cafe Spiaggia, 59
Caffe Pranzo, 90
Cape Cod Room, 16
Capt'n Nemo's, 98
Carlos & Carlos, 60
Carlos, 140
Carson's, 38
Casbah Armenian Restaurant, 103
Charlie Trotter's, 57
Chestnut Street Grill, 16
Chez Paul, 20
Chicago Chop House, 35
Chicago Hwe Kwon, 28
Chun Soo Chang, 114
City Tavern, 15
Club Lago, 63
Convito Italiano, 129
Courtyards of Plaka, 152
Cricket's, 14

D & J Bistro, 174
D. B. Kaplan's, 42
Dae Ho, 115
Daruma, 127
Davis Street Fish Market, 122
Delaney & Murphy, 168
Dianna's Opaa, 151
Dieterle's, 163
Ditka's, 37
Don Juan, 155
Don Roth's in Wheeling, 170
Don Roth's River Plaza, 10
Dragon Inn North, 132
Dynasty, 112
Ed Debevic's, 34
Edoya, 167
Edwardo's Natural Pizza Restaurant, 98
El Jardin, 78
Eli's The Place for Steaks, 40
Fernando's, 99
First Street Pier, 139
Foley's, 12
Fricano's, 91
Froggy's, 142
Frontera Grill, 49
Gandhi India Restaurant, 104
Gaylord India Restaurant, 66
Geja's Cafe, 46
Gene & Georgetti, 41
Gennaro's, 179
George's, 61
Giannotti, 164
Gin Go Gae, 113
Gino's East, 64
Gordon, 11
Grand & Wells Tap, 14
Greek Islands, 153
Gulfport Diner, 190
Gusto Italiano, 131
Harry Caray's, 36
Hat Dance, 48
Hatsuhana, 71
House of Hunan, 67
Hue, 27
Hunan Garden, 138
It's Greek to Me, 180
Itto Sushi, 96
Jean Claude's Cafe du Parc, 86
Jerome's, 74

Jilly's Cafe, 124
Jimmy's Place, 100
Jow Koon, 95
King Crab, 75
King Long, 134
Kotobuki, 107
L'Escargot on Halsted, 52
L'Escargot on Michigan, 52
La Boheme, 133
La Gondola, 23
La Strada, 25
La Tour, 45
Lanna Thai, 115
Lawry's The Prime Rib, 33
Le Francais, 172
Le Perroquet, 55
Le Titi de Paris, 169
Le Vichyssois, 175
Lindo Mexico Restaurant, 19
Little Bucharest, 92
Little Italy, 144
Little Szechwan, 141
Lou Mitchell's, 149
Mama Desta's Red Sea Restaurant, 26
Maple Tree Inn, 187
Mareva's, 100
Matsuya, 96
Meanderin' Mandarin, 144
Memories of China, 68
Metropolis, 43
Miami Bar & Grill, 47
Michael Stuart's, 13
Miomir's Serbian Club, 102
Mirabell Restaurant, 89
Monique's Cafe, 54
Morton's, 37
Mrs. Levy's Delicatessen, 148
My Place For?, 109
Mykonos, 166
New Japan, 127
New Taj Mahal, 94
Nick's Fishmarket, 18
Ninety Fifth, 44
Nuevo Leon, 182
On the Tao, 112
Pablo's Cafe, 79
Palermo's, 190
Palm Beach, 130
Parthenon, 154
Pasteur, 116
Philander's, 160
Portofino, 160
Prairie, 178

Index 199

Printer's Row, 179
Ragin' Cajun, 75
Randall's Ribhouse, 41
Ristorante Italia, 155
Roditys, 151
Ron of Japan, 28
Rosded, 106
Sai Cafe, 97
Sayat Nova, 64
Scoozi, 62
Seven Treasures, 181
Shaw's Blue Crab, 136
Shaw's Crab House, 17
Siam Square, 126
Spiaggia, 59
St. Tropez, 84
Star of Siam, 69
Star Top Cafe, 73
Su Casa, 50
Szechwan House, 67
Tallgrass, 193
Tania's, 80
Tap and Growler, 148
Tasty Eat, 104
Thai Villa, 105
That Steak Joynt, 34
The Bagel, 108
The Bakery, 80
The Berghoff, 22
The Butcher Shop, 32
The Charcoal Oven, 121
The Chardonnay, 83
The Cottage, 191
The Cypress, 161
The Dining Room at the Ritz-Carlton, 51
The Everest Room, 21
The Golden Ox, 89
The Grill Room, 130
The Palm, 39
The Pump Room, 32
The Red Lion Pub, 81
The Tower Garden and Restaurant, 121
The Village, 24
The Waterfront, 45
The Whitehall Club, 53
Timbers Charhouse, 138
Tokyo Marina, 117
Toscano, 183
Toulouse, 50
Uncle Tannous, 93
Vernon Park Tap, 185
Villa Marconi, 186

Village Tavern, 173
Walker Bros. Original Pancake House, 128
Winnetka Grill, 134
Yanase, 72
Yoshi's Cafe, 86
Yu Lin's Chinese Dumpling House, 142
Yugo Inn, 101
Zaven's, 20
Zincs, 150
Zofia's Polish Restaurant, 166
Zum Deutschen Eck, 88

SUBURBAN LOCATIONS

ARLINGTON HEIGHTS
Delaney & Murphy, 168
Le Titi de Paris, 169
Walker Bros. Original Pancake House, 128

BERWYN
Aqui mi Tierra, 77

CALUMET CITY
The Cottage, 191

CALUMET PARK
Gulfport Diner, 190

DEERFIELD
Ada's, 137
Ed Debevic's, 34
Hunan Garden, 138
Shaw's Blue Crab, 136

DES PLAINES
Edoya, 167
Mykonos, 166
Sayat Nova, 64

ELGIN
Dieterle's, 163

EVANSTON
Blind Faith Cafe, 123
Cafe Provencal, 125
Daruma, 127
Davis Street Fish Market, 122
Jilly's Cafe, 124
Lindo Mexico Restaurant, 19
New Japan, 127
Siam Square, 126

GENEVA
302 West, 162

GLENCOE
American Joe's, 135

GLENVIEW
Dragon Inn North, 132
Gusto Italiano, 131
Palm Beach, 130
The Grill Room, 130
Walker Bros. Original Pancake House, 128

HARWOOD HEIGHTS
Carson's, 38

HIGHLAND PARK
Aegean Isles, 140
Carlos, 140
First Street Pier, 139
Little Szechwan, 141
Timbers Charhouse, 138
Yu Lin's Chinese Dumpling House, 142

HIGHWOOD
Alouette, 143
Froggy's, 142
Little Italy, 144
Meanderin' Mandarin, 144

HINSDALE
The Cypress, 161

LAKE ZURICH
D & J Bistro, 174

LAKEMOOR
Le Vichyssois, 175

LANSING
Cafe Borgia, 192

LINCOLNWOOD
Bones, 120

LOCKPORT
Tallgrass, 193

LOMBARD
Carson's, 38
Greek Islands, 153

LONG GROVE
Village Tavern, 173

NILES
Zofia's Polish Restaurant, 166

NORRIDGE
Giannotti, 164

NORTHBROOK
Edwardo's Natural Pizza
　　Restaurant, 98
Ron of Japan, 28

OAK LAWN
Palermo's, 190

OAK PARK
Philander's, 160

ELMWOOD PARK
Portofino, 160

PALATINE
Amourette, 172
Gusto Italiano, 131

ROLLING MEADOWS
Gino's East, 64

ROSEMONT
Cafe de Paris, 165
Morton's, 37
Nick's Fishmarket, 18

SCHAUMBERG
Daruma, 127

SKOKIE
Carson's, 38
Edwardo's Natural Pizza
　　Restaurant, 98
The Bagel, 108
The Charcoal Oven, 121
The Tower Garden and
　　Restaurant, 121

WESTCHESTER
Morton's, 37

WHEELING
Billy and Company, 170
Bob Chinn's Crab House, 171
Don Roth's in Wheeling, 170
Edwardo's Natural Pizza
　　Restaurant, 98
Le Francais, 172

WILMETTE
Convito Italiano, 129
Walker Bros. Original
　　Pancake House, 128

WINNETKA
King Long, 134
La Boheme, 133
Winnetka Grill, 134

TYPES OF CUISINE

AMERICAN
302 West, 162
American Joe's, 135
Ann Sather's, 82
Arnie's, 43
Billy and Company, 170
Binyon's, 10
Bones, 120
Carson's, 38
Chestnut Street Grill, 16
Chicago Chop House, 35
City Tavern, 15
Cricket's, 14
Delaney & Murphy, 168
Ditka's, 37
Don Roth's in Wheeling, 170
Don Roth's River Plaza, 10
Ed Debevic's, 34
Edwardo's Natural Pizza
　　Restaurant, 98
Eli's The Place for Steaks, 40
Foley's, 12
Gordon, 11
Grand & Wells Tap, 14
Harry Caray's, 36
Jerome's, 74
La Tour, 45
Lawry's The Prime Rib, 33
Lou Mitchell's, 149
Metropolis, 43
Miami Bar & Grill, 47
Morton's, 37
Prairie, 178
Printer's Row, 179
Randall's Ribhouse, 41
Star Top Cafe, 73
Tap and Growler, 148
That Steak Joynt, 34
The Butcher Shop, 32
The Charcoal Oven, 121
The Cypress, 161
The Grill Room, 130
The Palm, 39
The Pump Room, 32
Timbers Charhouse, 138
Village Tavern, 173
Winnetka Grill, 134

ARMENIAN
Casbah Armenian
　　Restaurant, 103
Sayat Nova, 64

ASSYRIAN
Arbela, 111

AUSTRIAN
Mirabell Restaurant, 89

BRITISH
The Red Lion Pub, 81

CAJUN
Ragin' Cajun, 75

CARIBBEAN
Miami Bar & Grill, 47

CHINESE
Dragon Inn North, 132
Dynasty, 112
House of Hunan, 67
Hunan Garden, 138
King Long, 134
Little Szechwan, 141
Meanderin' Mandarin, 144
Memories of China, 68
On the Tao, 112
Seven Treasures, 181
Szechwan House, 67
Yu Lin's Chinese Dumpling
　　House, 142

CHOPS
Ditka's, 37

CONTINENTAL
Cricket's, 14
Jilly's Cafe, 124
Ninety Fifth, 44
The Bakery, 80
The Cottage, 191
The Tower Garden and
　　Restaurant, 121
Zaven's, 20

CREOLE
Maple Tree Inn, 187
Ragin' Cajun, 75

CUBAN
Tania's, 80

DELICATESSEN
Ada's, 137
D B. Kaplan's, 42
Mrs. Levy's Delicatessen, 148
The Bagel, 108

EASTERN EUROPEAN
Mareva's, 100

Index　　　　　　　　　　　　　　　　　　　　　　　201

ECLECTIC
Arnie's, 43
Bistro 110, 56
Charlie Trotter's, 57
City Tavern, 15
Jerome's, 74
Metropolis, 43
Printer's Row, 179
Star Top Cafe, 73

ETHIOPIAN
Mama Desta's Red Sea Restaurant, 26

FONDUE
Geja's Cafe, 46

FRENCH
Alouette, 143
Ambria, 85
Amourette, 172
Biggs, 54
Bistro 110, 56
Cafe de Paris, 165
Cafe Provencal, 125
Carlos, 140
Charlie Trotter's, 57
Chez Paul, 20
D & J Bistro, 174
Froggy's, 142
Jean Claude's Cafe du Parc, 86
Jimmy's Place, 100
L'Escargot on Halsted, 52
L'Escargot on Michigan, 52
La Boheme, 133
Le Francais, 172
Le Perroquet, 55
Le Titi de Paris, 169
Le Vichyssois, 175
Monique's Cafe, 54
Palm Beach, 130
St. Tropez, 84
The Chardonnay, 83
The Dining Room at the Ritz-Carlton, 51
The Everest Room, 21
The Whitehall Club, 53
Toulouse, 50
Yoshi's Cafe, 86
Zincs, 150

GERMAN
Dieterle's, 163
Mirabell Restaurant, 89
The Berghoff, 22
The Golden Ox, 89
Zum Deutschen Eck, 88

GREEK
Aegean Isles, 140
Courtyards of Plaka, 152
Dianna's Opaa, 151
Greek Islands, 153
It's Greek to Me, 180
My Place For?, 109
Mykonos, 166
Parthenon, 154
Roditys, 151

INDIAN
Bombay Palace, 65
Gandhi India Restaurant, 104
Gaylord India Restaurant, 66
New Taj Mahal, 94

ITALIAN
Bacchanalia, 185
Bruna's, 184
Cafe Borgia, 192
Caffe Pranzo, 90
Carlos & Carlos, 60
Club Lago, 63
Convito Italiano, 129
Fricano's, 91
Gene & Georgetti, 41
Gennaro's, 179
George's, 61
Giannotti, 164
Gino's East, 64
Grand & Wells Tap, 14
Gusto Italiano, 131
La Gondola, 23
Little Italy, 144
Palermo's, 190
Portofino, 160
Ristorante Italia, 155
Scoozi, 62
The Village, 24
Toscano, 183
Vernon Park Tap, 185
Villa Marconi, 186

JAPANESE
Daruma, 127
Edoya, 167
Hatsuhana, 71
Itto Sushi, 96
Kotobuki, 107
Matsuya, 96
New Japan, 127
Ron of Japan, 28
Sai Cafe, 97
Tokyo Marina, 117
Yanase, 72

KOREAN
Chicago Hwe Kwon, 28
Chun Soo Chang, 114
Dae Ho, 115
Gin Go Gae, 113

LEBANESE
Uncle Tannous, 93

LOBSTER
Morton's, 37
The Palm, 39

MEXICAN
Aqui mi Tierra, 77
Don Juan, 155
El Jardin, 78
Fernando's, 99
Frontera Grill, 49
Hat Dance, 48
Lindo Mexico Restaurant, 19
Nuevo Leon, 182
Pablo's Cafe, 79
Su Casa, 50

MIDDLE EASTERN
Arbela, 111
Beirut, 110

NORTHERN ITALIAN
Avanzare, 58
Cafe Spiaggia, 59
La Strada, 25
Spiaggia, 59

NOUVELLE CUISINE
La Tour, 45
Michael Stuart's, 13
Tallgrass, 193

PAKISTANI
New Taj Mahal, 94
Tasty Eat, 104

PANCAKES
Walker Bros. Original Pancake House, 128

PIZZA
Edwardo's Natural Pizza
  Restaurant, 98
Gino's East, 64

POLISH
Arcadia, 156
Zofia's Polish Restaurant, 166

RIBS
Carson's, 38
Randall's Ribhouse, 41

ROMANIAN
Little Bucharest, 92

SANDWICHES
Capt'n Nemo's, 98

SEAFOOD
Bob Chinn's Crab House, 171
Cape Cod Room, 16
Chestnut Street Grill, 16
Davis Street Fish Market, 122
First Street Pier, 139
King Crab, 75
Nick's Fishmarket, 18
Philander's, 160
Shaw's Blue Crab, 136
Shaw's Crab House, 17
The Waterfront, 45

SERBIAN
Miomir's Serbian Club, 102
Yugo Inn, 101

SICILIAN
Little Italy, 144

SOUL FOOD
Army & Lou's, 182
Gulfport Diner, 190

SOUTHERN
Blue Mesa, 76
Gulfport Diner, 190
Maple Tree Inn, 187

SPANISH TAPAS
Cafe Ba-Ba-Reeba, 87

STEAKS
Delaney & Murphy, 168
Ditka's, 37
Eli's The Place for Steaks, 40
Gene & Georgetti, 41
Harry Caray's, 36
Morton's, 37
The Palm, 39

SWEDISH
Ann Sather's, 82

THAI
Ananda, 70
Jow Koon, 95
Lanna Thai, 115
Rosded, 106
Siam Square, 126
Star of Siam, 69
Thai Villa, 105

VEGETARIAN
Blind Faith Cafe, 123

VIETNAMESE
Hue, 27
Pasteur, 116

YUGOSLAVIAN
Yugo Inn, 101

PRICE RANGE

INEXPENSIVE
Ada's, 137
Aegean Isles, 140
Arbela, 111
Arcadia, 156
Beirut, 110
Blind Faith Cafe, 123
Bruna's, 184
Cafe Borgia, 192
Capt'n Nemo's, 98
Chicago Hwe Kwon, 28
Chun Soo Chang, 114
Club Lago, 63
D. B. Kaplan's, 42
Dae Ho, 115
Don Juan, 155
Dynasty, 112
Ed Debevic's, 34
El Jardin, 78
Fernando's, 99
Gandhi India Restaurant, 104
Gennaro's, 179
Gin Go Gae, 113
Gino's East, 64
Gulfport Diner, 190
Hue, 27
It's Greek to Me, 180
Jow Koon, 95
Lanna Thai, 115
Lindo Mexico Restaurant, 19

Little Bucharest, 92
Little Italy, 144
Lou Mitchell's, 149
Mama Desta's Red Sea
  Restaurant, 26
Matsuya, 96
Mrs. Levy's Delicatessen, 148
Mykonos, 166
New Taj Mahal, 94
Nuevo Leon, 182
Pablo's Cafe, 79
Parthenon, 154
Rosded, 106
Seven Treasures, 181
Su Casa, 50
Tasty Eat, 104
Thai Villa, 105
The Bagel, 108
The Berghoff, 22
The Red Lion Pub, 81
Vernon Park Tap, 185
Villa Marconi, 186
Village Tavern, 173
Walker Bros. Original
  Pancake House, 128
Yanase, 72
Yugo Inn, 101

MODERATE
American Joe's, 135
Amourette, 172
Ananda, 70
Ann Sather's, 82
Aqui mi Tierra, 77
Army & Lou's, 182
Bacchanalia, 185
Billy and Company, 170
Binyon's, 10
Bistro 110, 56
Blue Mesa, 76
Bob Chinn's Crab House, 171
Bombay Palace, 65
Bones, 120
Cafe Ba-Ba-Reeba, 87
Cafe Spiaggia, 59
Caffe Pranzo, 90
Carlos & Carlos, 60
Carson's, 38
Casbah Armenian
  Restaurant, 103
Chicago Chop House, 35
City Tavern, 15
Convito Italiano, 129
Courtyards of Plaka, 152
D & J Bistro, 174
Daruma, 127

Davis Street Fish Market, 122
Dianna's Opaa, 151
Dieterle's, 163
Don Roth's in Wheeling, 170
Don Roth's River Plaza, 10
Dragon Inn North, 132
Edoya, 167
Edwardo's Natural Pizza Restaurant, 98
Eli's The Place for Steak, 40
First Street Pier, 139
Fricano's, 91
Froggy's, 142
Frontera Grill, 49
Gaylord India Restaurant, 66
George's, 61
Giannotti, 164
Greek Islands, 153
Gusto Italiano, 131
Hat Dance, 48
House of Hunan, 67
Hunan Garden, 138
Itto Sushi, 96
Jerome's, 74
Jilly's Cafe, 124
King Crab, 75
King Long, 134
Kotobuki, 107
La Gondola, 23
Lawry's The Prime Rib, 33
Little Szechwan, 141
Maple Tree Inn, 187
Meanderin' Mandarin, 144
Memories of China, 68
Metropolis, 43
Miami Bar & Grill, 47
Miomir's Serbian Club, 102
Mirabell Restaurant, 89
Monique's Cafe, 54
My Place For?, 109
New Japan, 127
On the Tao, 112
Palermo's, 190
Pasteur, 116
Portofino, 160
Ragin' Cajun, 75
Randall's Ribhouse, 41
Ristorante Italia, 155
Roditys, 151
Sai Cafe, 97
Sayat Nova, 64
Scoozi, 62
Shaw's Blue Crab, 136

Siam Square, 126
Star of Siam, 69
Star Top Cafe, 73
Szechwan House, 67
Tania's, 80
Tap and Growler, 148
That Steak Joynt, 34
The Butcher Shop, 32
The Charcoal Oven, 121
The Cypress, 161
The Golden Ox, 89
The Grill Room, 130
The Village, 24
The Waterfront, 45
Timbers Charhouse, 138
Tokyo Marina, 117
Toscano, 183
Uncle Tannous, 93
Yu Lin's Chinese Dumpling House, 142
Zincs, 150
Zofia's Polish Restaurant, 166
Zum Deutschen Eck, 88

EXPENSIVE
302 West, 162
Alouette, 143
Ambria, 85
Arnie's, 43
Avanzare, 58
Biggs, 54
Cafe de Paris, 165
Cafe Provencal, 125
Cape Cod Room, 16
Carlos, 140
Charlie Trotter's, 57
Chestnut Street Grill, 16
Chez Paul, 20
Cricket's, 14
Delaney & Murphy, 168
Ditka's, 37
Foley's, 12
Geja's Cafe, 46
Gene & Georgetti, 41
Gordon, 11
Grand & Wells Tap, 14
Harry Caray's, 36
Hatsuhana, 71
Jean Claude's Cafe du Parc, 86
Jimmy's Place, 100
L'Escargot on Halsted, 52
L'Escargot on Michigan, 52
La Boheme, 133

La Strada, 25
La Tour, 45
Le Francais, 172
Le Perroquet, 55
Le Titi de Paris, 169
Le Vichyssois, 175
Mareva's, 100
Michael Stuart's, 13
Morton's, 37
Nick's Fishmarket, 18
Ninety Fifth, 44
Palm Beach, 130
Philander's, 160
Prairie, 178
Printer's Row, 179
Ron of Japan, 28
Shaw's Crab House, 17
Spiaggia, 59
St. Tropez, 84
Tallgrass, 193
The Bakery, 80
The Chardonnay, 83
The Cottage, 191
The Dining Room at the Ritz-Carlton, 51
The Everest Room, 21
The Palm, 39
The Pump Room, 32
The Tower Garden and Restaurant, 121
The Whitehall Club, 53
Toulouse, 50
Winnetka Grill, 134
Yoshi's Cafe, 86
Zaven's, 20

NOTES

NOTES

Proof-of-Purchase
ISBN 0-89721-186-3